The British Raid on ESSEX

The British Raid on Essex

THE FORGOTTEN BATTLE OF THE WAR OF 1812

Jerry Roberts

WESLEYAN UNIVERSITY PRESS

Middletown, Connecticut

WESLEYAN UNIVERSITY PRESS

Middletown CT 06459

www.wesleyan.edu/wespress

© 2014 Jerry Roberts

Manufactured in the United States of America
Typeset in Minion by Tseng Information Systems, Inc.
Maps courtesy of Long Cat Graphics and the Connecticut
River Museum (LCG/CRM).

The Driftless Connecticut Series is funded by the
Beatrice Fox Auerbach Foundation Fund
at the Hartford Foundation for Public Giving.

Wesleyan University Press is a member of the
Green Press Initiative. The paper used in this book meets
their minimum requirement for recycled paper.

Hardcover ISBN: 978-0-8195-7476-3

Ebook ISBN: 978-0-8195-7477-0

Library of Congress Control Number: 2014931803

5 4 3 2 1

Front endpapers: This section of *Official 1813 Map of Connecticut,* sanctioned by the
General Assembly and created by Moses Warren and George Gillet, shows roads from
New London and Killingworth leading to Pettipaug and the Connecticut River. Detail.
(Hudson & Goodwin, 1813. Courtesy of the Connecticut Historical Society, Hartford,
Connecticut.)

Back endpapers: *Blockade Map* of New London and its vicinity, produced in 1813
by A. Doolittle, portrays British vessels off New London and Decatur's squadron already
up the Thames River. This map clearly shows the proximity of the Connecticut River and
Pettipaug to New London and the British Squadron. (Courtesy of New London County
Historical Society.)

To JENI, *for keeping us focused on the future,*
allowing me to spend my time digging up
the past, and to SKYE *and* CHURCHILL *for*
reminding me every day that like history, life
is a never-ending story.

CONTENTS

PROLOGUE

This is the story of two battles, the British Raid on Essex in 1814, and the effort to bring this untold chapter of American history into the light of day. The original struggle lasted less than twenty-four hours. The second has taken a bit longer.

The rediscovery of the British Raid on Essex actually began in Halifax, Nova Scotia back in April of 1980 with the chance meeting of two retired naval officers, one American and one Canadian. Longtime Essex resident, Commander Albert Dock, was attending a meeting of the North American Society for Oceanic History. Here he met Rear Admiral Hugh Francis Pullen, Royal Canadian Navy. When Pullen learned that Dock was from Essex, Connecticut he commented on what a small world it was. While doing some climbing around in his family tree Pullen had discovered that his great, great grandfather, John Skinley, had been in the Royal Navy. Along with twenty-three others he had received the Naval General Service Medal for his role in a small boat raid during the War of 1812. Seaman Skinley, as it turns out, had visited Al Dock's hometown on April 8, 1814 as part of the British Raid on Essex.

Commander Dock had heard of the raid of course, but lamented the total lack of facts associated with it. The event had survived only in the collective folklore of this quaint New England village. Aside from a handful of cannonballs kicking around town, and the annual Commemoration Day parade, no one knew much about it. That's when Admiral Pullen dropped his own little Canadian bombshell on Commander Dock. As a result of his research, Pullen had acquired copies of all the official dispatches and reports to the Admiralty that chronicled the raid in meticulous British detail from beginning to end. He asked Dock if he would like duplicates.

These documents, along with some additional local research, formed the basis for Commander Dock and his neighbor, Captain Russell Anderson, USNR, to put together a twenty-page pamphlet, which was published by the Essex Historical Society in 1981. In addition to their four-page narrative explaining the battle, the booklet contained transcriptions of a number of documents, both British and American, including the official report by Captain Richard Coote who had commanded the operation. Coote's report contained a blow-by-blow account of the raid as well as a list of the twenty-seven ships they had destroyed. It was a wonderful little publication that at last brought some documentation to the British Raid. But like the battle itself, it too slipped back into obscurity.

By 2009 as the Bicentennial of the War of 1812 approached, the Raid had not only been left out of the history books, it had also been left off the list of 1812 battle sites compiled by the United States Navy's History and Heritage Command. As Executive Director of the Connecticut River Museum at the time, I wondered why. The museum is located on the Essex waterfront, virtually on the spot where the British had landed. We decided to try and do something about it.

Taking on the challenge of picking up where the booklet had left off, we set out to peel away the mysteries surrounding the raid, separate fact from long-standing folklore and force state and national recognition of this brief but dynamic moment in our nation's maritime history. Thus began several years of research on both sides of the Atlantic, in archives large and small, and sometimes in the river itself. Like history, this project is a work in progress.

Had it not been for that chance meeting in Halifax, in 1980, it is probable that this incredible story would have remained consigned to the realm of folklore, truly the forgotten battle of the War of 1812.

The British Raid on ESSEX

Sir,

I have great satisfaction in transmitting to you a letter I received from Captain Coote of His Majesty's Sloop Borer, under whose directions I placed a division of Boats from His Majesty's Ships, La Hogue, Maidstone, Endymoin, and Borer, for which purpose of destroying a number of large Privateers and letters of Marque, building and equipping in the Connecticut River, and which Service by the judicious arrangements of that Officer, aided by the exemplary good Conduct, steadiness and gallantry of every Officer and Man employed with him, has been attended with complete success.

Your most obedient Servant,

Thomas Bladen Capel

Captain & Senior Officer off New London,

April 13, 1814

CHAPTER ONE

Forgotten Battle

The light was fading. Thirty-two-year-old Captain Richard Coote peered through his ship's glass, once again scanning the bluffs overlooking the river a mile to the south. His position was exposed. He was anchored in the Connecticut River, five miles north of its mouth and the safety of his warships. Darkness could not come soon enough. It had been more than three tenuous hours since he had rejected the American demand for surrender. He was now committed to this course of action, this gamble.

Coote's men had rowed up the Connecticut River, occupied the village of Pettipaug, a mile and a quarter north of their current position, and torched every ship in the harbor including several newly built American privateers. They had taken the two best vessels with them as prizes of war, the brig *Young Anaconda* and the schooner *Eagle*.

Young Anaconda now lay burning nearby. It had gone aground on the way out, forcing Coote to anchor the *Eagle* and transfer men and equipment before setting the brig ablaze. As he waited for the black of night to begin the final run downriver, he and his men continued to take sporadic musket fire from a wooded area on the adjacent shore. Over the past several hours the small group of American militia there had been cautious in their harassment. They were very aware that the British could send a boat filled with Royal Marines ashore to deal with them if needed. These were the blue jays nipping at the tail feathers of the hawk that had wandered into their airspace. But protected behind the bulwarks of the captured privateer, the small arms fire had proven to be more of a nuisance to the British than a real threat.

Through his glass, Coote could still just make out the large numbers of Americans on the commanding bluffs downriver. He had been watching them gathering there, tenaciously digging breastworks for the field pieces which had been arriving from Killingworth, Saybrook, Lyme and New London over the past several hours. By all estimates there were at least 500 Americans now assembled along the banks of the river to block the British escape, probably more. Attempting to run this gauntlet in daylight would have been suicidal. But with the strong outbound current and the blackness that the partially overcast skies would soon bring, the British had a fair chance of getting down the river and reaching their ships alive.

Off the mouth of the river, HMS *Borer* and *Sylph* carried forty-six guns between them, more than enough to counter anything the Americans could hope to muster on this coast. But they were over five miles away—five miles of open river along which hundreds of American militia, soldiers, sailors and marines had been gathering, preparing for revenge.

So far the raid had gone off incredibly well for the British. They had accomplished their mission without the loss or injury of a single man. They had penetrated six miles into the United States of America, taken control of a significant port town, destroyed virtually all of the enemy's shipping there and were now about to complete their escape. All Coote needed was the dark of night so he could get his men out safely. At least that was his plan.

At 7:00 p.m. Coote decided it was dark enough and ordered his men back into the ships' boats, which were clustered around the *Eagle*. At that very moment, less than a quarter mile away on the narrow back roads leading north from Saybrook, another race against time and the fading daylight was taking place. Twenty-five-year-old Lieutenant William Bull and his gun crew were pushing their team of horses as fast as their hooves would carry them. His orders were to get one of the State Corps brass six-pound cannons to the point adjacent to the enemy's position and bring it to bear on them before darkness stole the last chance they had of avenging the disaster in Pettipaug. Back up in the harbor, dozens of ships were still smoldering, adding the gray and black smoke of tarred rigging and wood to the already grim sky.

Earlier in the day, after receiving the first word of the British incursion, Captain Amaziah Bray, in command of the 2ⁿᵈ Company of Artillery, Connecticut State Corps, had raced from Killingworth to the fort at the mouth of the river on Saybrook Point with two of the Corp's four six pounders. The other two field pieces had been assigned to Saybrook, but they were not at the fort.

In civilian life, thirty-three-year-old Bray was a lawyer, but he had already become a bit of a local hero in this war. He and his men had been in action throughout 1813 exchanging gunfire with the Royal Navy while protecting coastal vessels that had run into Killingworth Harbor to escape capture by British ships and barges patrolling the Long Island Sound. They had engaged the enemy at the mouth of the Connecticut River as well. Yet this was very different. This was a major incursion far up the river. Pettipaug's shipping had been destroyed. Heads would roll. But right now all that mattered was getting a gun close enough to engage the enemy before it was too late.

That afternoon, not long after Bray's company had arrived at the fort, they had been ordered to move their field pieces further north to a position on the bluffs at Ferry Point, directly across from the men and guns digging in atop the hills on the Lyme side of the river. Here they had all become part of the massive trap that had assembled as Coote watched through his glass. Men had continued to arrive but most of the hastily mustered companies were still short handed. They needed all the help they could get. Lieutenant William Bull, acting as a volunteer in command of one of the guns from the Saybrook company, had joined Bray and the others on the bluffs, confidently prepared to blow the British out of the water as they came down the river. It hadn't mattered that there were no large guns in position to hit the British where they had anchored the captured schooner a mile upstream. There was only one way the enemy could get back to their ships and that was right down the middle of the river, between the men and guns positioned on either side. It was going to be like shooting fish in a barrel. But so far the British had not budged.

As evening approached, Generals William Williams and Jirah Isham had arrived across the river in Lyme with a large contingent of troops from New London. Major Marsh Ely had been in command of the local militia units throughout the day. Together, they assessed the situation. Breastworks had been dug into the high ground and field pieces positioned on both sides of the river. Captains Jacob Jones and James Biddle of the American warships *Macedonian* and *Hornet* had arrived from New London. Biddle had commandeered a sloop, crewed it with United States marines and got it into the river below Calves Island on the Lyme side. The fort down on Saybrook Point was now manned. The trap was fully set. Everyone was just waiting for the British to make their move.

But as the sun grew low, they all began to understand at last that Coote was not going to play along. The British were going to wait for darkness and there was the very real chance of missing them. The evening sky was overcast and there was a mist in the air. The moon would not rise until after 10 p.m. It would be a black night. Finally, the Americans realized they could no longer wait for the enemy; it was time to go and get them! Orders were hurried across the river for Captain Bray to get one of the field pieces up to a point adjacent to the enemy position and hit them where they were. It was time to force their hand and bring them down into the well-armed gauntlet before dark.

Lieutenant Bull was dispatched with one of the six pounders. It was not easy going, driving the team through the twisting back roads hauling the field carriage-mounted gun. At last Bull and his crew reached the river overlooking the enemy position. In the fading light, they coaxed the horses off the road over some open ground, through a wooded area and up a small rise overlooking the river. The small group of militia that had been taking potshots at the British from a stand of trees all afternoon was glad to see them. Now, at last, a weapon capable of inflicting some serious damage had arrived.

It was growing darker by the minute, but they could not engage the enemy just yet. Due to the disorganized nature of the day and the rush to get the gun into action on the Point, Bull arrived without the necessary complement of men or equipment normally required to handle the field piece. The gun carriage was quickly unhitched from its limber, and muscled into position overlooking the river. Bull turned to look out over the blackening water . . . there they were: the burning brig and the anchored schooner with the ships' boats alongside. The Americans were astonished at how close the British were. This was going to be a point blank situation. But they could not fire yet.

Lacking proper match rope, the crew was forced to quickly kindle a small fire and create glowing coals to heat an iron brand with which to touch off the gun's powder. Seconds and minutes were slipping by. Darkness was descending rapidly now. Bull could see the British moving about, transferring men and equipment from the anchored schooner into the boats along side. There were men with torches on the captured privateer. Clearly they were going to set it alight and begin their run down the river in the barges at any moment.

Bull helped load the gun, which ate up more precious seconds: tamping the powder cartridge down into the breach; inserting the three and a half inch, six-pound iron ball down the barrel; priming the touch hole with fine powder from a brass flask. Men were fanning the coals to get the brand glowing red-hot. Bull had sighted the barrel towards the 106-foot, 250-ton American privateer *Eagle*, now a British prize. It had already started to catch fire. He could see the last of the enemy sailors and marines embarking back into the large ships' barges that had brought them up the river the night before. He could see the officers with their cocked hats giving orders, preparing to get underway. It was now or never. The crew readjusted the field piece on Bull's orders, swinging the trail of the carriage with pikes and bringing the gun to bear directly on the boats. The barrel needed no elevation. This was a direct shot.

If this had been an hour earlier Coote would have sent marines ashore to overwhelm the American position. But the British were now committed to a new timeline. They had to get free of the burning schooner and underway before the Americans could hit them. Bull pulled the brand from the fire and carefully brought it down over the touchhole. There was a split second hissing sound as the priming powder burned through to the cartridge.

The field piece erupted, belching flame as it rolled back in recoil. The gun's explosive report quickly returned an echo from the hills on the far side of the river three quarters of a mile away. The six-pound iron round shot whistled over the boats just missing everything and everyone as it skipped across the water toward the dark and distant shore. Perhaps the militia near Bull's gun let out a tentative cheer as they intensified their musket fire. This is what they had all been waiting for. Bull's crew quickly sponged the barrel and reloaded. How many rounds could they get off before the enemy got underway or were swallowed in darkness? On the bluffs, a mile to the south, hundreds of men who had been waiting all afternoon for the action to start, understood the time had come; it would be their turn soon. Fire, brimstone, redemption!

Again the gun unleashed its tongue of fire and another sharp report echoed across the water. This second ball did not fly out across the river. It found its mark amongst the boats. Its report was instantly accompanied by the sound of shattering wood and the muffled yet unmistakable cry of human agony. Bull and his crew reloaded as quickly as possible . . . the night was falling and this was the moment of retribution.

It had all started just twenty hours earlier.

On the night of April 7, 1814, a raiding force of 136 British sailors and marines had rowed six miles up the Connecticut River from two warships anchored in Long Island Sound. The raid was one of the most audacious small boat operations in naval history, resulting in the largest single loss of American shipping during the War of 1812. It was all there, burning ships, blazing cannons, a well-paid traitor, mysterious Masonic handshakes, a boy hero, spilled rum and a long lost sword. Yet, two hundred years later these dramatic twenty-four hours were all but forgotten.

LOSER'S DAY
Essex, Connecticut, originally known as Pettipaug, is a village almost too quaint and picturesque to believe. First settled in 1648, its Main Street runs from a small traffic circle at the top of town down a gentle slope lined with historic houses and a continuous canopy of old oaks, maples and chestnuts, to the waterfront at the end of the peninsula that defines the village. The harbor is actually formed by a wide spot in a bend in the river. Three coves within its

western shore create the peninsula upon which the village was settled. Two hundred years ago it was called Pettipaug Point.

During boating season the harbor is filled with several hundred moorings where sailing vessels and powerboats swing to face the incoming and outgoing tides, which are the daily interface between the river, Long Island Sound and the open Atlantic. The Connecticut is the largest river in New England. It begins with a tiny spring-fed lake a few dozen yards from the Canadian border, 400 odd miles to the north of Essex. After reaching the village the river flows another six miles to its mouth on Long Island Sound, which in turn is connected directly to the Atlantic Ocean through the Race, just 15 miles to the east. At its other end, ninety miles to the west, the Long Island Sound connects to New York Harbor, through Hell Gate and the East River, with the broad Atlantic lying just beyond.

Main Street Essex is less than half a mile long but at least twenty-four of its houses predate the War of 1812. Several of these were built before the Revolution. In the middle of the town stands the iconic Griswold Inn, known to locals as simply, "the Gris." The original structure was built in 1801 as a residence by Captain Richard Hayden and his new bride. He was part of a family shipbuilding dynasty started by his grandfather Uriah who had built the colonial warship, *Oliver Cromwell*, near the foot of Main Street during the Revolution. At the time it was the largest full-rigged ship built in Connecticut. In 1806 Richard sold his five-year-old home to Ethan Bushnell and then built the first brick building in town just a few doors closer to the waterfront. Bushnell opened a tavern with an inn and it has been in business in one form or another for the past 200 plus years.

The taproom itself is much older. Built in the mid 1700s across Main Street as the village's first schoolhouse, it was later moved and joined to the back of the inn. It is said that the first British cannonball fired into the town passed directly through the structure — in one side and out the other — one of many scars left by the battle that the history books forgot. Another of the inn's many undocumented yet plausible oral traditions is that British officers used it as a field headquarters during their occupation of the town.

Every Monday, this room, with its ancient-looking plaster-and-lath vaulted ceiling, is packed with devotees of maritime music as the *Jovial Crew* belt out sea shanties in an almost tribal, Celtic atmosphere. This has been going on as long as anyone in town can remember — a primal link to the village's seafaring heritage. The faithful pound on tables, drink Revolutionary Ale and sing their lungs out even in the winter when the tourists and snowbirds are long gone. The inn has witnessed the comings and goings of the village for two centuries.

Patrons have included local ship builders and seamen, tinkers, tailors, sailors and soldiers returned from war, yachtsmen from the boats in the harbor, leaf peepers and bed-and-breakfast weekenders from New York City, tour-bus tourists, you name it. The place has seen hard times such as when the last steamboats left the river in 1931 and good times such as when the boat yards turned out high-end wooden yachts. Katharine Hepburn grew up just down the road in Fenwick at the mouth of the river and continued to live there, calling it her only home, for the rest of her long and colorful life. The local theater where she got her start is still open for business in nearby Ivoryton.

From the grand old trees to the white picket fences, Essex is the quintessential New England village, quiet and subdued, low-key, apparently frozen in time; a real life Brigadoon halfway between New York and Boston.

The village originally served as Saybrook's blue water port and business center. By 1700, vessels from the village were trading with other colonies along the eastern seaboard as well as the West Indies. Like many other villages along the river and the Connecticut coast, Pettipaug provided foodstuffs, livestock, barrel staves and other materials to the sugar cane plantations in Jamaica, Barbados and the other islands, in return for sugar, molasses and rum. Molasses was also distilled into rum locally and all of these commodities were traded within New England, and most notably Britain, in return for manufactured goods and luxury items not yet produced in the colonies.

In support of this growing trade Pettipaug became a significant shipbuilding town. The three large coves that shape the peninsula are now lined with high-end homes, marinas and yacht clubs; but they were once dominated by shipyards, sail lofts, blacksmith shops, warehouses, chandleries and other businesses supporting the maritime trades. The town even had a 900-foot ropewalk that paralleled the upper end of Main Street. If you wanted to make a very long piece of rope for ship's rigging, you needed a very long building. Pettipaug had one.

Between 1700 and 1860 over 600 vessels were built here. Each house along Main Street bears a little plaque bestowed by the Essex Historical Society denoting when it was built and by whom. A casual stroll tells the story. Virtually all of the houses were homes to ship builders, master mariners, or the proprietors of other trades directly related to the sea. The fact that these were intermarried dynasties is made clear by the dominance of a small group of names including Post, Pratt, Hayden and Starkey. From this quiet little corner of New England the captains of Connecticut built their empires and ventured to the far corners of the globe. This was no provincial backwater; it was a seaport six miles up a river that was the gateway to New England's interior in one direction, and to the world with its seven seas in the other.

Today Essex is a sleepy yachting center and a low-key sanctuary for those willing to venture off of I-95's beaten path. The residents are old school and insular, quietly living in a place where history has been made for three centuries. You can still feel it in the air; palpable, as they say. It's the best-kept secret around and the locals would just as soon keep it that way.

Yet every year, for the past fifty years, something very quirky happens on Main Street on the second Saturday in May. The local fife and drum corps, the Sailing Masters of 1812, lead a parade of about a dozen other corps, all kitted out in the uniforms of the Revolution and the War of 1812, from the top of town down to the waterfront. There are no high school marching bands or crepe-covered limousines or floats. No majorettes or scout troops with banners, just fifes, and drums, and a few bagpipes thrown in for good measure. This is an authentic New England experience, not a fabrication to attract tourists.

The parade is officially known as Commemoration Day, or more colorfully, Burning of the Ships Day. But many locals simply call it Loser's Day. Until recently, almost no one in town, or anywhere else for that matter, could tell you what it was all about, except that it had something to do with the British burning the town a long time ago and stealing all the rum. But as it turns out, the British did not burn the town or steal any rum at all. They came to burn the privateers of Pettipaug.

The British raid was big news at the time. Over ninety papers across the nation chronicled the grief, mortification, mudslinging and blame gaming that followed. Fortunes were lost, dynasties imperiled. Yet within a decade the facts behind the story had faded into obscurity. The village became a separate town from Saybrook and changed its name from Pettipaug to Essex in 1820. The whole convoluted episode survived only through folklore, a few misinformed mentions in a handful of magazine articles, a couple of poorly researched books . . . and a parade that few people understood. Two centuries later, as the nation prepared to recognize the bicentennial of the War of 1812 the British Raid on Essex might just as well never have happened. But it did.

CHAPTER TWO

Decatur's War

President Madison's Republican-dominated Congress declared war on Great Britain on June 18, 1812. The British did not want this war and neither did New England—especially Connecticut, Massachusetts and Rhode Island. Not a single Federalist voted in favor of going to war. Some historians contend that the War of 1812 was simply part of the larger power struggle between America's two major political parties, the Jeffersonian Republicans who dominated the agrarian South and expansionist West, and Federalist New England whose economy was based on manufacturing and maritime trade. That, of course, meant trade with Great Britain.

There have been stacks of books written exploring why the United States declared war on the greatest military power on earth, which also happened to be its best merchant-trading partner. Freedom of the seas and outrage over impressment are the most defensible reasons. For years the British had been boarding American vessels and removing crewmen who were pressed into forced service in the Royal Navy. Their justification was to recover deserters, but thousands of American citizens were removed from American ships—a major slap in the face to United States sovereignty and national pride. The desire to push the British out of Michigan and Ohio in order to push the Indians out of the way as the United States expanded westward was perhaps less righteous but presumably more important to those who lead us to war. The justification was that the British were stirring up Indian attacks and atrocities against American settlers. The notion that the United States might take this opportunity to *finish* the Revolution and liberate Canada while we were at it seems to have been more of an afterthought than a cause. It sounded good on paper; it just didn't work out all that well.

In any case, aside from a bit of attention during its bicentennial, the War of 1812 has been consigned to the B-list of American history. It ended after two years and eight months of costly fighting on land and at sea—not to mention the incalculable expense of disrupted trade—with a treaty that returned everything to prewar status quo. In the end, both the United States and Great Britain simply came to realize it was not worth continuing the conflict. So they stopped. Nobody really won, except perhaps the Canadians; and nobody really lost, except of course the Native Americans. They fought with the British and then watched them leave the playing field soon after the war ended, leaving the door to the west wide open.

Yes, there were some high points for the young United States, mostly at sea; but sandwiched between the glory of the Revolution and the national tragedy of the Civil War this indecisive second conflict with the mother country has never quite grabbed the public imagination. Thank god for Captains Isaac Hull and Stephen Decatur with their single-ship victories over the Royal Navy, and General Andrew Jackson at the Battle of New Orleans . . . better late than never. Throw in Captain James Lawrence's, "Don't give up the ship," "The Star Spangled Banner" and a renewed sense of national identity and it all starts to look pretty good. Never mind the fact that America's three attempts to "liberate" Canada were decisively beaten back, not so much by British regulars as by Canadian militia. This ended the question of annexation once and for all and it's why the American flag has fifty stars rather than fifty-one. Let's not even mention that the enemy burned Washington. Yes, it was just as well that both sides were willing to call the whole thing off and get back to business.

In Europe the second American war with Great Britain was just a sideshow to the *real* war. Over there 1812 was all about crushing Napoleon. Tchaikovsky's soundtrack was written for *their* War of 1812, not ours.

Leaving the big picture to others, the British Raid on Essex was the indirect result of a very specific component of the naval war waged along the New England coast. It was a fact that in 1812 Britain had the most powerful navy on earth. The United States had a few good warships and some promising officers, but clearly Britannia ruled the waves. In 1812 the British army may still have been bogged down in Europe but their navy had soundly defeated the combined French and Spanish fleets at Trafalgar in 1805. So it was largely the Royal Navy that prosecuted the war until the army was free to join in after Napoleon's defeat at the battle of Leipzig and the fall of Paris forced him to abdicate the French throne on April 11, 1814. Ironically this was just four days after the British Raid on Essex.

When the War of 1812 began, thirty-three-year-old Captain Stephen Decatur was already a bona fide American naval hero. At twenty-five he had become the youngest captain in the history of United States Navy. He had demonstrated his zeal and professionalism in the Quasi-War with France and the first Barbary War off the coast of North Africa. In 1804, he carried out a dramatic small-boat raid aboard a captured Barbary corsair renamed *Intrepid*

Commodore Stephen Decatur was already an American hero before the War of 1812. His capture of HMS Macedonian *added to his fame, yet he and his squadron spent much of the war blockaded in New London by British naval forces. (Courtesy of Mystic Seaport.)*

United States and Macedonian. *This 1814 engraving by Benjamin Tanner based on a painting by Thomas Birch depicts Decatur's victory over the British frigate* Macedonian *off the Azores on October 25, 1812. The prize was brought into New London and the ship was recommissioned into the US Navy after extensive repairs in New York. (Courtesy of Mystic Seaport.)*

and burned the American frigate USS *Philadelphia*, which had itself been captured by the corsair fleet and was being held in Tripoli Harbor. No less a naval icon than Admiral Horatio Nelson himself had called Decatur's raid, "the most bold and daring act of the age." Not a bad thing to have on your résumé.

Once President Madison declared war, Decatur wasted no time getting into action in command of the forty-four-gun frigate *United States*. On October 25, 1812, off the Azores, in a brilliant display of seamanship, Decatur soundly defeated the thirty-eight-gun frigate HMS *Macedonian* and brought his badly shot-up prize back to New London. By early April 1813 Decatur and the *United States* were in New York ready to get back to sea. Here the ship had gone through months of delays waiting for materials to repair her battle damage, which necessitated a new main mast. Also in the harbor and still finishing its extensive rebuild was Decatur's prize, the *Macedonian*. Two other American warships, the brigs *Hornet* and *Argus* were in the harbor as well.

On April 9th Decatur took the *United States* and *Argus*, through the Verrazano Narrows and out to Sandy Hook, New York as his first step to getting out into the open sea again. Here he found his way blocked by the powerful seventy-four-gun ship-of-the-line, HMS *Valiant* under Captain Robert Dudley Oliver, along with the frigate, HMS *Acasta*. Recognizing the potential of Decatur and the four American warships now in New York Harbor to wreak more havoc in the Atlantic, the British were determined to keep them bottled up.

Decatur decided to wait for wind conditions that would better favor his break out. Meanwhile the British had closed the other entrance to New York, the mouth of Long Island Sound ninety miles to the west. Here the seventy-four-gun *Ramillies* and the frigate *Orpheus* had begun patrolling Block Island Sound and the waters off Montauk Point.

On May 10th *United States* was joined by *Macedonian*, now recommissioned into the United States Navy under Captain Jacob Jones. But within a few days Decatur, assuming there were additional British warships waiting for him just over the horizon, decided on a new plan. He took the ships back up into New York Harbor and on May 18th headed up the East River, planning on making the passage through Hell Gate and the Sound, and breaking out into the Atlantic through the Race at the far end. He believed his chances against the older HMS *Ramillies* were better than a shoot-out with the newer *Valiant*.

The *Ramillies* was a veteran of some of the greatest naval actions in recent times and her commander, Captain Sir Thomas Masterson Hardy, was not just another Royal Navy officer. He was "Nelson's Hardy," Admiral Nelson's flag captain aboard HMS *Victory* at the Battle of Trafalgar on October 21, 1805, when the Royal Navy secured dominance of the seas for the next 100 years. After being shot on deck by a French sniper while setting a fine British example of officers not taking cover under fire, Nelson was brought below decks where he later died in Hardy's arms. Nelson's legendary last words, after asking that the nation take good care of his mistress, Lady Hamilton, were, "Kiss me Hardy."

Hardy would have known all about Decatur, and like every British officer would welcome the chance to challenge him at sea.

As the two American frigates made their way through the East River the *United States* went aground, causing them to miss the favorable wind and tide

Captain Jacob Jones (above), commander of USS Macedonian, *and Captain James Biddle* (opposite), *commander of USS* Hornet, *brought American marines and sailors from Decatur's squadron in New London to assist efforts to prevent the British from escaping the Connecticut River on the evening of April 8ᵗʰ. (James Biddle engraving by T. Gimbrede for* Analectic Magazine, *published by M. Thomas; Jacob Jones engraving by D. Edwin after the portrait by Rembrandt Peale, Courtesy U.S. Naval Historical Center.)*

combination needed to pass through Hell Gate for another five days. Here the *Hornet*, under command of Captain James Biddle, and the privateer *Scourge*, joined them.

Decatur was now de facto commodore of an ad hoc squadron, united in their desire to get past the British and back into the war. Ironically, both Captains Biddle and Jones had been officers aboard USS *Philadelphia* and had spent eighteen months as prisoners in Tripoli while Decatur carried out his famous raid to destroy their captured ship. On October 17, 1812 Jones was in command of the eighteen-gun USS *Wasp* with Biddle as his first lieutenant when they captured HMS *Frolic* while attacking a British convoy. Four hours later *Wasp* was in turn captured by the seventy-four-gun, HMS *Poictiers*. The *Wasp*, renamed *Loup Cervier* was put into service with the Royal Navy and later played a role in the aftermath of the British Raid on Essex.

Just after getting through Hell Gate during an electrical storm on May 24th, the *United States* again went aground and was simultaneously struck by lightning. The vessel's shattered main royal mast came crashing to the deck followed by Commodore Decatur's broad pennant. They were all lucky the ship's powder magazine did not explode. As the squadron shook itself off and made its way into the Sound, HMS *Valliant's* Captain Oliver realized that Decatur had slipped out of New York Harbor through the back door. Not wanting to miss the glory of taking on this American legend, he pulled rank on Hardy and ordered *Ramillies* and *Orpheus* to take his place off of New York while he took *Valliant* and *Acasta* and raced along the outside of Long Island in an attempt to beat Decatur's squadron to the far end of the Sound. Hardy was livid, but orders were orders.

Decatur won the race but jeopardized his lead by anchoring south of New London to do some additional repair work and gun practice. On the night of May 31st he held a war council in his wardroom and planned the squadron's final breakout for the first light of dawn. On the morning of June 1st with a favorable north-northwest wind, Decatur led his squadron through the Race and set a course to pass north of Block Island and then into the open Atlantic. They had seen the two British warships off Montauk, but they were twenty miles to leeward and therefore offered no immediate threat. Due to faulty intelligence, however, Decatur believed there were more British warships in the area than there actually were, including Hardy with *Ramillies*. As they approached Block Island Sound, perhaps spooked by the ships coming up from Montauk Point, all three American captains believed there were additional British warships positioned ahead to intercept them. In a decision that is still not fully understood, the normally bold Stephen Decatur ordered his ships to come about and head back toward the Race and the protection of New London with its two forts, Griswold and Trumbull. This actually gave *Valliant* and *Acasta* a chance to cut them off. With *United States* now in the rear of the retreating ships, *Acasta* managed to get off a shot or two from its bow chaser. The *United States* returned fire from her stern guns. After a dramatic chase the American ships made it into New London. The British followed them as far as the Race and then anchored between the forks of Long Island, slamming the door shut on Decatur's hopes of reaching the Atlantic. During all the excitement, the privateer *Scourge*, captained by Samuel Nicoll had managed to thread the needle and make it out to sea.

Although safe within the well-protected harbor, Decatur was trapped again. All the British had to do now was conduct a tight blockade off New London for the duration of the war. And they did. Before long, Hardy and *Ramillies* were back off New London with a squadron to keep Decatur and his vessels from causing any further trouble. Unlike New York, New London does not have a viable back door. Decatur secured his ships upriver, safely above New London, but pursued various schemes to attempt an escape. The most celebrated of these was his attempt to take the squadron out of the river under cover of darkness in December 1813. The passage was aborted when mysterious "blue lights" were seen and presumed to be signals from someone in New London warning the British that the Americans were on the move. Despite two hundred years of speculation it has never been confirmed that the lights were in fact signals. Decatur also attempted to coordinate an escape plan with American "torpedo men" attempting to blow up ships of the blockading squadron.

BLOCKADE

The British had already identified the western end of the Long Island Sound, including the Race and the waters off New London and Block Island Sound, as a logical choke point. Controlling Long Island Sound enabled the British to put a stop to the once impressive flow of produce and products coming out of the Connecticut River Valley from reaching ports along the New England coast. Here, American commerce could be intercepted and British vessels could replenish their water casks at Block Island, which became an unofficial British outpost. British ships could also receive both supplies and intelligence from neutral vessels and even specially-licensed American coasters. It has been said that the packet ship *Juno* was allowed to continue its regular trips to New York City, and that she supplied the British with newspapers on a regular basis. With their ships' barges and other small craft the Royal Navy conducted almost daily patrols and small raids along this coast all of which put increased pressure on Connecticut port towns and what was left of coastal trade.

Now, the presence of Decatur and the American squadron in New London focused additional British attention on the area. With the powerful blockading squadron on their doorstep many New Londoners feared an invasion. As the months dragged on, despite his fame and glory, Decatur's welcome began to wear a little thin.

Yet even this offered new opportunities to some. In March of 1813, two months before Decatur's arrival in New London, President Madison had issued An Act to Encourage the Destruction of the Armed Vessels of War of the Enemy. It offered to reward any citizen half the value of any British warship they could destroy by any means. This represented a potential fortune and by June the opportunity had unleashed a succession of attempts to destroy British ships off New London using everything from explosive-laden vessels, floating bombs (then known as torpedoes) and even semi-submersibles and submarines. The British considered these as acts of civilian terrorism encouraged by the United States government. This was far outside the accepted protocol of civilized war at sea. Today we call it asymmetrical warfare.

THE PRIVATEERS OF PETTIPAUG

By early to mid 1813, British pressure on maritime commerce had already prompted some shipbuilders and investors to look toward privateering. In port towns like Pettipaug—where fortunes were tied to the sea—ships and seamen, shipyards and shipwrights sat idle. Rather than waiting for the war to end, shipbuilding dynasties like the Haydens, Starkeys and Pratts turned to building and outfitting these government-licensed, privately owned warships. There were certainly risks for those involved, but it was a great way for any nation to supplement its regular navy through private enterprise. Patriotism is a wonderful thing, but there are few motivators as powerful as the potential of monetary gain.

Government-sanctioned privateering had been going on for centuries and was employed by most nations including global super powers such as England and France. It was used extensively by both sides during the American Revolution, with Connecticut right in the thick of it. Privateering came in two basic forms. The most common was the letter of marque. The idea here was that a merchant ship, whose primary task was to carry cargo, could be armed and licensed to capture enemy ships when and if the opportunity arose for it to do so. Privateer commissions, on the other hand, were in essence licenses to operate privately owned warships whose primary task was to wage war against an enemy's shipping for profit. These ships did not carry cargo and

To *Captain*   *commander of the private armed*

called the

INSTRUCTIONS

FOR THE PRIVATE ARMED VESSELS OF THE UNITED STATES,

1. **THE** tenor of your commission under the act of Congress, entitled " An act concerning letters of marque, prizes, and prize goods," a copy of which is hereto annexed, will be kept constantly in your view. The high seas, referred to in your commission, you will understand, generally, to extend to low water mark; but with the exception of the space within one league, or three miles, from the shore of countries at peace both with Great Britain and with the United States. You may nevertheless execute your commission within that distance of the shore of a nation at war with Great Britain, and even on the waters within the jurisdiction of such nation, if permitted so to do.

2. You are to pay the strictest regard to the rights of neutral powers, and the usages of civilized nations; and in all your proceedings towards neutral vessels, you are to give them as little molestation or interruption as will consist with the right of ascertaining their neutral character, and of detaining and bringing them in for regular adjudication, in the proper cases. You are particularly to avoid even the appearance of using force or seduction, with a view to deprive such vessels of their crews, or of their passengers, other than persons in the military service of the enemy.

3. Towards enemy vessels and their crews, you are to proceed, in exercising the rights of war, with all the justice and humanity which characterize the nation of which you are members.

4. The master and one or more of the principal persons belonging to captured vessels, are to be sent, as soon after the capture as may be, to the judge or judges of the proper court in the United States, to be examined upon oath, touching the interest or property of the captured vessel and her lading: and at the same time are to be delivered to the judge or judges, all passes, charter parties, bills of lading, invoices, letters and other documents and writings found on board; the said papers to be proved by the affidavit of the commander of the capturing vessel, or some other person present at the capture, to be produced as they were received, without fraud, addition, subduction or embezzlement.

By command of the President of the U. States of America.

Jas Monroe   *Secretary of State.*

Official instructions to licensed American privateers signed by Secretary of State James Monroe. (Courtesy of Mystic Seaport.)

were operated along the same lines as naval vessels complete with uniformed officers. In both cases what separated privateers from piracy was the fact that they were licensed by a government to attack and capture only the shipping of their declared enemies in time of war. Privateers flew the national flags of their own countries . . . most of the time.

Of course the idea was not to *sink* an enemy ship. The plan was to capture it, put a prize crew on-board and sail it to a friendly port where it would be declared a legitimate capture by an Admiralty Court and then put up for auction through a prize agent along with its cargo. After government fees and the agent's commissions were paid, half the profit would go to the owners of the vessel, which was often a consortium of ship owners (to diversify the inherent risk) and the other half would be divided between the officers and crew as stipulated by the articles signed by those involved. The very effective incentive of the system was that officers and seamen alike had the opportunity to gain significant financial reward from an aggressive and successful voyage. The downside was, of course, that failure to successfully capture enemy prizes resulted in no payment for the crew and potential financial ruin for the investors. Worse yet, there was also the cold, hard fact that privateers were always high priority targets of an enemy's navy, which would understandably want to rid the seas of these predators of their own nation's merchant marine.

It goes without saying that privateers would always avoid attacking an enemy warship for the obvious reason that they would most likely not survive that experience. The plan was to capture merchant shipping laden with moneymaking cargo. Even so, the success rate, in fact, the survival rate, of privateers was not high. Of the 515 American privateers that operated during the War of 1812 only 42 percent were able to make successful captures, while 49 percent were themselves captured by the Royal Navy. These statistics do not even take into account privateers lost at sea, or the significant number of prizes that were recaptured by the British before they reached a safe port. Still, there were those willing to accept these odds. Pooled ownership spread the risks between multiple investors while shipbuilders who simply made their money by selling privateers to others avoided the odds altogether. The privateers lying at Pettipaug Point were a mixture of both.

It was no secret to the British or anyone else that Pettipaug was a shipbuilding town and that vessels were being built or outfitted as privateers and letters of marque there. It's not as if the British needed spies walking around the village to know what was going on. The fact is, newly built privateers were being openly advertised in newspapers for all to see and it was well known that British officers of the blockading squadron routinely received the American papers off New London. Among several ships for sale in the February 8th edition of the *New York Gazette & General Advertiser* were two vessels in Saybrook (Pettipaug) openly listed as privateers. One was a "well-modeled" pilot-boat built schooner, the other a pilot-boat built brig. Both were touted as fast sailors, the brig equipped to carry twenty guns. So yes, the British knew privateers were being built and fitted out in Pettipaug. Everyone did. But everyone also knew that the navigational challenges of the Connecticut River, beginning with the massive sandbar at its mouth, made the village immune to British attack. You just couldn't get a warship up there. So how did it happen?

There have always been two basic explanations for why the British raided Pettipaug. The first is obvious. We were building privateers and they knew it. Pettipaug was just a stone's throw from New London where the British had plenty of maritime resources keeping Decatur bottled up. The idea of destroying a group of privateers at their source rather than having to hunt them down one by one on the high seas was very appealing. If it could be done.

The other explanation is that the raid was carried out in direct retaliation for civilian attacks on the blockading squadron encouraged by the president's bounty. This was the same justification given for the bombardment of Stonington four months later.

President Madison's offer to reward citizens for sinking enemy ships had stirred up a real hornet's nest of activity in the New London-Stonington area based out of the Mystic River. Entrepreneurs prepared to gamble lives and money on the commodity of destruction arrived from as far away as New York City with a range of "infernal machines" as the British called them. Even the celebrated inventor, Robert Fulton, supplied torpedoes for some of the attempts to blow British warships out of the water for profit. All of this resulted in numerous attacks on the blockading squadron. One of these would lead directly to what we now call the British Raid on Essex.

On the night of March 24, 1814, a group of men lead by Captain Jeremiah Holmes, an extraordinary man who would later play a major role in the defense of Stonington, attempted an attack on the seventy-four gun HMS *La Hogue* off New London. They perhaps thought it was Hardy's flagship *Ramillies*, but Hardy had been called away to the British base at Halifax. *La Hogue* was the flagship of Captain Thomas Bladen Capel who had arrived as Hardy's temporary replacement. His squadron also included the frigates *Endymion* and *Maidstone*. Decatur had a new jail keeper.

As an American seaman, Holmes had been illegally pressed into service by the Royal Navy in 1804 and trained as a gunner's mate, seeing quite a bit of action at sea. He escaped in 1807 and made it back to Stonington. He was now one of the young bucks combining innate Yankee ingenuity with a strong entrepreneurial spirit in pursuit of destroying a British warship for President Madison's bounty. In Holmes' particular case, there was also a score to settle with the Royal Navy.

The torpedo used on this occasion was concocted by a mysterious man named Mr. Riker from New York. It consisted of a thirty-foot tin cylinder, seven inches in diameter, filled with seventy-five pounds of gunpowder and kept afloat with buoys. Operationally, it was towed four hundred feet behind a boat that used the tidal current to bring the device up against its target as the towboat maneuvered it into position. A twelve-foot crossbar fitted with hooks was meant to snag the enemy ship's hull and trigger the powder. Although an earlier attempt had failed when the towrope fouled and the contraption sank, the attack on the night of March 24th produced better results. The device did not actually make contact with the warship's hull but snagged its anchor line, triggering an explosion under the ship's bowsprit. The blast set off a mighty geyser and soaked a few British sailors as the column of water came crashing down on the foredeck. Although the attempt on *La Hogue* made a big splash both figuratively and literally it failed to damage Capel's ship. But it got his attention.

Captain Capel was not a man to be trifled with. Born the fourth son of the fourth Earl of Essex in 1776 he was entered onto the pathway of the officer class and apprenticed to the captain of HMS *Phaeton* at age six. He was a midshipman by the time he was sixteen and a full lieutenant at twenty. He served aboard Admiral Nelson's flagship at the Battle of the Nile and was soon after made commander and then full post captain. He had become part of Nelson's inner circle and commanded HMS *Phoebe* at Trafalgar. Capel clearly was not amused by Holmes' attempt to blow up his flagship off New London.

Eleven days after the British raid on Pettipaug, the April 19th edition of the *New England Repertory*, published in Boston, stated,

> We are informed from New London that an unsuccessful Torpedo expedition for blowing up *La Hogue* was fitted out at or near that place a day or two previous to the burning of the vessels at Pettipague and that it was understood the avowed object of the enemy was to retaliate for this attempt.

The timing of the raid so soon after a well-documented attempt by locals to sink the British command ship off New London, certainly justifies the revenge theory, and the privateers being built there clearly offered a tempting target. But it was not that simple. To get upriver the British needed more than a reason, more than a desire to sink privateers, more than the urge to avenge an attack on the squadron's flagship. To get up the Connecticut River and destroy the shipping in Pettipaug, the British needed local knowledge. They needed a pilot. They needed a traitor.

THE TRAITOR

Of all the elements that surround the British Raid on Essex perhaps the one that has produced the most colorful speculation, and fueled decades of folklore, is the true identity and motivation of the American who helped guide the British upriver.

There has *never* been any doubt that there *was* a traitor. Although neither Capel nor Coote mentioned the payoff of an American pilot in their reports, their boss did. Vice Admiral Alexander Cochrane, Commander in Chief of all British Naval forces operating on the North American station at the time of the raid, sent a dispatch to the Admiralty in London accompanying Coote's after-action report. Cochrane stated,

> Be pleased to acquaint my Lords Commissioners of the Admiralty that the Expedition under Captain Coote against the Enemy's Shipping in the Connecticut River having proceeded from information obtained from an American who volunteered his personal risk and conducted the Boats to the scene of action upon the promise of a very handsome reward should the Expedition prove successful, the Captains of the Squadron off New London, convinced of the importance of the Service rendered to Government subscribed for him one thousand Dollars, which I have directed their being reimbursed, and, as an inducement to others to come forward upon like occasions, I have directed a further Sum of One thousand Dollars to be sent to the Honourable Captain Capel to be given to the Person.

The equivalent economic value of $2,000 dollars in 1814 was nearly several hundred thousand dollars in 2013 terms. We are not talking about the dollar-for-dollar inflation rate over two hundred years, we are looking at the economic value of $2,000 in an age when people earning a good deal less than $300 a year could live comfortably, own a substantial home and raise a large family. This payment clearly underscored how important the British felt the services of the traitor were. But who was he?

Speculation ranges from a local man motivated by jilted love; a British spy disguised as a clam digger; Captain Coote himself disguised as a clam digger; local sea captain Jeremiah Glover; to a mysterious character known as Torpedo Jack!

The clam digger theory started up just a couple of days after the raid with a report from the April 14th edition of the *Middlesex Gazette*:

One or two men, with the enemy, whose countenances were recognized by the inhabitants as those who had several times called at the point to sell fish and clams, did considerable damage, by robbing the inhabitants and wantonly destroying property.

This sort of thing was mentioned in several contemporary accounts.

From the *Connecticut Gazette*, New London, Apr. 13, 1814:

Their conduct towards the inhabitants was unexceptionable, except that some cloths and plate were taken by a person supposed to be an American, who it was conjectured acted as a pilot and guide; and had frequently been there with fish for sale.

This was, no doubt, the genesis of speculation that Coote himself had come ashore and visited the village disguised as a fishmonger. The idea was melded into *Sea Lady*, a *Hardy Boys*-style chapter book for young readers written by Julie Forsyth in 1956.

Although it is highly unlikely that Captain Coote was peddling clams in Pettipaug, the folklore surrounding some of these stories is not as far-fetched as it sounds. There is pretty good circumstantial evidence that British officers did reconnoiter ashore in disguise. The small boat raids that were taking place on a regular basis were certainly used to take soundings and gather local information, which at times meant going ashore. Coote himself had at times disguised HMS *Borer* as a disheveled merchant vessel.

According to the *Connecticut Gazette*, June 12, 1813, Lieutenant McDonald of HMS *Valiant* landed at Black Hall, the former residence of Governor Griswold in Lyme, and requested some refreshment. "Capt. Griswold furnished him with such articles for a cold collation as his house afforded. After partaking of which, they retired, having conducted with perfect decorum."

And then there is the jilted lover theory. In the 1939 historical novel, *The Splendor Stays*, by Marguerite Allis, which liberally mixes fact with fiction, the traitor turns out to be a disgruntled local youth. He had been told off and threatened by the real life Captain Elisha Hart for attempting to court his daughter Mary, one of the celebrated seven Hart sisters of Saybrook. Apparently the young man had been a fisherman, but Mary's father called him, "a lowly red-headed clam-digger" not worthy of a daughter of the Hart seafaring dynasty. According to the story, in a mixture of class revenge and the misguided hope of raising his social standing funded by a fat British payoff, he sells out his town and pilots the raiding force up the river. Of course his red head is recognized on the night of the raid and his romantic aspirations don't work out.

In 1981, Marion Hepburn Grant—yes, Katharine's sister—wrote *The Hart Dynasty of Saybrook*. This non-fiction book chronicles the Hart family including the seven daughters of Captain Elisha Hart, one of whom married Captain Isaac Hull who had defeated HMS *Guerriere* while in command of USS *Constitution* earlier in the war. According to the segment of the book that covers the British Raid on Essex, the ill-fated romance of the fourth sister, Mary Ann, is explained,

> [O]ne of Elisha's seven beautiful daughters, she had fallen in love with a local youth who became a "Blue Light", or American traitor. After the English attack, he was accused of accepting a large bribe and piloting the enemy up the Connecticut to Pettipaug. When the young man failed to defend himself and disappeared from town, broken-hearted Mary Ann became a recluse.

According to the book Mary Ann never married and died of a broken heart.

More logically, some modern suspicion has been cast on local captain Jeremiah Glover. He claimed to have been abducted by the British while trying to parlay the release of his sloop that was tied alongside one of the privateers, which the British were planning to take. It is a virtual certainty that Glover was not in any way guilty of guiding the British up the river, he was in Pettipaug when they captured him. But did he, as some have speculated, make a deal to pilot them out in order to save the sloop upon which his livelihood depended? According to a post mortem of the raid in the *New York Commercial Advertiser*, Glover's sloop was one of only two vessels that were not destroyed.

And then of course there is Torpedo Jack.

James Tertius de Kay's *The Battle of Stonington, Torpedoes, Submarines, and Rockets in the War of 1812*, published in 1990, chronicles the British blockade of New London and the civilian attacks on the British squadron that indirectly led to both the raid on Pettipaug and the bombardment of Stonington four months later. In de Kay's account, Torpedo Jack first appeared on March 24th, the night of Holmes' attack on HMS *La Hogue*; the attack that has been blamed for inciting the raid on Pettipaug, two weeks later, even though Pettipaug had nothing to do with it. The attack occurred at two thirty in the morning. The British squadron immediately sent out picket boats to search for the terrorists but Holmes and his torpedo men had managed to elude capture and disappeared into the night.

But a mysterious American rowing a boat with muffled oars was picked up by a picket boat from HMS *Maidstone*, part of the squadron off New London. The man immediately proclaimed his innocence but he was slapped in irons. The prisoner was nicknamed Torpedo Jack by the crew. In those days, any floating bomb was called a torpedo and, Jack, or Jack Tar, was standard parlance for British sailors. When threatened with his life for committing terrorist acts against the Royal Navy, Jack changed gears and offered to guide the British up the Connecticut River where everyone knew there were privateers being built and fitted out. According to this account, although never documented in any of the Admiralty papers, the capture of Torpedo Jack on March 24th offered Capel an opportunity to strike the privateers of Pettipaug. Not only would it be the perfect payback for the attack on *La Hogue*, but destroying a nest of privateers was a very worthwhile endeavor in its own right.

Despite a lack of solid documentation, or even a proper name, Torpedo Jack emerges as the most likely suspect. It seems that Captain Capel had his man.

CHAPTER THREE

The Raid

Now armed with a willing pilot, Capel quickly put together a bold plan. Pettipaug lay a full six miles up the Connecticut River which was well known for its deceptively shallow areas and challenging navigation. But the real problem facing Capel and whatever force he might send was the massive sand shoal, which lay at the mouth of the river. It prevented any hope of getting warships up to Pettipaug.

The Saybrook Bar is the reason that to this day the Connecticut is one of the only major rivers in the world not to have an industrial port city at its mouth. As the swiftly flowing river carries natural sediment down its 410-mile course it is stopped cold twice a day at its mouth by the incoming Atlantic tide. The sediment is dropped and over centuries has built up the Saybrook Bar. Although the river's mile-wide mouth looks inviting, it is deceptively shallow. Before a proper channel was cut in the late 1800s, the average depth at the mouth of the river was only eight to ten feet. Larger ships built upriver, such as the *Oliver Cromwell*, had to wait for a moon or spring tide to get over the bar. In the case of the thirty-six-gun frigate *Trumbull*, also built during the Revolution, they had to wait eighteen months for a high enough tide. Even then, large casks had to be fitted alongside the hull and pumped full of air to decrease the vessel's draft.

With large warships drawing in the order of eighteen to twenty-four feet, it was clear that the idea of bringing the full weight of the Royal Navy up the Connecticut River was not possible. In 1814 the Saybrook Bar stood squarely in the way of a raid on Pettipaug. But the Royal Navy had already had several hundred years to perfect the fine art of problem solving. Capel decided to assemble a raiding force of officers, sailors and marines from his squadron and send them up the river in ships' boats deployed from warships anchored just off the bar. These were oar-powered vessels, but not simple rowboats. Barges and pinnaces were capable of carrying more than thirty men each and could be armed with powerful carronades in their bows. They were both the liberty launches and amphibious assault vessels of their time. Small boat actions, as they were called, were the backbone of some of the most daring raids of the age of sail. Although considered risky duty and normally relegated to lieutenants and sometimes commanders, Admiral Nelson himself was involved

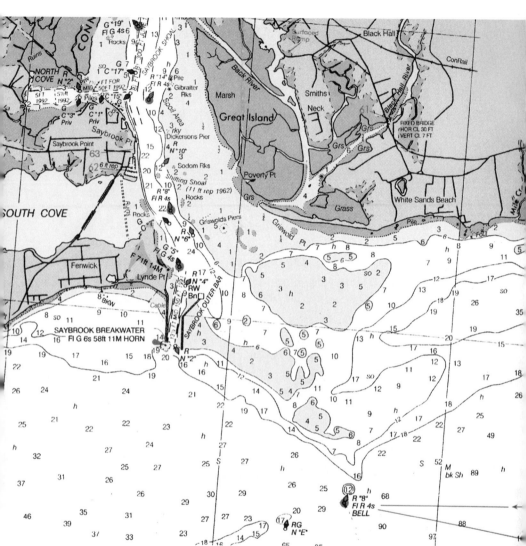

This modern chart shows the shallow depths created by the great Saybrook Bar. Long before the creation of the dredged channel protected by breakwaters, this natural obstacle prevented the British from entering the river with large warships but also gave the residents of Pettipaug, six miles to the north, a false sense of security. (National Oceanic and Atmospheric Administration, NOAA.)

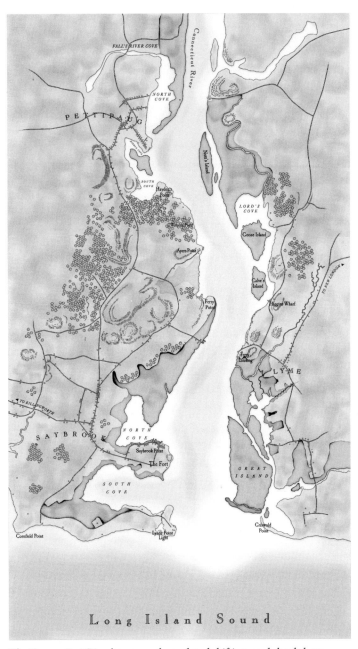

The Connecticut River's narrow channel and shifting sand shoals have always presented navigational challenges. Pettipauge Point is located six miles to the north of the river's mouth. (LCG/CRM.)

in a small boat action in 1797 at Cadiz, which nearly cost him his life. Now on April 7th, 1814 all Capel needed was the right man to lead the assault into enemy territory, far from the protection of his squadron.

Any of the officers of the blockading squadron would have given their eye teeth to lead the raid. Although it would be extremely dangerous, representing potential capture or even death, it also represented potential glory and almost certain promotion for those involved. Capel chose Commander Richard Coote, the thirty-two-year-old captain of the sixteen-gun brig HMS *Borer*. Coote had already captured or destroyed twenty-two American vessels in 1813 alone. He was also the first man to sail a warship through the rock-infested Fisher's Island Sound, a potential but hazardous shortcut from New London to the open Atlantic via Block Island Sound. Coote was a rising star in the Royal Navy and just the sort of man Capel needed to pull off his daring plan.

Richard Coote was a commander by rank, but because he was the commanding officer of a warship, he was called Captain by tradition. In all British reports, even those made by Admiral Cochrane and the secretary of the Admiralty in London, Commander Coote is referred to as Captain. All midshipmen aspire to become lieutenants, lieutenants have their eyes on commanders' ranks, and commanders aspire to be made post captains, a coveted rank that meant an officer was on the ladder to become an admiral if he performed well, lived long enough and didn't offend the wrong people. Coote was already well on his way up that ladder.

The idea of sending dozens of men six miles into enemy territory without the direct fire support of warships was not taken lightly. They could be trapped, captured or killed. But the opportunity to destroy a nest of American privateers was well worth the risks involved. In any case, the Royal Navy and officers like Thomas Capel or Richard Coote were not in the business of avoiding risk.

With Coote selected as the operational commander he would have worked with Capel to quickly plot out the details. The bulk of the raiding force was selected from the officers and crews of three larger ships from the squadron off New London. These included Capel's own flagship, the seventy-four-gun *La Hogue*, the fifty-gun *Endymion* and the thirty-two-gun *Maidstone*. Coote would bring a handful of his own men from *Borer*. As sunset approached on the evening of the 7th, the men and boats from each of the ships involved were sent over to join the *Borer* for the run to the mouth of the Connecticut River about fifteen miles to the west.

From the logbook of HMS *La Hogue*: "at 6 sent the Barge & 1st Yawl to the Borer: 7.30 mustered at Quarters. Borer weighed & stood to the Westward."

The log of the *Maidstone* reads simply, "At 6:30 sent a boat manned & armed to the *Borer* on service."

The log of the *Endymion* was even more explicit: "6:30, out Barge sent her manned & armed with the Boats of the squadron in Company with the *Borer* & *Sylph* under the Command of Capt Coote to destroy the enemy vessels in the Harbour of Saybrook."

The boats from the participating warships were put in tow of the *Borer*, which set sail at 7:30 p.m. as the black of night settled in over Long Island Sound. The *Borer* was accompanied by the twenty-gun ship, rigged, sloop-of-war, HMS *Sylph*, which could provide communication with the squadron and extra firepower at the mouth of the river if needed. Of course, Coote also had Capel's secret weapon aboard, the American traitor.

GOING IN

After a two and a half hour transit, the two vessels arrived off the mouth of the river at nine thirty on the night of the 7th, just as the moon had begun to rise. Within fifteen minutes Coote brought HMS *Borer* to anchor off the Saybrook Bar and was making fast work of dispatching the raiding force into the five ships' boats, which had been towed from New London. The *Borer's* own gig was offloaded and would take part in the raid. With Coote personally leading the raid, his senior officer, Lieutenant John Farrant, was left in command of *Borer*. It would have been tough duty for this officer, already a veteran of numerous major actions—including the Battle of Trafalgar, during which he was wounded—to watch 136 other men row off toward probable glory.

One member of the *Borer's* crew embarking on the raid had a unique relationship with his commanding officer. Fifteen year old Basil Elliott had been expelled from Hammersmith School in London in 1812, a potential embarrassment to his well healed family. But his older sister Mary had appealed to her fiancée, Captain Richard Coote, to take him to sea as a midshipman. He now accompanied his future brother-in-law who no doubt planned to keep him under his wing during the operation.

It was an impressive little armada. From the *La Hogue* were three ships' boats totaling sixty-eight men; a barge with thirty men commanded by Lieutenant Henry Pyne, a pinnace with twenty-nine men commanded by Lieutenant William Parry and a gig with six men under acting Lieutenant Fisher.

The ships' boats are deployed off the mouth of the river. (Monochrome reproduction of watercolor sketch by Victor Mays.)

From *Maidstone* was a barge with twenty-nine men commanded by Lieutenant Matthew Liddon. From *Endymion* was another barge with thirty men under Lieutenant Arthur Fanshawe. Coote was probably aboard Borer's own gig with six of his men, although he may have been in one of the larger boats.

A practical addition to the force was Assistant Surgeon Bowden of the *Endymion* who volunteered to accompany the expedition and whose services, as noted later by Coote himself, proved extremely useful. In all, the raiding force was made up of one hundred thirty-six officers and men, which included a detachment of at least forty marines commanded by Lieutenant Walter Griffith Lloyd of *Endymion*. Lloyd had three additional Royal Marine lieutenants under him. That brought the total number of lieutenants to nine. Along with the seven midshipmen who also participated in the raid, the ratio of officers to men was robust to say the least. No doubt every officer from all four of the participating ships would have readily volunteered for this dynamic operation.

The marines were equipped with sea service muskets, a shorter version of the Long Pattern musket commonly known as the Brown Bess. Firing a .72-caliber lead ball and fitted with bayonets these were the stock and trade of the Royal Marines assigned to ships. Sailors carried the standard issue figure-of-eight 1804 boarding cutlass and pikes or axes as needed. In addition to the men, officers would have carried their own swords and .56-caliber flintlock sea service pistols. The barges and perhaps the pinnace would have been equipped with either nine or twelve pound carronades mounted in their bows capable of throwing solid round shot, grape shot, or canister. It is probable that one or more of these boats carried a larger, twenty-four pound carronade. There was nothing in the Connecticut River that could have hoped to challenge such a concentrated force of men, weaponry and professionalism. Nothing, but the current and the wind.

The mission had been planned so the ships could anchor and deploy their boats well after sunset. They would reach Pettipaug by about one in the morning, do their work and be coming back down the river at the break of dawn before any serious counterforce could be mustered. However, during the weeks of early spring the Connecticut River experiences a phenomenon known as the *freshet*. As the 400-mile watershed, which freezes during the winter months, thaws and gives up its stored water, the river swells and the downbound current increases for several weeks. This seaward flow is so strong it overpowers the incoming tide and sends a massive plume of fresh water out into the Sound. On the night of the 7th, although the nautical almanac called for a flood tide that would have helped carry the British up the river, the water was still flowing toward the sea. This would be tough to row against but at least the southeast wind would have favored the trip upriver. Perhaps Coote had originally intended to get the barges under sail, but once in the river, the wind was coming out of the north, directly against them along with the current. It was going to be a long haul up to Pettipaug, but they were now fully committed.

The first American to notice anything out of the ordinary was the lighthouse keeper at Lynde Point, overlooking the very mouth of the river. According to the logs of the ships back in New London, the day had been fine and moderate but the evening seems to have been clouding up, partially ob-

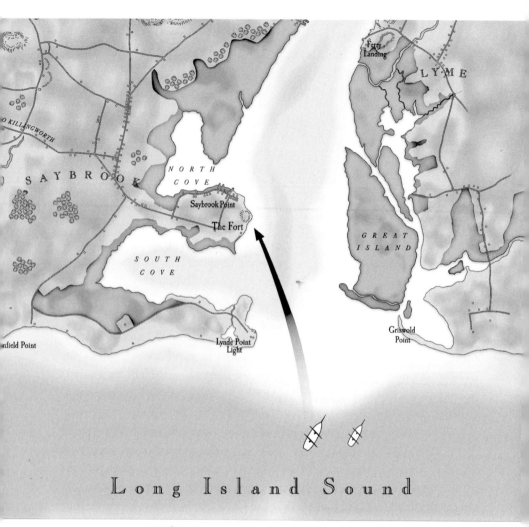

At 9:45 p.m. on April 7th the British anchor off the mouth of the Connecticut River and deploy six ships' boats stopping at the fort on Saybrook Point. (LCG/CRM.)

scuring the rising moon. It is uncertain what the keeper might have seen or perhaps even heard at this hour, but most accounts agree he saw something. *Connecticut Spectator*, Middletown, CT. May 17, 1814:

> Before 11 o'clock, on the evening of the 7th of April, six British boats were discovered coming into the mouth of Connecticut River, by the keeper of the Light-House, who immediately gave notice to the inhabitants of Saybrook Point, or platform, which is about one mile above the light-house.

Indeed Coote makes it clear in his report that the first object of the mission was to land a detachment of marines at the fort on Saybrook Point to disperse any garrison and spike the guns in order to eliminate their threat on the way back down the river. It was sometimes called the Old Platform, a large natural rise overlooking the river, a plateau from which several cannons could effectively control whatever came or went. The fort had been armed with a battery of cannons and a garrison through the first eighteen months of the war. The guns had engaged several small British harassment raids on fishing vessels and coasters sheltering in the mouth of the river. Now it had to be neutralized and it was up to Lieutenant Lloyd and his marines to do it. As the rest of the boats stood off in the river, the marines assailed the mound. Reaching its summit they found no garrison, no guns, no munitions, just a flagpole. Two years into the war, the mouth of the Connecticut River had been left completely undefended. Although the fort had been manned through the previous December a classic chain-of-command and funding turf-war between Connecticut and the federal government had left it without men or munitions at this critical moment. The government was willing to pay for the Saybrook garrison only on the condition that these troops came under federal authority. Connecticut refused to agree to this, leaving the fort unmanned until the situation could be resolved. If the fort had in fact been manned and armed with a battery of six pounders that April night there is a very good chance the British raid could have been thwarted right then and there. But it wasn't. Although it is probable the British knew that the river was undefended—an empty fort could hardly have been kept a secret—they had to land there to be sure.

The first fort, built in 1635, had played a significant role in the English settlement of the river. During the Pequot Wars it withstood a vicious six-month siege. But on the night of April 7, 1814 the fort on Saybrook Point did not save the privateers of Pettipaug. The *Connecticut Spectator* reported, "By

12 o'clock, a considerable number of the enemy were seen in the old fort at Saybrook Point where it appears they found nothing, neither met with opposition."

Within eyesight of the gun mound was the village and docks of Saybrook. A few dozen houses would have been within earshot, but considering the lateness of the hour and the probable stealth of the marines it is hard to say who might have recognized that the War of 1812 was coming up the Connecticut River. It wasn't the first time. According to the *Connecticut Gazette*, on June 27, 1813 Saybrook had requested gunboats and private guns for the fort after four British barges chased two small American vessels as far as the lighthouse and fired into the town. "Long shot were thrown from the barges among our dwelling houses, which have been picked up."

Throughout 1813 as small coastal vessels made their way through Long Island Sound, British sloops of war or barges inevitably chased them down. They would put into places like Killingworth Harbor, now known as Clinton, or the mouth of the Connecticut River where they could expect some protection from the brass six pounders of the State Corps of militia. But the night of April 7, 1814 was different. This was a raid in force and once the British left the fort astern and continued upriver, their destination could not have been mistaken: Pettipaug with its shipping, ship building, and newly built privateers.

Local legend suggests that a teenage boy was sent on horseback to warn Pettipaug that the British were coming. It is not clear whether the lighthouse keeper or the people on Saybrook Point sent him. Whether he existed or not he has been heralded in the mythology that evolved around the raid as "the boy Paul Revere of Saybrook."

According to local reports, the marines cut down the American flag pole as a calling card and then got back into their boats and continued to row north against wind and river. If true, there is a certain irony in that back in 1633 the English had cut down a pole bearing a Dutch coat of arms as they sailed up the river to build their first permanent settlement in Windsor.

Out in the river, progress was slow. At best, these large boats were barely making two knots of headway against the wind and current. It would have been backbreaking work for the men on the oars, but that was part of being a sailor in the Royal Navy in the Age of Sail — any navy for that matter. It took them another three hours to reach the harbor at Pettipaug Point around three thirty on the morning of April 8th.

Essex harbor is formed by a wide bend in the river. On the eastern side is

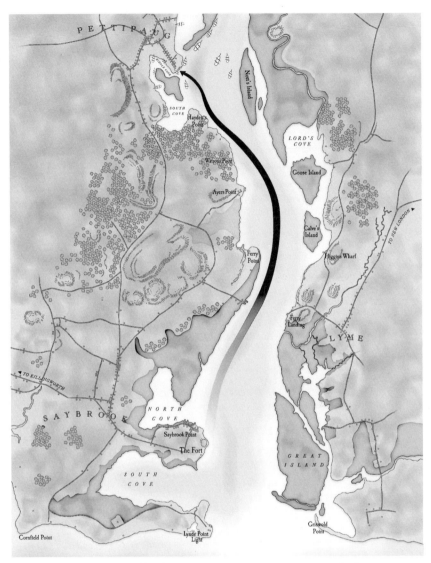

The British row up river and land at Pettipaug Point at 3:30 a.m. on April 8th.
(LCG/CRM.)

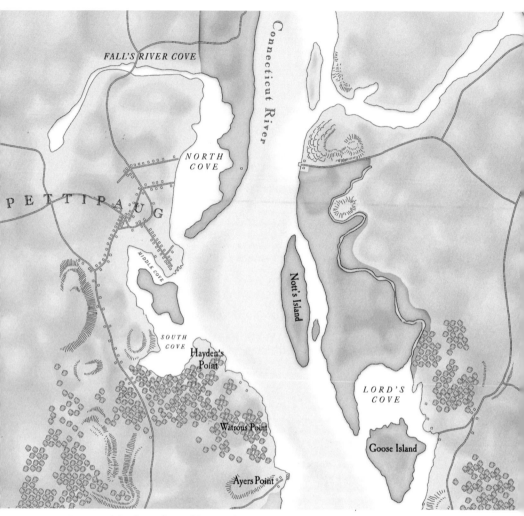

Pettipaug's harbor is framed by a wide bend in the Connecticut River. North, South, and Middle Coves define Pettipaug Point. (LCG/CRM.)

the long and thin Nott Island, running north and south with a small channel behind it. On the western side is Pettipaug Point, the peninsula formed
by North, South and Middle Coves. Hayden's Point defines the southern end
of the harbor. To the north, the river narrows again and disappears around
a bend at Brockway Landing, nearly three miles upriver. North, South and
Middle Coves are in essence inner, more protected harbors with the area
between Hayden's Point, Nott Island and Pettipaug Point defining the main
harbor.

Skirting the eastern end of the village was a wooden bulkhead against
which ships were tied. In the main harbor, and in the coves, other ships swung
at their anchors or moorings. The village's two main shipyards were the Hayden yard, just south of where Main Street reaches the waterfront, and the
Williams yard, a mile above the town up in Falls River Cove at the far end of
North Cove. There were at least three smaller yards as well, the most note-
worthy being Noah Starkey's shipbuilding operation in South Cove. Several of
these yards sheltered partially completed vessels still in their building stocks.

It is unlikely that there would have been any lights showing from the village
at this hour. Navigating by whatever glow the moon provided, Coote would
have just perceived the masts and dark hulls of the ships moored in the river.
The pilot would have nodded towards the point where a landing would give
the quickest access to the main street enabling the marines to rapidly deploy
into the town. Coote must have wondered what kind of resistance they would
be facing.

We do not know exactly how many men were on the waterfront as the
British rowed into the harbor. The American records are as patchy and disorganized as was their defense. No one would have ever expected the British
to come this far up the river. There were only thirty or so dwelling houses in
the village, which did not have its own discrete militia company. Pettipaug,
was part of Saybrook, so the mustering grounds, as well as all contingency
plans, would have been centered closer to the mouth of the river. More than
half of the men in the company lived over two miles from the village, and if
they had received any alarm at all they would have just as likely headed to Saybrook to wait for orders, as move toward Pettipaug. At this hour any response
would have been ad hoc and chaotic. According to those in the village, there
had been only a half hour warning before the British arrived. Others stated
that the inhabitants had no knowledge that the enemy was near until some of

Detail of ships' boats on Connecticut River. (Courtesy of Victor Mays/CRM.)

the vessels were already on fire. Clearly there had been no time to assemble and organize an effective defense within the village.

It is fairly safe to say that as the British rounded Hayden's Point and turned toward the waterfront there would have been only a mixed group of defenders, perhaps a dozen or so men, but probably not more than twenty. Some would have been militiamen, others simply volunteers. None of them were prepared for this. Local militia were required to show up with their own weapons, often fouling pieces, and twenty rounds of ammunition. The State Corps were equipped with government issued .69-caliber Springfield model 1795 muskets. The defenders most likely assembled on the rise overlooking the river between the Samuel Lay House on Main Street and the bulkhead. This would have provided the best high ground, about eight feet above the harbor. To their right the old West Indies warehouse, built in 1754, jutted out into the water adjacent to the landing at the foot of Main Street. Just beyond this, the Hayden shipyard with its large storehouse, dwelling house and building stocks overlooked the harbor and a number of ships on the wharves and at moorings. On their left, North Cove stretched over a mile into the darkness. Directly in front of them, the harbor spread east to Nott Island and south to Hayden's Point. Despite the defused moonlight the harbor would have been a dark void at 3:30 in the morning. The small group of impromptu defenders peered into the night looking for some sign of whatever they were up against. What should they expect? A boatload of British sailors? Two boats? Certainly no warship could be coming up the river. This was all new.

Apparently no officers had shown up yet. Captain George Jewett, in charge of the 1st Artillery Company, a prominent attorney, village selectman and the master of the local Masonic Lodge was not there, even though he lived right on Main Street. In his report to the Governor a few days later he wrote, "So few of the Inhabitants had any notice of their approach; and so sudden was the landing, that the marines were in many of the Houses before the Inhabitants were out of their beds." That still does not explain where he was that night. Perhaps he was elsewhere trying to muster his artillery company closer to Saybrook Point, or perhaps, as some have suggested, he was "indisposed."

According to the *Yankee*, in Boston, "An officer who commanded in the militia was called upon to turn out a force to oppose them, but he was either sick or pretended to be so."

The men on the waterfront were on their own. Apparently they did have a four-pound field piece, which would have given some level of confidence. It was quickly loaded and readied for action, as were all of their muskets. But what were they up against? Was this for real or just some kind of false alarm; the result of some panic mongers down on Saybrook Point? The British could not come this far upriver. Nothing like this had ever happened before. It is easy to imagine all of this going through the heads of these civilian soldiers hurriedly assembled there on the waterfront, without orders or leadership, or much of a clue as to what they were about to experience.

From the British perspective there would also have been some apprehension among the boats' crews. What would they find waiting for them on the waterfront? A well-equipped militia with several pieces of artillery that might have benefited from several hours warning? After all, it had been over three hours since they left the fort at the mouth of the river. Yet Coote and his officers held all the best cards. They would have known that no one really expected a raiding force to appear this far inland. There would not have been a contingency plan for this. As the American militiamen peered out into the darkness and did their best to prepare for a totally unknown threat, the British were fully prepared. Riding with them in those six boats was over two hundred years worth of the professionalism and discipline of the Royal Navy. The lieutenants were quietly keeping their men steady, reminding the oarsmen to keep the noise of the muffled rowlocks to an absolute minimum. It was important not to give themselves away just yet. Perhaps they could even make the landing undetected. That would be ideal.

In each of the larger boats, the marines rechecked their sea service muskets: hammers cocked, flint in place, extra cartridges at the ready. The gunner's mates had already loaded the carronades mounted on swiveling carriages in the bows. These weapons could do serious damage. They had shorter, lighter barrels than the long guns mounted in the broadsides of warships. They were not accurate long-range weapons at all, but they were versatile and effective. Whether the boats were equipped with nine or twelve pounders, they would have had the choice to load with solid or grape shot. Grape was a collection of one-inch iron balls held together in rope and canvas bindings. When fired, the bindings would be blown apart as the shot left the muzzle allowing the projectiles to spread out like large scale shot gun pellets. Grape was designed to clear a ship's decks of men. It was destructive stuff.

Some reports have suggested the British fired first, as they rounded Hayden's Point. It is possible, but it would have been a long shot and achieved nothing except to tip the defenders off. Coote reported it was the Americans who fired the first shots. It is likely the British would have wanted to get as close to their landing site as possible before making their presence known.

Did the defenders hear something? Did someone see the darker shapes of the boats in the moon glow? A trigger was squeezed. A flintlock sprang down onto the striking plate. Powder ignited—exploded in the barrel—propelling its lead shot into the harbor. The silence was shattered. Other muskets began to discharge into the night, their muzzle flashes contrasting the darkness around them. Whether an order had been shouted or it was a spontaneous reaction, the shooting had begun. Whoever was manning the field piece brought their slow match to the touchhole unleashing a brilliant tongue of flame, a sharp report, and launching a four-pound iron shot, the size of a hardball, whistling out into the harbor. There could have been no hope of accuracy but perhaps this show of force would scare off whoever was out there. The first shots had been fired. The quiet game was over.

The British returned fire.

THE LANDING

[O]n approaching it we found the town alarmed, the Militia all on the alert, and apparently disposed with the assistance of one 4 lb. Gun to oppose our landing . . . however after the discharge of the Boats' Guns, and a volley of Musketry from our Marines, they prudently ceased firing and gave us no further interruption.

— CAPTAIN RICHARD COOTE

Coote's cool, matter-of-fact assessment of his arrival on the Essex waterfront is typical of his entire report. No problem, no drama.

The muzzle flashes of the American guns gave the British a clear picture of where the defenders were, and perhaps even how many. When they returned fire with the marine's sea-service muskets and the boats' guns it would have made an impressive statement. Forty large-caliber muskets discharging, obviously coming from several different boats, followed by the explosive firing of three or four carronades made the balance of power very clear to the defenders on shore.

The fact that there are no reports of anyone on either side having been killed or injured at this point is a testament to the total lack of accuracy of these weapons, especially when fired blindly at night. Or perhaps it indicated the fact the British had not come to kill people, just burn ships. If they had fired grape shot, or even solid shot directly into the Americans it is hard to imagine there would not have been bones smashed, blood spilled and several fatalities.

It seems the British gunner's mates had aimed high, not into the defenders. Reports have it that the first cannonball reached the schoolhouse halfway up Main Street. Another ball was found in the hillside at the far end of town just below the Baptist Church, built there in 1811, almost half a mile inland. In the collection of the Connecticut River Museum are two pieces of shot said to have been removed from the far inside wall of the Samuel Lay House, about 150 feet from shore, just behind where many of the defenders would have gathered. One of them is a one inch, iron ball and the other a half-inch lead ball. A piece of grape shot and a pistol round? Another lead ball was found lodged in the staircase of the 1804 Ephraim Bound House, 325 yards up the street, directly across from the Griswold Inn. The ball found in the hillside above the town was said to be a twenty-four pound iron shot—a larger carronade than one would expect to be carried in the British barges. Yet in the Dauntless Club, which now occupies Uriah Hayden's house adjacent to the landing site, a twenty-four pound ball is still being used as a doorstop. A brass plaque identifies it as having been fired into the town by the British during the raid. Add to these the three or four additional balls in the museum's collection attributed to the raid and you get the picture. The British had brought some significant firepower and heavy metal to town.

What happened next is all a blur from the American perspective, and became fodder for countless newspaper debates in the weeks to come. As Coote observed, after the volley his men unleashed from the harbor, the Americans gave no further resistance. The militia and volunteers realized they were hopelessly outgunned and outmanned. They fell back from the waterfront and withdrew into the village as the British boats approached the landing at the foot of Main, now completely unopposed.

American Mercury, Hartford, April 12, 1814:

> We learn by our informant the following particulars: that the six barges arrived with muffled oars at Pettipauge, about three o'clock on Friday morning last, they landed about 270 soldiers and marines who immediately rushed into the village, posted sentinels and took possession of it. A few patriotic citizens behaved like men. They seized their arms and accoutrements and repaired immediately towards the scene of action, singly, by pairs, and half dozens, but want of union, regularity and officers, rendered their services ineffectual, so they generally returned as they came, only not quite so swift.

Were the defenders of Essex too quick to abandon the waterfront? Should they have held their ground and provoked an all out fire fight which they could not hope to survive? That is a question that would haunt the town for decades to come. As people woke to the sound of gunfire from the harbor they stepped onto the street to find the militia heading the other direction, followed within a few minutes by approaching Royal Marines.

Some of the six boats most likely came ashore on the landing at the foot of Main Street, a gap where the bulkhead that lined the end of the peninsula met the West Indies warehouse which sat atop a wharf jutting out into the harbor adjacent the Hayden shipyard. Others may have come alongside the wharves with men disembarking directly onto them. It was just after three thirty in the morning. The Royal Navy had arrived. Once the raiding force hit solid ground they got down to business. According to Coote:

The mobilization included local militia and State Corps of Artillery later joined by additional militia, volunteers, soldiers, marines and naval personnel dispatched from New London. (Courtesy of Victor Mays.)

The Marines were formed immediately on landing under the skilful direction of Lieut Lloyd of that Corps, took up a position as to command the principle Street and to cover the Seamen which employed in their respective Duties.

Lloyd would have calmly marched his men up Main Street at least as far as the Bushnell Tavern. With bayonets fixed and charges loaded they were quite capable of dealing with any last minute resistance. They quickly established defensive positions with pickets in case the militia got a second wind once their officers showed up and directed them to put up a show of counter force. But this did not happen. As the marines began searching the houses nearest the waterfront for guns, keeping an eye out for any signs of trouble, the seamen and their officers prepared to go about the business that had brought them here. Within fifteen minutes of stepping ashore Captain Richard Coote was in command of Pettipaug Point. It was Good Friday, 1814.

Providence Patriot, April 16th: "It has been the custom of the steady habit(ed) people of Connecticut, for some years past, to appoint Good Friday to Fasting and Prayer."

Was Capel's decision to launch the raid on Pettipaug timed to catch the steady habited people of Saybrook and Pettipaug off guard?

CHAPTER FOUR

In the Heart of the Enemy's Country

As the militia moved away from the village, they encountered scattered late arrivers moving toward the point in ones and twos. They told them there were no officers, no orders. They withdrew from the village hoping to regroup and find some leadership. Should they take to the high ground above the village and keep an eye on the enemy, or make their way down to their normal mustering grounds, two miles to the south, closer to Saybrook Point? No one had planned for this.

People who had somehow slept through the initial commotion were now hurriedly getting dressed and trying to figure out what was going on. How did the Royal Navy get this far up the river? What did they want? Were they going to ransack their homes and torch the town?

Connecticut Spectator, May 17, 1814:

> The inhabitants had no knowledge that the enemy were in the river, not more than thirty minutes before they were landed and had possession of the Point; and several of the inhabitants had no information that the enemy were near until some of the Vessels were on fire; there was not time after the alarm was given, to get the women and children off from the point, before the enemy were landed and amongst us, and commenced the burning and destroying vessels on the stocks, and on the water.

From the *History of Middlesex County, Essex-War of 1812*, J.B. Beers & Co., NY 1884:

> [M]any of them knew nothing of it until the flames from the burning vessels, which lit up the country for miles around, awoke them from their slumbers. Fear and consternation seized the people. Aged women and little children hurried off to Centerbrook, taking such valuables as they could gather, expecting that their homes were to be burned and fearing that the men would be put to death or taken prisoners.

The scene was chaotic as some men fell back from the village and others scrambled to round up their wives and children. At this point no one had any idea what was going to happen next.

DEAL, OR NO DEAL?

At some point, not long after the marines had secured the town and the seamen were beginning to set about their work, there was an encounter that has cast to this day a long shadow over the village. Coote says nothing of it in his report but on the American side it has been mentioned in dozens of accounts. No one was taking minutes so there is a lot of room for speculation, interpretation and even, "spin," depending on who is telling the story and why. Along with the true identity of the traitor, and the lack of an organized defense, this is the most controversial and often debated part of the saga.

In simple terms it is generally understood that Captain Coote, or one of his officers, informed an impromptu gathering of citizens that the British had come with sufficient force to carry out their orders which were to destroy the shipping in the harbor. Coote had not come to burn the town or harm anyone if it could be avoided. But reading between the lines there was another side to this coin. If his men were molested, they would defend themselves with deadly force and the town would be burned. This basic story was covered in a number of papers after the raid. Some were more definitive than others, but the concept of some sort of understanding being reached is relatively consistent. In some cases the story is told with a degree of empathy and understanding toward the villager's plight. In other cases it was told less charitably; implicating cowardice and willful capitulation.

American Mercury, Hartford, April 12:

> The officer . . . stated that his orders were to burn the vessels in the harbor, and not molest the inhabitants, but if any of the soldiers were insulted or killed, they had orders to burn every house in the village.

Connecticut Gazette, New London, April 13:

> Capt. Coote informed them that he was in sufficient force to effect the object of his expedition, which was to burn the vessels; and that if his party were not fired upon, no harm should fall on the persons of the inhabitants, or the property unconnected with the vessels, and a mutual understanding of that purport was agreed to. The enemy immediately after commenced the act of burning the vessels.

On the evening of April 11th, just three days after the raid, the sloop *David*, arrived in New York after two days sailing from Killingworth. Its master, Captain Bushnell, brought the first news of the raid to reach the city. It made the morning papers and was pretty damning of the local citizenry.

The *Columbian*, NY, April 12, 1814:

> From Killingworth we have no other report of the British Incendiary ex-pedition, than one copied from the morning papers . . . and that is equally incredible and disgraceful to the inhabitants. That 250 men should land at the place in the night and set fire to the shipping, is not to be wondered at. But that they should remain on shore till the next evening, by which time five thousand men might have been collected in arms to assail them is truly astonishing. The inhabitants of the Old Platform it seems treated their visitors with great civility and witnessed their divisions with great sangfroid. Some reports go so far as to speak of terms and agreements be-tween the British and Saybrook folks, by virtue of which the former were suffered to destroy or carry off the floating property unmolested, provided they did no injury to the goods and chattels of the people on shore. The subject however, is disagreeable: and we cannot but hope that subsequent intelligence and information will in some degree remove from our fel-low citizens the base and truckling spirit imputed to them in the present transaction.

The people of Pettipaug defended themselves in the May 17th edition of the *Connecticut Spectator*, published in Middletown. This defiant manifesto, in-cluded in full in the appendix, was picked up by a number of newspapers in-cluding the *New York Evening Post* on April 23rd:

> We the undersigned, inhabitants of Pettipauge Point and the vicinity, having heard of many incorrect assertions from individuals, and several strong statements published in Newspapers respecting the unfortunate af-fair that happened at this place, on the 8th day of last April, take this oppor-tunity of making a fair and candid statement of the circumstances which took place at that time.

After addressing a number of other points they squarely confronted the issue of a deal:

> We have heard that it has been stated, by some individuals, that the in-habitants of Pettipauge Point, made an agreement or compromise with the

enemy not to resist, if they would spare their houses and other buildings. No such agreement, we believe, was ever made; neither was it heard by the inhabitants of Pettipauge Point, until some time after the affair happened. And we think every such assertion ought to be treated with Contempt.

The Monday morning quarterbacking of the *American Mercury* and the other papers that rushed to judgment was all well and good, but on April 8th from the perspective of the villagers, the math was pretty simple. Option one: stay out of the way and the British will burn the ships and leave without damaging the town or injuring its people. Option two: take potshots at them in which case the marines will open fire and torch the homes. These were seasoned troops who had been at war with France for the best part of two decades. They could be civilized and orderly, but they were also quite capable of meting out death and destruction. It was a lousy choice, but it was the best deal the people of Pettipaug were going to get that night.

In point of fact there was no actual deal, and this is the big difference between folklore, hearsay and factual history. There was no unilateral capitulation as suggested by some newspapers written by people who had not been there that evening. There was no vote or show of hands, or organized decision by the village leadership to leave the British to their work in exchange for Coote's promise not to harm the town. There *was* no village leadership that night and there were no viable options.

CONSPIRACY THEORY

In addition to the whole controversy surrounding "the deal," there has long been a more sinister rumor that goes beyond justifiable acquiescence under threat of death and destruction. Some have suggested that the reason George Jewett was unaccounted for that night is that he was secretly negotiating an off-the-record deal with Captain Coote. The insinuation is that Jewett, Master of the Mount Olive Masonic Lodge, had reached out to Coote, a brother Freemason as the story goes, to exchange American capitulation for a British promise of not damaging anything but ships. Worse still, it has even been suggested this was all set up before the raid. The problem with all of this very cloak-and-dagger conjecture is that there has never been a shred of evidence to support either scenario. There is no need to look for a conspiracy theory here. The British simply planned and executed a bold and well orchestrated raid, caught the Americans totally off guard, and once they had landed with overwhelming force, the people of Pettipaug had no practical option but to get out of the way. For all of this the village of Essex would live under a cloud of censure for decades to come.

Jewett himself was roundly attacked by the papers for not being accounted for during the entire twenty-four-hour span of the British raid. His greatest accusers were two local men, Obadiah Spencer and Gideon Dickinson, who published a scathing "eye witness" account in the May 31, *American Mercury.* Jewett defended himself vigorously and questioned the political motives and honor of his accusers in the June 8th edition of the *Connecticut Spectator:*

> We thought at the time we gave the official account of the attack on Pettipauge, that the democrats would let the affair rest in silence. But Mr. Babcock's Mercury of the 31st ult. came out with a long string of bitter invective, which is proved to have been written by two infamous illiterate fellows, who, in the course of their remarks implicated the officers of the state government, of the state troops, and in short; every institution, of the State. In this account 'by an Eye Witness,' Capt. Jewett, and the company which he commands, have been most shamefully vilified. We conclude Mr. Babcock, will now, consign this false statement, with a host of others, to the repository of democratic fallibility.

But it is still not clear exactly where Jewett was. He may have been elsewhere doing what he could to organize his scattered militia company or he may in fact have been, "unusually and unpleasantly indisposed" as reported by the *American Mercury.* We will probably never know.

The accusations and defense, exemplified by the complete article in the *Mercury* and the town's response in the *Spectator* are included in the appendix. It went on for weeks and to some extent still does. Did the people of Pettipaug actually make a deal to save their homes in exchange for their ships, and their honor? Or did they do the best they could do under the circumstances? Four months later, when Washington was attacked and burned, the government and the president himself were forced leave in great haste. Yet the nation shook off any stigma and moved forward. Should Essex be any different? Two hundred years later you can call it Commemoration Day if you like, but many still have another name for it.

A better question to ask might simply be, why didn't the British burn the village? This was war after all. They sure had a go at Stonington four months later. To this there is a simple answer. The last thing Captain Coote wanted was a street fight in the back alleys of Pettipaug. He wanted to burn the ships and get out before large organized reinforcements arrived. His best chance at accomplishing this, and guaranteeing the safety of his men, was to not force the villagers into a no-option choice that would leave them no alternative but to fight back. As long as the people believed they were not going to be killed or their houses destroyed they would be far more inclined to take a rain check on heroics. If the British had started burning houses all deals, real or implied, would have been off.

THE BURNING

To make a short story of it, we were employed in burning vessels from daylight, at about half-past four, till noon. — LIEUTENANT PARRY, HMS LA HOGUE

Parry's timeline was a bit off but his point was clear: the British made good use of their time ashore. They landed at 3:30 a.m. and left the waterfront at 10 a.m. This was not a lot of time to destroy a harbor full of vessels, but they set to it with systematic zeal. As the Marines secured the town, the lieutenants and midshipmen broke the men up into teams and moved off to torch ships on the building stocks and along the wharves. They came equipped with incendiary material, which doubtlessly included torches, tarred oakum and pitch. Some would have carried flint-striking kits and probably whale oil-fueled boats' lanterns. Perhaps "blue light" signal lamps, which used a compound burned in open containers, may have also been used to provide temporary light or to ignite tinder for burning the ships.

Although almost everything aboard a ship is flammable—including the wooden hulls, the tarred rigging, the oakum-calked decks and the canvas sails—getting them burning was not as easy as throwing a torch on deck. Before each vessel was set ablaze, every effort was made to record the rig, tonnage, location, state of completion and anticipated purpose—merchantman or privateer—and when possible, the ship's name. Ships that had already been registered would have their papers aboard, their name and hailing port on their stern and their tonnage carved into the deck beam at the main hatch. For vessels that had not yet been completed, any officer was capable of estimating a vessel's tonnage, which was not its weight but the volume of its hull calculated by its length, beam and depth. As evidenced by Coote's detailed list of ships destroyed, meticulous records were kept as the burning proceeded. This was not chaos; it was organized destruction.

Essex from the air, a modern Brigadoon. *Looking southeast with Long Island Sound in the distance, Middle and South Coves are to the right and the lower end of North Cove is on the lower left. Nott Island can be seen directly across from the village. The Steamboat Dock building, at the foot of Main Street, is on the waterfront just beyond the red-sided Essex Boat Works. (Image by Tom Walsh, Shoreline Aerial, © 2014.)*

View from the hill. This photograph was taken from the steeple of the Congregational church in Essex circa 1890. This vantage point, on the hills behind the village, offers a similar perspective to the modern image above. (Courtesy of Essex Historical Society, Essex, Connecticut.)

The annual Commemoration Day fife and drum parade is hosted by Essex's own Sailing Masters of 1812. A dozen or more fife and drum corps from the region march down Main Street with the event culminating on the waterfront at the British Landing Site. (Photograph by Jerry Roberts.)

Panoramic view of Essex Harbor circa 1900. A steamship is approaching from the south. The West Indies warehouse, which the British entered, is on the waterfront. Just beyond, the Hayden homestead and the foot of Main Street are clearly visible. (Photographer unknown, CRM.)

Griswold Inn, 2013.
(Photograph by Jerry Roberts.)

Built in 1801 as the home of Captain Richard Hayden, this house was sold in 1806, and by the time of the British raid, had become the Bushnell Tavern. It later became the Griswold House as photographed here, circa 1865. Note the addition on the back. This is the old school house through which a British cannonball is said to have passed. Still in operation as the Griswold Inn, the establishment has been in business, in one form or another, for over two centuries. (Courtesy of the Paul Foundation, Essex CT. © 2000 Griswold Inn Collection.)

Departure. *This watercolor by Victor Mays depicts the deployments of ships' boats from HMS Borer at 9:45 p.m., April 7ᵗʰ, 1814. (Victor Mays/CRM.)*

This circa 1890 photograph, looking south toward Long Island Sound, shows the raised mound known as the Old Platform at the end of Saybrook Point. Although its battery had seen action earlier in the war, the British found it unmanned and without guns or munitions. (Courtesy of Connecticut Historical Society, Hartford, Connecticut.)

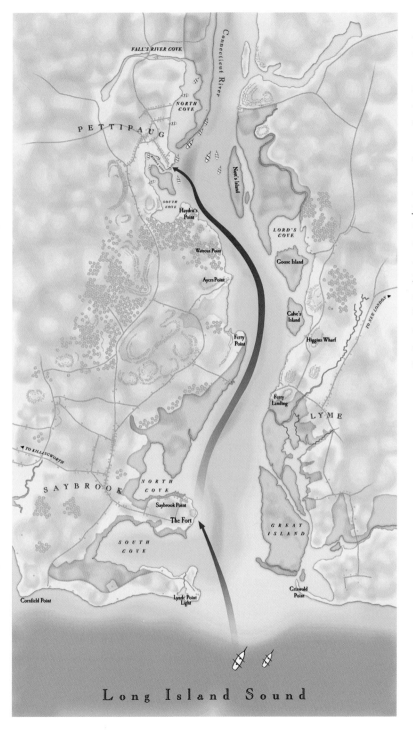

Going In. *The British anchored off the mouth of the river at 9:45 p.m., April 7th. They deployed 136 men in 6 ships' boats and proceeded upriver. After stopping at the old fort at 11:00 p.m. the boats continued north to land at Pettipauge Point at 3:30 a.m. on the 8th. Here they burned twenty-five vessels between 4:00 a.m. and 10:00 a.m. (LCG/CRM.)*

This depiction of Pettipaug in 1814 was recreated by Robert VanKeirsbilck from the 1881 birds-eye-view of Essex by O.H. Bailey & Co., Boston, Mass. Note the West Indies warehouse and the British landing site at the foot of Main Street and the 900-foot ropewalk at the top of town. (LCG/CRM.)

In shipbuilding towns such as Pettipaug, vessels were built in the open on stocks like this schooner depicted by Richard L. Brooks. (CRM.)

In this image, circa 1890, the West Indies warehouse (left) and the Hayden shipyard building are still intact at the landing site at the foot of Main Street. The British would have entered these and other waterfront buildings to remove ship's stores. (Courtesy of Essex historical Society.)

Both the Uriah Hayden homestead (left) and the red brick, Hayden-Starkey store (ship's chandlery; below left) are still standing directly adjacent to the waterfront. The Hayden Homestead, now the Dauntless Club, can be seen in the vintage image above. (Photographs by Jerry Roberts.)

Published in England in 1813, this cartoon by William Elmes characterizes American efforts to destroy British vessels off New London using floating bombs, known as torpedoes, as well as submarines and other "infernal machines." The British considered such unconventional warfare as dishonorable tricks and one such attack lead directly to the raid on Pettipaug. (Eon Images, eonimages.com.)

This section of the twenty-two-foot mural by Russell Buckingham, commissioned in 2006 by the Connecticut River Museum, depicts the British landing at the foot of Main Street. Although there are no known portraits of Coote, the central figure represents the British commander. To Coote's left is Lieutenant Parry. The Royal Marines commanded by Lieutenant Lloyd are shown on Coote's far right. (Courtesy of Russell Buckingham/CRM.)

As the crews fanned out, one by one, the vessels began to burn, sending columns of pungent black and gray smoke into the predawn darkness and casting orange and yellow reflections upon the water. Coote mentions that when ships were found tied alongside the wharves, they were "warped" out into the stream.

The reference to warping the vessels is very telling. Coote is informing us that they did not just run around recklessly torching ships along the docks. After recording a vessel's information, the seamen would use its deck windlass or capstan and heavy line to literally pull it off the docks either to a mooring or the ship's own anchor which could be hauled out and dropped with one of the barges. Smaller vessels could be warped off by hand. But why bother to cast the burning ships off? Again, it was because they did not want the burning ships to set the town ablaze. The best insurance Coote had against his men being fired on was to not cross this line. He was there to destroy ships, especially the privateers. If the town was torched intentionally, or even caught fire accidentally, the citizens would have had good reason to start shooting at the British. The whole thing would have rapidly devolved into chaos, a shoot-out on Main Street, and an inefficient atmosphere for completing the task at hand. Much better for Coote to keep his word, keep the carrot and stick thing going and get his work done. The British did not burn Pettipaug because it was in their own best interests not to. In fact, on more than one occasion British officers actually helped extinguish fires that had begun to spread from burning ships to a few waterfront buildings.

Norwich Courier, April 13, 1814: "Two vessels on the stocks were set fire to but were extinguished by the enemy when it was found that the fire was likely to communicate to the adjacent buildings."

From the May 17th *Connecticut Spectator*,

> After finding that a sufficient force could not be collected in time to save the property from destruction, some of the inhabitants, whose buildings were much exposed to the fire, went back to the Point, to try to save their buildings from the general conflagration with the vessels. Mr. Richard Powers, whose house had just taken fire from a vessel being on the stocks, made enquiry of the commander whether he might endeavor to save his house?

His request was granted by the officer. Clearly the residents interfaced with the British regarding the fate of their homes. The *Spectator* continues, "Capt.

Timothy Starkey, jr. asked the officer if he should spare the houses and stores from the flames? His answer was, that he did not know what might happen."

For the time being whatever unspoken understanding was reached served both parties well. It spared the villagers their homes and prevented a no-win, close quarters bloodbath. It certainly allowed the British to focus on the work at hand. Yet the willingness to spare homes and private property was about to change. Just five days before the raid, Admiral Alexander Cochrane had taken command of the North American Station. Over the next several months, he would show a much harder hand, ordering the bombardment of Stonington, the burning of Washington and the attack on Baltimore.

Meanwhile, Lieutenant Lloyd's marines maintained their pickets, patrolled the streets and kept a sharp eye for any sign trouble. They had to remain vigilant against the very real possibility of an attempted surprise attack by a counterforce of American militia. It is not known how far the British ventured within the village. Local legend suggests that Bushnell's tavern served as a command post as it was centrally located in the heart of the village. It is likely that the Royal Marines ventured as far north as the ropewalk but it was not destroyed during the raid. Lloyd probably wanted to keep his defensive perimeter concentrated to protect the lower end of the peninsula.

In addition to burning vessels, the seamen entered the chandleries and warehouses along the waterfront and the lower end of Main Street. According to Coote's report, "Several Stores were found to contain large quantities of Cable, Cordage, Sails & Spirits which were either destroyed or removed."

Near the foot of Main Street, seamen entered the West Indies warehouse and the Hayden shipyard storehouse, both filled with valuable ship's stores and materials typical of any port town. Directly adjoining the shipyard was the Hayden-Starkey Store, a ships chandlery and one of the few brick structures in the village. This was one of the buildings from which many items were removed including heavy rope, known as cordage. It is said that while some of it was removed to the dock to be loaded into the ships' boats, some was dragged into the street in front of the chandlery where, "This wretch, without orders, destroyed a large new cable by cutting it with an axe." The culprit was reported to have been an American, suspected of being the pilot who guided the British up the river. People seemed resigned to the British burning their ships and taking ship's stores, but the wanton destruction of good rope by an American traitor was infuriating. The same person is said to have also stolen some silver-plate, but it was recovered by British officers and returned to its owners.

Although there is no specific evidence that the British removed cordage from the ropewalk at the top of town, it would have been an obvious temptation. Another temptation may have been the large quantities of spirits mentioned by Coote. It was reported in Albert Dock and Russell Anderson's booklet that the British "stole" seven hogsheads of rum. A hogshead was a large, wooden cask capable of holding roughly 65 gallons of spirits. At that time every English and American soldier, sailor and marine was issued a half pint of rum a day as part of his "compensation." Mixed with water, sugar cane or molasses and lime juice it became grog. In rough terms, 7 hogsheads equate to 455 gallons or 7,280 daily rations. That is a lot of rum. It would have been worth a good deal of money. Coote justified taking rope and sails and other maritime supplies as legitimate targets of war and certainly worth something to the Royal Navy. Considering its importance to ships' crews, rum may have also been considered a legitimate navel supply to be confiscated. But the British did not take the 7 hogsheads of rum.

Reexamining the original newsprint from which Dock and Anderson transcribed this account, it is clear that they misread the word "stove" for "stole." That is a critical difference. The British smashed the rum, they didn't take it. The *Norwich Courier*, April 4, 1814 reported the barrels were not ordered "stove-in" simply to be destructive, but to "protect" the seamen from possible temptation.

As the first loom of dawn began to bring some light to the harbor at around 4:30 a.m. the officers set out with men and boats to burn vessels at anchor or on moorings just off the point. This is apparently when Coote identified the two ships he decided to take.

RESISTANCE

When the militia had departed after their initial stand on the waterfront, the viability of continued physical resistance within the town went with them. Yet, while the invaders and the invaded seemed to have maintained some sort of mutual, non-aggression arrangement, there was resistance of a more practical kind. While many packed their wagons and got out of town, several men and boys made attempts to save some of the vessels. A few accounts mention ships being towed into more remote locations in attempts to hide them while other efforts were made to extinguish ships that had already been set afire. In Middle Cove, a ship owner was reported to have put out fires on some of the ships and then lit bonfires nearby to "deceive the plunderers."

In the Williams yard, several smaller boats were intentionally sunk to protect them from enemy torches. This is the same yard where sixteen-year-old Austin Lay attempted to put out fires aboard the *Osage* despite repeatedly being threatened by British officers.

Although there are no contemporary accounts of physical resistance, gunfire or violence within in the village during the British occupation, there are two mysteries that suggest that some stories remain untold. First, when the Ephraim Bound House, built on Main Street in 1800, was being renovated in 1964, a lead musket ball was found lodged in one of the interior beams. The caliber of it indicates it was fired from a pistol not a musket. The shop is over 325 yards from the waterfront and it would have been impossible for a ball that size to have been fired by the British from out in the harbor. So how did it get there? Were shots actually fired in town after the landing?

Even stranger is this newspaper account published in 1893 recalling the old ropewalk that once paralleled the far end of Main Street:

> No one can remember or is living now when the rope walk was built, but it was there in 1812 because it was just in front of the old rope walk that George Harrington was shot by the British. He died many years ago, though not from the effects of the shot.

Was Harrington somehow hit by a random shot fired from the harbor as the British arrived? That is unlikely because the ropewalk is over 350 yards from the shore and the British would have fired from at least another 300 yards out in the harbor. So do these accounts suggest some limited skirmishing took place *in* the village? In 1899 Samuel Comstock published an account of the raid, which includes the passage, "In the course of that April day a few squads of men went gunning, and some desultory shots were fired." He also mentions that the brave defenders "huddled in the rope walk." Since no official accounts on either side mention any exchange of gunfire after the initial landing it is impossible to determine whether all of this is simply speculation or evidence of unrecorded events.

SPILLED RUM AND THE FORGOTTEN SWORD

If you read enough of the contemporary reports, and some additional accounts produced over the past 200 years, it is clear that a lot happened in and around town while the British were burning ships and searching warehouses. Most of this was not documented in official reports. When looking over these events it is important to discern fact from folklore. Many accounts contain a mixture of both.

There are many descriptions of people attempting to save their property in a variety of ways, from straight out placation to appeals based on an assumption of Freemason brotherhood. According to the *History of Middlesex County*, compiled in 1884 by J.B. Beers and Co.,

> One man, desiring to conciliate the officers, brought out a waiter with decanters of rum and glasses. One of the officers drew his sword and with one sweep cut off the necks of the decanters and smashed the glasses.

This story, whatever its origins, seems to have inspired a mention in Stuart Rankin's *Maritime History of the Town of Essex* which won first place in the Dauntless Club essay competition for students of Pratt High School in 1928. Young Mr. Rankin seems to have taken in a wide range of oral histories while also accessing old newspaper accounts in the local library. Although everything he wrote must be taken with a grain of salt, much of it is based on contemporary accounts. Of spilled rum he writes,

> The Haydens and the Starkeys were notorious Tories. One of the Starkeys owned a store on Main Street, and as the British marched up the street, he placed decanters of rum upon his porch. Bowing low, he said, 'Help yourselves, gentlemen, help yourselves.' The British commander whipped out his sword and with one stroke swept every decanter off the porch saying, 'I can buy all the drink that I want for my soldiers.'

There were certainly people in the area who sympathized with the British, but if the Haydens and the Starkeys were such well-known Tories, it did them little good that night. Between them they lost by far the lion's share of the ships that were destroyed.

According to an account titled, "A Pettipauge Anecdote" published in the *Providence Patriot*, on May 11th, a similar attempt to win British favor proved just as fruitless,

When the British marauding party lately landed at Pettipauge, the owner of a large ship on the stocks, known as a violent federalist, approached the British commander, and with much assurance, pointed out his ship, and hoped that would not be destroyed, as he was a warm friend of the British, and had opposed his own government and their wicked unjust war with all that lay in his power. 'Sir,' replied the British officer, 'the man who opposes his own government in time of war, deserves neither the confidence nor protection of any government.' The ship was burnt.

Reports of Freemasons making appeals to the British, believing many of the officers were also part of this secret society, appeared in numerous news accounts after the raid including this one in the April 15th edition of the *Salem Gazette*: "In the late attack on the shipping at Pettipauge, one man who had a vessel on the stocks, saved her by making known to the officer that he was a Freemason."

Rankin also referenced Freemasonry at work, "A vessel belonging to Mr. Judea Pratt of New York was saved because he gave a Masonic sign, and Lt. Coutts, recognizing it, ordered the ship to be left untouched."

The article in the April 15, 1814 edition of the *Salem Gazette* seems connected to a lengthier story published in 1955 in the *Hartford Courant Magazine* by Captain Jeremiah Whittaker. There were no references or footnotes citing original source material. According to the article, Nehemiah Hayden, of the Hayden ship building dynasty, who lived in one of the Main Street houses directly across from the Griswold Inn, had already watched several of his ships go up in smoke as the British burned everything afloat. In a shipyard at the entrance to North Cove was another ship in which he had a financial interest, un-launched on the stocks. When he saw that one of the burning parties had gathered kindling and set a fire under the hull, Captain Hayden strode up to the ship and began to scatter the fire with his boot. The officer in charge of the party warned him away and ordered his men to reset the fire. At this point, Hayden supposedly noticed a Masonic emblem on the officer's uniform. He quickly let the officer know that he too was a brother Mason and appealed on the grounds of fraternal bonds that the officer should spare his ship. According to the story, the officer made the command decision to call off his men.

Captain Hayden was so grateful he invited the young officer and his small company to his house for a taste of rum. The men cut across the back lots to the rear door of the captain's home and then down a set of steps to the cellar for the drink. According to some supposed tradition of good manners, the officer stood his sword against the wall at the top of the steps. At some point later when they emerged and rejoined the fray, the sword was forgotten. The story has it that the sword was then left where it stood and handed down from owner to owner every time the house was resold. Again, this is a story without provenance. It is doubtful that any British officer would have agreed to enter an enemy's basement to share a drink of rum during a combat operation. Furthermore, Masons did not wear badges on their uniforms. This was a secret society after all, not the Boy Scouts. The story of the forgotten sword makes for a great bit of folklore, yet this whole scenario seems rather unlikely.

But, was there a sword? In 2011, eighty-five-year-old Bud Lovell, who had once owned the Griswold Inn and the house in which the sword was supposedly left, swore to me the sword had been there, that he had seen it and held it, but it had disappeared at some point. Today the house has been heavily renovated and reinvented as the Griswold Inn's Goods and Curiosities shop. It is filled with modern treasures, reprints of old maps and vintage photos of Essex along with other collectibles for the upscale, bed-and-breakfast tourists. But the sword and the stairs that once lead to the cellar are long gone. It would be very easy to dismiss all this as folklore and hearsay, but there in the grainy photo that accompanied the *Salem Gazette* article, the sword is clearly shown standing on its tip, leaning in a corner next to the cellar steps. It seems there *was* a sword in the house; it's just not clear how it got there.

Fact or fiction, this was not the only sword the British left behind.

In 2010, a sword was brought into the Connecticut River Museum by Geoff Nielson, a man with a passion for history who enjoyed discovering treasures in local antique shops and donating them to the museum. On this particular day I met Geoff in the museum lobby with curator Amy Trout. Nielson presented the well corroded but recognizable sword complete with an oak cradle that he had proudly made for it. Etched into a shiny brass plaque that he had ordered and screwed to the base were the words, "Revolutionary War, Sailor's fighting boarding cutlass excavated from river bottom at Essex Harbour, Connecticut."

He knew this was special so he was really eager for our feedback. As I looked at the sword my heart truly began to pound. I have been in the history business for more than half of my life; I have seen and helped find amazing things. I have strolled the behind-the-scenes storage areas where curators' fantasies fill the air with the smell of old wood and the ethereal vibes of true history. But this one really had me going. I looked back up to Geoff, then Amy, both waiting for my thoughts. "Geoff," I began, "I have to tell you that this is not an American sailor's fighting cutlass from the Revolution." I could see he was crestfallen. He had no doubt spent several hundred dollars on the sword. He had personally crafted the oak mount and ordered the inscribed plaque. He had brought it to us out of shear generosity and a love of history.

Now I was standing there telling him the story he had been sold along with the sword was not true. He was an old fire chief and this must have felt like a class A false alarm. But his pain did not last longer than the time it took me to form the next words. "Geoff, this is a hundred times more important to us than what your plaque says." It was an 1804 pattern Royal Navy, boarding cutlass, also known as the Nelson Figure of Eight, because the Admiral favored its straight blade and simple design. The hand guard is stamped out of a single sheet of steal like two conjoined circles and bent around the grip to protect both the palm and knuckles during a skirmish. It is also called the Trafalgar Cutlass, because it was what Britannia's jolly tars fought the decks with on that glorious day. This was the personification of British naval history, and the most logical way it had ended up on the bottom of Essex Harbor was during the British raid on Pettipaug on April 8, 1814. This was the proverbial needle in the haystack, in this case preserved by two hundred years of river mud, now delivered to our doorstep. Geoff grinned and told me I had made his day. The feeling was mutual.

CHAPTER FIVE

The Ships

Burning a harbor full of vessels was no simple task. The vessels in Pettipaug came in many shapes and sizes ranging from small twenty-five- to seventy-ton sloops, to schooners, brigs and full-rigged ships ranging from one hundred fifty to four hundred tons. In terms of size the vessels ranged from fifty-five feet to over one hundred twenty feet long. Some were tied up to the wharves and bulkheads; others were on moorings while a few were still on building stocks under construction. Because of the virtual shut down of merchant trade along the coast, many vessels had been laid up, meaning that they had been partially de-rigged and in some cases housed over—the construction of a temporary roof over the decks of a ship to protect it from weather and prevent rot during long periods of inactivity. Coote's report lists numerous ships with their spars on deck, another sign of a ship being laid up, waiting for better times.

There were four basic types of vessels in Pettipaug Harbor. Sloops were single-masted gaff-rigged vessels ranging in size from forty-five- to fifty-feet long. Schooners were two-masted gaff-rigged vessels ranging from fifty to one hundred feet. Brigs were square-rigged two-masted vessels ranging from sixty to one hundred ten feet and full-rigged ships were three-masted square-rigged vessels ranging from seventy-five to one hundred twenty-five feet. The sloops and schooners had fore-and-aft rigs, which made them more capable of tacking to windward than square-rigged vessels. The general term "sloop" should not to be confused with the naval term "Sloop-of-War" which applied to warships with a single gun deck and carrying eighteen cannons or less. These were generally ship-rigged but some like the *Borer* were brigs.

As with most events surrounding the raid, there are contradictory records concerning the actual burning of the ships. Captain Coote's report includes a detailed account listing the twenty-seven ships they burned by name, tonnage, rig, location and state of completion or readiness for sea. One can imagine the lieutenants busily writing down all this information as their men set about getting them alight. Contemporary American newspaper accounts also include lists and partial salvage records compiled after the raid, including their original value and their salvage value, if any. Even among American

Basic rigs: sloop, schooner, topsail schooner, brig, full-rigged ship. (Commodore S.B. Luce, U.S. Navy, Seamanship. The Equipping and Handling of Vessels Under Sail or Seam. *New York: Van Nostrand Company, 1891.)*

accounts there are several contradictions in names, tonnages and the actual number of ships destroyed. Two hundred years later, trying to rectify the American lists with Coote's report remains a challenge.

One problem is that the British counted every ship they set fire to, whether it had a name or not. If it did not, they simply listed its rig and tonnage. Some American versions do the same and easily reach or exceed the number reported by Coote, while other tallies only counted vessels that were completely destroyed and omitted those on which the fires had been extinguished and the vessel had been saved, or rebuilt after being salvaged.

Coote's List of Burned Ships

Captain Coote's list of ships destroyed which was included with his report to Capel. [The source, ADM 1/506, p. 280, Document 3 – D, wrongly lists the date as April 9th.]

List of (27) Vessels destroyed in Connecticut River on the 8th of April (1814) by the Boats of His Majesty's Ships La Hogue, Maidstone, Endymion, Borer

Name	Rig	Tons	Built For	Guns	State & Condition Location
Young Anaconda*	Brig	300	privateer	18	Completely Fitted, Lying at the town
Connecticut	Schn	325	privateer	18	Completely Fitted, Lying at the town
Eagle*	Schn	250	privateer	16	Completely Fitted Lying at the town
Not named	Schn	180	privateer	16	Ready for launching (on the stocks)
Not named	Schn	150	privateer	14	Planked up & frame laid (on the stocks)
Not named	Sloop	90	packet		Ready for launching (on the stocks)
Not named	Brig	250	Merchantman		Ready for launching (on the stocks)
Factor	Schn	180	Merchantman		Ready for launching (on the stocks)
Osage	ship	400	E. India Trade	20	Masted & housed over, at wharf a mile above town
Atalante	Ship	380	E. India Trade		Masts & spars on board, at wharf a mile above town
Superior	Ship	320	letter of marquee	16	new & housed over, at moorings above the town
Guardian	Ship	320	letter of marquee	16	Masted & housed over, at moorings above the town
Unknown	Ship	250	Merchantman		Masted. Spars on board, at moorings above town
Unknown	Ship	300	Merchantman		Masted. Spars on board, at mooring above town
Felix	Brig	240	Merchantman		Masted. Spars on board, at moorings above the town
Cleopatra	Brig	220	Merchantman		Masted. Spars on board, at moorings above the town
Unknown	Brig	150	Merchantman		Completely rigged & fitted
Hatton	Schn	200	Merchantman		Completely rigged
Emblem	Schn	180	Merchantman		Lower masts in, Lying below the town
Emerald	Sloop	55	Cargo of wood		Ready for sailing, Lying below the town
Mahrata	Sloop	50	Ballast		Ready for sailing, Lying below the town
Nancy	Sloop	25			Ready for sailing, Lying below the town
Mars	Sloop	50			Ready for sailing, Lying below the town
Comet	Sloop	25			Ready for sailing, Lying below the town
Thetis	Sloop	80			Ready for sailing, Lying below the town
Unknown	Sloop	70	Ballast		Ready for sailing, Lying below the town
Unknown	Sloop	70	Ballast		Ready for sailing, Lying below the town
Total: 27		Total tonnage: 5,110			Total of Guns pierced for: 134

A number of boats, cables, cordage, sails, Moulds, shipwrights tools, working sheds destroyed

signed Richard Coote Commdr.

[*vessels Coote says were taken down the river by the British and later burned]

According to Lieutenant Parry, daylight came at 4:30. Nautical twilight, when the horizon can first be seen, began at 4:20. Civil twilight, when it is light enough to really see and do things, began at 4:54. Actual sunrise would begin at 5:22. Coote wanted to be back in the river as early in the new day as possible, before the enemy could organize in force. He had already lost precious time coming up the river against the wind and current and certainly did not want to be caught in the village in broad daylight facing a general mobilization. The race against time had begun the moment the British anchored off the mouth of the river and now the clock was ticking louder than ever.

Yet the dawn brought new opportunities. In addition to the vessels close at hand, the light of day revealed additional ships above the town. Coote elaborated, "As the day opened many others were seen on slips and at moorings higher up the river, and those were promptly set fire to by a small detachment under Lieuts Pyne and Fanshaw."

From the *Connecticut Gazette*, New London, Wednesday, Apr. 13, 1814: "A party of 14 men in the meantime were sent a quarter of a mile above the point, who put fire to several vessels which were on the stocks." These would have been vessels still being built in the lower end of North Cove, but there were still bigger fish to fry.

THE *OSAGE*

At the far end of North Cove, a mile above the village lays Falls River Cove. The Falls River has long been a source or waterpower for small mills and the cove was the location of the Williams shipyard. Here, two of the largest vessels constructed in Essex up to that time had been recently built, the *Atlanta* and the *Osage*, both full-rigged ships. According to Coote's report they were both lying at a wharf a mile above the town, which would have put them at the Williams yard. After the long row up North Cove, during which they would have diverted to deal with additional vessels along the shore, the two lieutenants and their torching crews reached these two ships and set about their destruction. Ironically, the *Osage* would become one of the better-known ships in the long history of this shipbuilding town—despite the fact that it never got to sea.

Coote's report says she was quite new, masted, but housed over. He lists her as being intended for the East India trade, which would explain why she was pierced for twenty guns. The term *pierced for* refers to how many gun ports

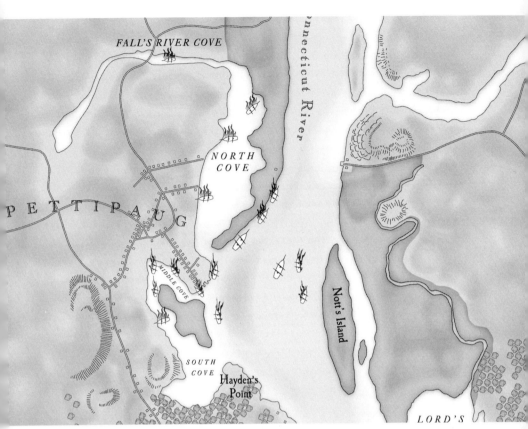

From 4 a.m. to 10 a.m. ships are burned in the harbor and coves around Pettipaug while the British occupy the village. (LCG/CRM.)

a vessel had been built with, not that it actually had cannons aboard at the time. The gun ports underscore the fact that a full decade into the nineteenth century, merchant vessels still needed their own protection in some waters. The ability to carry twenty cannons would also mean her owners could have sailed the *Osage* under a letter of marque as a commerce raider if they chose. But more likely she was destined to remain laid up until the war ended and trade resumed. The fact that she was housed over suggests the owners were not planning on putting her in any kind of service any time soon.

Some accounts suggest the *Osage* was out in North Cove at the time the raid began, but was towed into the inner cove while it was still dark in hopes of hiding her from the British who were still a mile to the south dealing with vessels closer to the village. Other reports suggest the *Osage* had not yet been launched and was still on the building stocks when the British reached the village. In an effort to save her, Captain Williams rallied the shipyard workers who knocked out the stops and let her slide into the cove.

Whatever the case, she was found in Falls River Cove and burned. She is remembered today not for being the largest ship built in Pettipaug up to that point, but for the efforts of a teenager to save her with a bucket and water. Sixteen-year-old Austin Lay became the boy hero of the British Raid for his legendary attempts extinguish flames aboard the *Osage* once she had been set afire. Although he was repeatedly stopped by the British and removed from the ship, he was tenacious and made at least three attempts to fight the fire despite the threat of having his tongue cut out. Decades later, eighty-three-year-old Lay still had his tongue and was still telling his story to another generation of Essex school children lest they forget the night the British came to town and were met with youthful Yankee pluck. He is buried in Riverview Cemetery overlooking North Cove where as a teenager he attempted to save the now legendary ship.

The *Osage* also became the single largest surviving artifact of the raid. For several decades her massive burned-out carcass was a local landmark and was harvested for its much-treasured wood, which was mostly oak and chestnut. In 1914 locals equipped with axes, chain, rope and tackle and a team of oxen removed much of what was left of her. In 1934 the shifting of spring ice revealed the last remnants of the wreck's massive keel, which was then dragged from the cove.

To this day, scattered about town, are fireplace mantels, walking sticks, iron spikes, chess sets, and other bits of folk art made from her bones. For generations the local high school's yearbook was called the *Osage* and there was an Osage Inn on West Avenue in Essex. Two large timbers, still charred by fire are now displayed in the Connecticut River Museum along with cannon and musket balls, the 1804 boarding sword and other artifacts from the raid.

Back in Falls River Cove, even today, despite the mansions that have sprung up around its southern rim, the massive planks of the old wharves of the Williams shipyard can still be discovered in the mud and overgrown tangle of its northwest shore. An unfinished mast lies submerged in the shallows, all within a couple hundred feet from where the *Osage* was burned on the morning of April 8, 1814.

Austin Lay at 83, in 1881. *As a teenager, Austin Lay had repeatedly attempted to save the ship* Osage, *an act of defiance that made him a legend in Essex. He lived until 1891, still retelling his story to new generations of local youth. (Courtesy Essex Historical Society.)*

In 1934, Samuel Hunt dragged the last major piece of Osage's *massive keel from Falls River Cove, although smaller timbers probably still remain buried in the soft muddy bottom. (Courtesy of Essex Historical Society.)*

HOW FAR?

Coote himself has left the door open to conjecture as to how far afield his men actually went to burn ships. If you look at his comprehensive list, which gives a fair accounting of where the ships were, the first to be put to the torch were those along the bulkheads and wharves in the village, and those un-launched on the stocks nearby. As dawn came, more were discovered in the coves and at moorings in the harbor. The farthest ships he specifically mentions were those, "Lying at a wharf a mile above the town." These would be the *Osage* and the *Atlanta* up in Falls River Cove.

On the other hand, later in his report Coote writes, "The object of the expedition being fully accomplished by every vessel within 3 miles of the town being either destroyed or in our possession, the party were at 10 o'clock embarked with the most perfect order."

Because Coote mentioned three miles, it has been suggested that the British went beyond Essex and perhaps upriver as far as Brockway's Ferry Landing, which is almost three miles above Pettipaug Point on the east side of the river. There is *no* documentation of any ships being burned there, either in the newspapers or the American or British lists of ships burned. Yet, in the local historical society there is some oral history suggesting that if the British burned ships in Pettipaug, they would have also burned those at Brockway Landing. It seems unlikely that Coote would have dispatched a boat to row out into the open river and proceed three miles upstream, against the freshet, beyond the concentrated protection of British forces in the village. Still, based on Coote's sweeping statement, it is possible and suggests the potential value of further research.

MYSTERY SHIPS

The British did not burn all the ships in Pettipaug. As the light of dawn allowed Captain Coote to assess additional vessels in the harbor, two of them caught his eye and he made a decision that would greatly affect the course of events to follow. These were two large, newly built, privateers—one a schooner, the other a brig. They were completely fitted out and ready for sea and Coote decided to take them down the river as prizes of war. He dispatched Lieutenants Parry and Liddon, each with a group of seamen, to take possession of them, get them ready for sea and load them with the ship's stores confiscated from the warehouses.

Coote lists the brig as the 300-ton *Young Anaconda*, pierced for eighteen guns and the schooner as the 250-ton *Eagle*, pierced for sixteen. Again, despite the gun ports, the cannon themselves would not have been aboard. Fighting vessels built in the Connecticut River were sailed around to New London, or more often New York, to be armed, provisioned and to sign aboard their crews.

Why did the British bother trying to take two American vessels down the river? The Royal Navy did not particularly need two more ships. Why not just burn them? The answer is simple. Captain Coote, as well as all of the officers and men with him, lived in an age when navies recognized that sometimes it took more than the love of king and country to fully motivate men to risk their lives in battle and put up with life aboard ships in the Age of Sail. Sometimes it took the possibility of personal financial gain. In this particular case it was the prize system. This was the naval equivalent to privateering and was employed by most navies including England, France and the United States. Just as with privateers, the idea was not to sink an enemy ship but to defeat it, capture it and put a prize crew aboard to sail it to a neutral or friendly port where it would be condemned and sold, or commissioned into the navy that had captured it. As motivation to officers and men alike a percentage of the value of a captured ship would be paid to the officers and crews of the capturing vessel. Decatur's capture and recommissioning of HMS *Macedonian* is a classic example for which his own share was $30,000. The prize system was a powerful incentive, giving even the lowliest seaman a financial stake in victory and a chance for officers to become quite wealthy over the course of their careers. The likes of Nelson, Hardy and Decatur had already benefited greatly from the system. Coote had no doubt already sent many captured vessels into the prize system and stood to come out of the war financially well rewarded for his zeal. The capture of the *Eagle* and the *Young Anaconda* represented money in the bank to everyone involved in the raid.

Coote's decision would radically change the course of the raid and cause the British to spend far more time in the river, and expose themselves to far more enemy fire than originally planned. In fact, one can argue that had they chosen not to take the captured vessels with them they could have been back down the river and aboard their ships by midday. But men like Coote had not built their careers on playing it safe and no one would have argued with his decision to try and take the two vessels out. As their shipmates were busy destroying all of the other vessels in the coves and harbors, Lieutenants Parry and Liddon and their men got down to the business of getting the captured enemy ships ready to sail down the river. Rafted up alongside the schooner was a smaller vessel, a sloop whose owner would add a new twist to the story.

The true identities of the two privateers that Coote attempted to take down the river have defied attempts to resolve. Coote said they were the schooner *Eagle* and the brig *Young Anaconda* yet none of the American lists include these names. None of them name another vessel on Coote's list either, the schooner *Connecticut*, also a large newly built privateer ready for sea. The British took the *Eagle* and the *Young Anaconda* with them and burned the *Connecticut* in the harbor along with twenty-four other vessels. Perhaps.

The *American* newspaper reports all simply refer to the ships Coote took with him as "the schooner and the brig." No names given. All of the American lists include a vessel named the *Black Prince*, a large, newly-built schooner, pierced for twenty guns and ready-made for privateering. Coote never mentions the *Black Prince*. Several modern accounts have suggested that it was in fact an advertisement for this privateer in the February 8th *New York Gazette & General Advertiser* that first attracted the British to Pettipaug and lead directly to the incursion even though the *Black Prince* is not specifically named in the ad.

Two respected local historians, Don Malcarne and Tom Stevens were also both adamant that the *Black Prince* was one of the two vessels Coote captured. Both the *Eagle* and the *Black Prince* were schooners. Is it possible they were one and the same? Did the newly built *Black Prince* not yet have a name board? If it hadn't been registered through the customs house at Middletown it would not yet have papers. Is this why it was not named in the *New York Gazette & General Advertiser*? Perhaps Coote simply found this yet unnamed schooner and called it *Eagle* because it had an eagle carved on the transom or figurehead. Interestingly, by tonnage and gun ports, the schooner *Connecticut* is a better match for the *Black Prince* than the *Eagle*. The true identity of the *Eagle* and the *Connecticut* remain a mystery.

As for the other prize Coote took out, the brig, *Young Anaconda*, there may be a similar explanation. Although none of the American lists have a ship of this name, they do all include an un-named vessel described as a "New Cutter brig," or a "Pilot Boat built Brig." So does the advertisement in *New York Gazette*. The tonnage and the number of gun ports match up relatively well to those Coote gave for the *Young Anaconda*. If these were the same vessel, where did Coote come up with the name?

Coincidentally or not, an American privateer named *Anaconda* had been built up the Connecticut River in Middletown for New York owners and had been captured by the Royal Navy in 1813. The word *Young* was often used as a prefix referring to a second, or replacement vessel. Was the new "Pilot Boat built Brig" meant as a replacement for the captured *Anaconda*? Or did Coote simply call it *Young Anaconda* because he had seen the original, which had been refitted in Halifax for Royal Navy service?

Was the *Eagle* really the *Black Prince*? Was the *Young Anaconda* the "New Pilot Boat built Brig"? We may never know. As the two vessels were prepared for sea, the burning continued.

CHAPTER SIX

Getting Out

CAPTAIN GLOVER

While Lieutenants Parry and Liddon were busy with the prize crews preparing the *Eagle* and the *Young Anaconda*, which were anchored in the harbor, they saw a dory being rowed out from shore showing a white flag. The man putting his back to the oars was none other than Captain Jeremiah Glover, a person who would become one of the key figures of this saga. Glover owned a small sloop with which he made his living on the sea. He and his wife lived in the village and he would have been just as surprised and alarmed as anyone to wake up finding the British in his harbor. So as dawn broke he made his way down to the waterfront to see if anything had happened to his sloop, which he had tied alongside one of the newly built privateers in the harbor. As Glover arrived, British officers and seamen already occupied the schooner, and they were busy preparing to get underway. This was the vessel Coote refers to as the *Eagle*. Glover stood there with a small group of his neighbors, observing the spectacle taking place in the harbor. What should he do? What he did, and where that led him is quite an amazing story, all the more so because we have it in his own words:

> While the enemy were burning and destroying vessels, at and near Petti-pauge Point, I was induced by the advice of my neighbors and friends, to take a white flag and go aboard of my small sloop to endeavor to prevail with the commander not to have her burnt. When I came alongside of my sloop which was lashed to the cutter built schooner that was in possession of the enemy, the commander demanded of me what I wanted or wished? I told him that the sloop was my property—that I was a poor man, and that I had no other means of supporting myself and family, but by what I could earn in that vessel; and that I hoped and trusted that he had feelings for the poor and unfortunate, and that he would restore me to my vessel. His answer was "Well, old man, if you behave well, perhaps we shall let you have her. Soon after I was on-board, I was solicited to pilot the schooner down the river. I told them I was no pilot."

The officer, in all likelihood, Lieutenant Liddon, wasn't going along with it. Captain Glover was obviously a man who made his living with his boat and would have known this river like the back of his hand. The officer insisted that Glover pilot them out. Even if the British already had a traitor, Torpedo Jack for instance, providence had just delivered an experienced Connecticut River captain right to their doorstep. Getting six rowboats up the river was one thing, but getting two large sailing vessels back out was another matter altogether. Still, Glover refused and told them he would rather abandon his vessel and asked that he be allowed to return to shore. The officer had had enough and ordered him to come aboard the schooner where he was taken prisoner. This was just the beginning of Jeremiah Glover's truly extraordinary adventure. When it was over, several days later, he went straight to a local magistrate and swore out an affidavit giving a detailed account of his experience and had it published in several papers, just in case anyone wondered what he was doing with the British all that time.

This affidavit now provides us with an American witness, a local sea captain on-board with the British during their escape. As historians, we couldn't ask for more. But can we trust his story? Was he the innocent man he claimed to be? If Glover was telling the truth, we have an American in the river with the British and we can compare his account with Captain Coote's. Glover could fill in some important gaps without British bias. On the other hand, if Glover turned out to be *the* traitor, or at least *another* traitor, his entire account is unreliable—a cover story for his guilty role in the destruction of twenty-seven American ships. He may not have been the one who guided the British *up* the river, but did he in fact agree to pilot the British *down* the river in order to save his sloop and perhaps earn a reward for his efforts? In the end, with a bit of solid research, it can be definitively proven that he was exactly what he said he was, an innocent man caught up in an extraordinary moment in history.

For one thing, the judge who took Glover's affidavit made it clear that he believed the local captain was telling the truth. Then we need to ask, what happened to him after the war? Did he pocket a large English payoff and leave town? A look at the census records reveal that Jeremiah Glover was still in Pettipaug in 1820, when the village changed its name to Essex. He was still there in 1830, and 1840. In fact he continued to live a quiet life right there in Essex with his wife until he finally passed away at the ripe old age of 86. His neighbors never ostracized him on suspicion of treason. He was an innocent man.

The absolute proof, if more was needed, took some serious sleuth work in the Admiralty archives in England. These days, an incredible amount of re-search can be done online, but there are times when actual documents have to be dusted off and sifted through. During the research needed to secure national recognition for the British Raid on Essex, the Connecticut River Museum had commissioned a researcher in the UK. We wanted to see the logbooks for all five of the British warships directly involved, for a period of two weeks leading up to the raid, and a month afterwards. These books had never been transcribed or even photocopied or microfilmed. It took someone with a digital camera going through the books page by page, photographing the left- and then the right-hand pages for each day. But as fate would have it, the book that mattered most, the log of HMS *Borer*, Captain Coote's own ship, is missing from the Admiralty archives. However, the *Borer's* muster book has survived. This is the record of who came aboard, when they did so, where they came from and why. On April 8, 1814, listed as taken prisoner in Saybrook (Pettipaug) is one Jeremiah Glover. Glover was captured as he tried to save his sloop, which was tied to the *Eagle*. Later that night, after the raid, he was logged into *Borer's* muster book as a prisoner. It also recorded that he was released four days later, on Tuesday the 12th of April, on Fisher's Island off New London, just as his affidavit stated. After the war, this absolute proof of his innocence, written in Royal Navy ink, was filed away and forgotten for the next two hundred years.

PARRY HOLDS THE KEY

With Glover's innocence proven beyond a doubt, we now have two empirical accounts written by men who were actually on the boats taken from Petti-paug, Glover and Coote. We would soon discover a third eyewitness who would help unlock one of the last great secrets of the story, the true identity of the man who sold out Pettipaug.

It was time to go back to de Kay's, *Battle of Stonington* and find out where he had come up with Torpedo Jack. The source given for the account was, "Joseph Goldenberg's article in the November, 1975 issue of *Mariner's Mirror*."

The *Mariner's Mirror* (UK) is published quarterly by the Society for Nau-tical Research under the patronage of the Duke of Edinburg. We managed to secure a photocopy of the article, which was stamped, "Marine Historical Association," the old name for Mystic Seaport. Even in black and white the title page was impressive with its ornate, over-the-top engravings of sea ser-pents, quadrants, octants and astrolabes, a crowned lion and a griffin—and

*Admiral William Parry, from his memoirs published in 1857. As a Lieutenant in 1814,
Parry commanded one of La Hogue's boats. His first hand accounts chronicle the capture
of Torpedo Jack and many details of the Raid on Pettipaug. (Longman, Brown, Green,
Longmans, & Roberts, 1857.)*

what appear to be a bunch of wizards peering into a round mirror with great interest. It looked like something Captains Cook or Nelson might have had on their wardroom bookshelves.

Pages 385 through 398 of the *Mariner's Mirror* contain an article entitled, "Blue Lights and Infernal Machines: The British Blockade of New London," by Joseph A. Goldenberg in 1975. It was all there: the story of Decatur's escape from New York and entrapment in New London, the terrorist attacks on the British squadron, and of course the capture of Torpedo Jack. So where did Goldenberg come up with all of this? His listed source is, "Edward Parry, Memoirs of Sir W. Parry, Kt. 42."

So who was W. Parry and where did *he* come up with Torpedo Jack? The name Parry sounded familiar to all of us involved in the project. It was epiphany time. Wasn't there a Parry mentioned in Coote's report to the Admiralty? There was. Lieutenant William Parry was one of the British officers taking part in the raid. He was third in seniority and commanded the pinnace from HMS *La Hogue*. He was the officer Coote had put in charge of getting the *Young Anaconda* ready for sea. As it turns out, he had written down everything just a few days after the raid, from the capture of Torpedo Jack to his whole experience going up the river in the ships' boats, the burning of the ships in Pettipaug and the saga of the trip back down.

Even before the British raid, Parry had already made a name for himself. In 1813 he published, *Nautical Astronomy by Night*, a subject critical to navigation at sea. It became a standard reference within the Royal Navy for years to come. After the war he became deeply involved with arctic exploration, leading expeditions, which included fellow veteran of the raid on Pettipaug, Lieutenant Matthew Liddon. Parry eventually made Rear Admiral and was subsequently knighted in 1829. In 1857 his son, the Reverend Edward Parry, Chaplain to the Lord Bishop of London, had his father's entire memoirs published.

TORPEDO JACK

After tracking down a copy of the book we now had Parry's first-hand account—transcribed by his son, but often written in his own words—of the capture of Torpedo Jack and its direct connection to the British Raid on Essex:

On more than one occasion, the enemy had endeavoured to destroy the British ships by means of "torpedoes," a species of "infernal machine;" and, during one night in April, an attempt of this kind was made on *"La Hogue,"* then lying off New London. "This," he writes, "ended in smoke, or rather in no smoke at all, for all the effect was the ducking of half-a-dozen people by the column of water forced up in the explosion." At the same moment, the *Maidstone* frigate detected a boat containing one man who pretended to have come off for the purpose of selling provisions. The lateness of the hour, however, and his muffled oars, combined with something uncommon in the appearance of the man himself, raised the suspicions of the Captain, who detained him in irons. The man would not allow that he had any share in the attempt to blow up the ship, but after a few days, offered, in consideration of being set at liberty, to pilot the boats of the squadron up to Pettipague Point, in the river Connecticut, where several American privateers and letters of marque were lying. "Torpedo Jack," as the sailors had dubbed their captive, was willing to prove the honesty of his intentions, by going himself, handcuffed, in one of the boats. An expedition was planned accordingly, consisting of six boats from: *"La Hogue"*, *"Maidstone"*, and *"Endymion"* under the orders of Captain Coote, of the *"Borer"* brig.

Torpedo Jack was real. But who was he? That bit of information would take yet another Hail Mary pass, from across the broad Atlantic.

OUTWARD BOUND

The object of the expedition being fully accomplished by every Vessel within 3 Miles of the town being either destroyed or in our possession, the party was at 10 o'clock embarked with the most perfect order and regularity in presence of a very numerous population. — CAPTAIN RICHARD COOTE

By 10 A.M. Coote had decided his work was finished and it was time to leave the shore. As the marine pickets were drawn back in to defend the embarkation, the harbor was filled with sooty columns of smoke and a pungent haze from the twenty-five vessels that had been put to the torch, some on the stocks, some at the wharves, some on moorings in the harbor, and the ship that the best efforts of Austin Lay had failed to save. The wreck of the *Osage* continued to burn a mile to the north graphically marking the extent of the British incursion.

Lieutenant Lloyd and his marines, bayonets fixed and at the ready, were the last to leave, covering the sailors as they loaded into the ships' boats the remaining materials they had removed from the warehouses. They rowed out to the two captured privateers anchored in the harbor. The officers took a very careful roll call of the men under their charge and reported back to Coote that all were accounted for. These men were from four different ships and no one wanted to leave anyone behind. As the marines finally left shore and joined the others in the harbor they would have been fully prepared to deal with any sudden acts of bravery from the good citizens of Pettipaug tentatively gathering on the waterfront.

There were no parting shots fired from either side, each no doubt glad that this moment had finally come. The Americans looked out at their smoke-filled harbor, the burning hulks and the enemy preparing to leave it all behind. This was not the moment for futile last-minute heroics. Coote could still send the marines back onto the waterfront if needed. The ship's barges still had carronades able to mete out death and destruction. No one had been hurt thus far, and both sides seemed content to keep it that way for the time being. Instead, those on the shore stood anxiously awaiting the enemy's departure so that they could get about the business of saving the vessels that were not yet totally destroyed and salvaging what they could. Their trial by fire was nearly over. For Coote and his men on the other hand, the real trial was just getting started.

Captain Richard Coote was now transitioning from one phase of his operation to the next. During the trip up the river he had employed stealth and surprise under cover of darkness. During the occupation of the town and the burning of the ships he had wielded overwhelming force in the presence of a confused and disorganized population. Now all the tables were turning. It was the broad light of day. Coote and his one hundred thirty-five officers and men were aboard two stolen privateers at anchor in the middle of Pettipaug Harbor, six miles from the safety of their own warships. He knew that by this time the villagers would have had more than six hours to spread the alarm. Eleven hours had lapsed since they had first landed at the fort on Saybrook Point. He accepted the fact that he would soon be facing more than disorganized local first responders. He clearly understood that the federal and state troops garrisoned in New London, along with the crews of Commodore Decatur's ships were only fifteen miles away and would have been mobilized. The Americans would soon show their strength. It was time to get out.

Getting back down the river would be no simple task. Rowing up under cover of darkness was one thing, but the British were now going to attempt to sail two large prizes of war down the river in the stark light of day through the heart of a fully-alarmed country. And that was not the only challenge Coote faced: nature and timing still had significant roles to play.

As the British prepared to leave the harbor, conditions were generally in their favor. The wind was from the northeast which meant it would have been on their port beam as they left harbor and on their quarter as they headed down the river. This would have meant a broad reach, which was ideal for both the schooner and the brig. On top of this, the combination of spring freshet and an outgoing tide meant the river was flowing quite strongly in the direction they wanted to go.

There were now dozens of people watching and waiting for the British to depart—wondering what was going to happen next. There is no doubt that some of the men serving in the local militia had made their way along the Saybrook road and then out onto Hayden's Point where they could keep an eye on the British. A few others finally arriving from the south may have also begun to make their way along the shore to the river near the harbor.

In addition to Glover, who was now confined aboard the *Eagle*, one of our best American witnesses to the events that unfolded is known to us only as, "A gentleman from Lyme." He was watching from a wharf across the river as the British prepared to depart the harbor. His detailed account was published in the April 29, 1814 edition of the *Salem Gazette* in Massachusetts, originally carried in a Middletown paper on the 20th; twelve days after the raid. Two hundred years later, after having reviewed the plethora of news accounts and more than a dozen memoirs and official reports, we have learned that like Captain Coote, with his concise and measured account of the raid, the Gentleman from Lyme, was a man who's observations we can trust.

A gentleman from Lyme has stated to a Friend in this city that he lives about a mile from Higgin's wharf in Lyme: that on the 8th inst. About 7 o'clock, A.M. he was informed that the British were at Pettipauge: that he immediately repaired to the wharf . . . that on his arrival he discovered the vessels at Pettipauge on fire, at the distance of about three miles, and the enemy on board a schooner, apparently intending to return immediately, the vessel, men and movements being clearly discernible with a glass.

The last time Higgin's Wharf appeared on any map was in 1890. In its place now is the Old Lyme Marina and Boat Yard about three miles downriver from Essex on the eastern side. From the dock, using a vintage ship's glass the harbor is clearly visible including the details of boats on the moorings. Our witness could easily have seen the vessels ablaze off Pettipaug Point, and amongst them, the schooner *Eagle*, which the British were preparing along with the brig *Young Anaconda* to make their run for Long Island Sound.

At last, with a growing number of people turning out to witness their departure, Coote ordered the anchors hauled. The great escape had begun. There was no turning back now. "At 11 AM we weighed with the Brig *Anaconda* and *Eagle* Schooner and proceeded with them some distance down the River."

But already the wind had begun to shift.

Under ideal circumstances, on a broad reach in open water with all sails up, either of these vessels could have sailed at five to six knots and would have been able to cover the six miles to the mouth of the river in not much more than hour. With a boost from the outbound flow of the river and the falling tide they would have covered this distance even faster. But these were not ideal circumstances. For one thing, they were probably towing the large ships' boats.

As the British rounded Hayden's Point, the wind was no longer with them. It was shifting from northeast to southeast and by the time they were in the river and heading south they were facing a headwind. Instead of a relatively fast reach down the river they were now faced with having to tack back and forth in the narrow channel. Both of these vessels were classified as sharp pilot-built, a modern design developed to be handy in tough conditions. But no ship can do well against the wind in a confined area where they cannot take full advantage of their "making" tacks before having to come about onto the less favorable or "losing" tack. In addition to the wind being against them, the down-bound current now presented a new set of challenges.

To steer a vessel, it must be moving through the water quickly enough for the rudder to have sufficient leverage to provide steerageway. With the wind now coming up the river slowing their speed through the water to perhaps a couple of knots, the flow of the river coming from behind made their rudders sluggish at each tack. The two vessels, particularly the brig, became slow in answering their helms. In simple terms, the vessels were not only making very little headway, they were increasingly cumbersome and hard to control in a river that can be unforgiving. Although it looks wide enough, the navigable channel is relatively narrow. Even today, well marked with buoys and even dredged at times, smaller sail and power boats still go aground on a regular basis each summer. In some places they encounter sand or mud, but

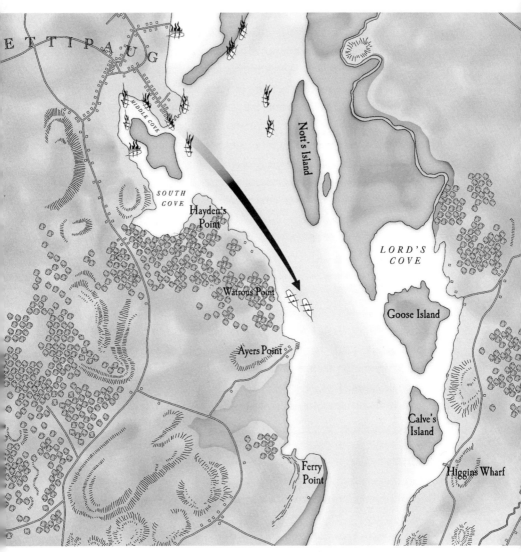

As the British leave Pettipaug with the two captured privateers, conditions on the river would pose challenges that would change the course of their withdrawal. (LCG/CRM.)

in a few others there are hull-cracking rocks just below the surface. For the British there was also the fact that these ships were new and had never been under sail before. They were probably not fully ballasted which made them tender, or "crank," and even more difficult to control. Add to all of this, the fact that, in a situation where the wind is opposing the tide, the river can become choppy and its cross currents and eddies more pronounced. Progress was slow and perhaps the two prizes were beginning to feel more like liabilities. Yet these ships were worth a lot of money to every man aboard. No one would have second-guessed the decision to try and take them out.

As the British tacked their way downriver they were no doubt being watched. Along the wooded shoreline stretching south from the point, a few scattered clusters of militia were most likely making their way on foot, pacing the captured prizes on their way toward the Sound.

Coote now had a clear view down the river and would have scanned both banks with his ship's glass. With the pall of smoke hanging above the harbor behind him, his focus would have been directed to the high ground that overlooked the river on both sides, about three miles south of his position off Hayden's Point. Instinctively, he would have known this was where the Americans would cast their net to try and prevent his escape. Today these sixty-foot bluffs are spanned by the Baldwin Bridge, which carries over a hundred thousand cars and trucks along I-95 every day. In 1814 there were no bridges on the Connecticut River, but these bluffs offered a commanding choke point, which, if used effectively, could make escape nearly impossible.

MAJOR ELY

The senior American officer in the area was Major Marsh Ely, commanding the Third Brigade, Connecticut Militia in Lyme. For the balance of the day he would be the man in charge of assessing the situation on the eastern side of the river, trying to pull scattered, under-strength units together and deciding where to best deploy whatever help he could muster. We do not know when Ely first learned the British were in the river, but by the light of dawn anyone within several miles of Pettipaug would have known something was seriously wrong there. The black and gray columns of smoke, from the twenty-five vessels that had already been torched, hung in the air over the harbor off the point.

By dawn, word from the *Old Platform* at Saybrook Point would have spread through communities on the west side of the river along with news of the actual landing in Pettipaug. At what point someone first rowed across to spread the word on the eastern side we do not know. It wasn't really necessary. Even without direct communication, the situation was obvious. As the Gentleman from Lyme reported, all it took was a look through a ship's glass from Higgin's Wharf or the hills of Lyme, and the devastation in Pettipaug was clear. By 10 a.m. when the British had been wrapping up their operations in the village, some of the members of the militia companies on the west side of the river, in Killingworth and Saybrook, would have begun to muster; while on the other side of the river Major Ely had already sent word to New London requesting all the help that could be sent. From the moment he first learned that the British were burning ships in Pettipaug he would have been looking for information, trying to get some communications established and deciding where best to allocate his resources. In Lyme, at Higgin's Wharf and Ferry Landing there seems to have been no dithering or shortage of energy. Very early on, the citizenry and the militia were working together to prepare to repel the enemy if they should come across the river and to stop them when they tried to make it back downstream. The Gentleman from Lyme reported:

> [T]he first object of the inhabitants at Lyme was to secure the vessels lying there: that they immediately provided a field piece and two ship guns – the militia collected expeditiously, and suitable preparations were made to wait on the enemy on their return.

Even by 9 a.m. Ely would have realized it was too late to try to coordinate an assault on the British in Pettipaug. He had not yet established communications with militia units across the river. The British would likely embark before there was any chance of reaching them. So the real decision was where best to try to assemble men and guns further down the river. On the eastern shore there was no solid ground where men and field pieces could command the river. Behind Nott Island was Lord's Cove and stretching south of that were marshy wetlands, which included Goose and Calves islands. Only behind these do the hills of Lyme rise up onto solid ground. There was really no practical place to get men and guns to the river and into a position to shoot at anything until the hills just south of Higgins Wharf rose up to become part of the bluffs now spanned by the Baldwin Bridge.

On the western side there was plenty of solid ground all along the river, which included some cleared grazing land and wooded areas. Hayden's Point directly overlooked Pettipaug Harbor. It is probable that as dawn broke some

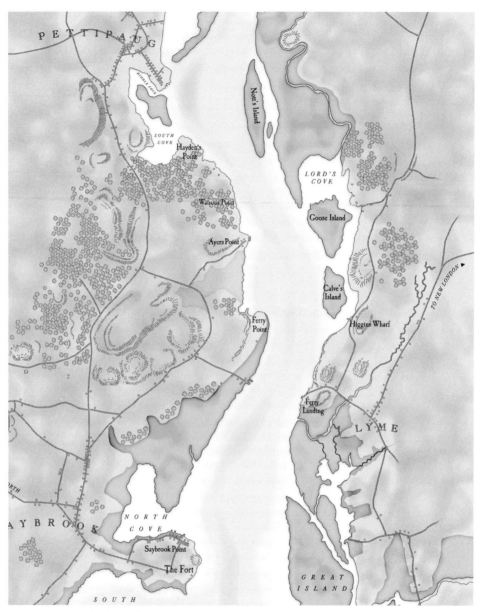

Major March Ely was faced with the daunting task of pulling together resources and organizing defenses on the eastern side of the river and coordinating with efforts on the western side in order to thwart British efforts to escape. (LCG/CRM)

small groups of men, perhaps even those who had left the waterfront as the British landed the night before, were already assembling there watching the harbor but lacking field pieces, or coordination. South of Hayden's Point is Watrous Point, not really much of a point but it certainly offers some high ground sloping back from the river. There were no roads leading into this area, most likely just some ox cart paths used for collecting wood. By 1814 the old growth hardwood forests in the area had long been cut down for ship-building and heating homes during cold New England winters. Building a medium-sized ship took several acres of hardwood and the average home ate up about 17 cords of wood a year. Pettipaug had already been building ships, and heating homes for well over a hundred years. Only scattered second-growth stands of trees and orchards lined much of the river along with farm-land and grazing meadows.

Further south, about a mile and a half below the village, was Ayers Point. It offered proper commanding views to both the north and south with cleared high ground, a small cluster of houses and a decent lane connecting it to the road running between Saybrook and Pettipaug. But the obvious choice for where to best try and stop the British from getting out of the river was the high ground on both sides at its narrowest point. On the Lyme side these were the sloping bluffs between Higgins Wharf and ferry landing. On the western side more commanding bluffs ran from Ferry Point south to the Saybrook ferry landing. This was the natural chokepoint that if properly armed could cause some real damage to anyone trying to come down the river. With Higgin's Wharf and the Lyme ferry landing as staging areas, and the perfect view corridor up the river from the bluffs between them, Major Ely set about organizing the available forces.

CHAPTER SEVEN

In the River

Sometime between 11:00 a.m. and noon Major Ely and those working to prepare defenses a mile further downriver may have looked north and observed the British as they rounded Hayden's Point and turned south. It must have been a bit surreal to witness the two newly built American privateers coming out of Pettipaug, under sail for the first time, knowing they were now crewed by British officers and men. They had arrived in rowboats. They were going out with warships. Yet anyone watching would have also observed that the wind was fighting them, and their progress was slow. Tacking to windward downriver meant an endless series of short runs forcing the ships to get dangerously close to the banks in an attempt to make all the headway they could before throwing the helm hard over and tacking back into the river. Every foot of progress was paid for with lost time. Time was not on Coote's side.

The British needed to get out as soon as possible, before the tide turned against them along with the wind, and before the Americans had a chance to complete their defenses on the bluffs. It was easier said than done. After struggling against the wind with the ungainly ships, they had only made a mile's worth of progress by 12:30. Coote complains in his report that the *Young Anaconda* with its square rig was proving extremely difficult to keep in the channel. . . .

And then it happened. Probably during a tack close to the western side of the river, the brig made contact with the soft mud and sand bottom and ground to a halt. Glover, as prisoner aboard the *Eagle*, estimated the grounding took place about a mile and a quarter below Pettipaug Point, which would put it somewhere between Watrous and Ayers Points. The schooner was immediately anchored nearby. This was a game changer.

For Major Ely, and any other American who happened to be looking, the sight of the captured vessel grounding to a stand-still must have felt like a godsend. Moments before it looked as if the enemy was going to tack downstream past American defenses still too disorganized to guarantee success. But that was no longer the case.

It was time for Captain Richard Coote to come up with a new plan. Once again, he would have picked up his glass and looked to the south, to the bluffs

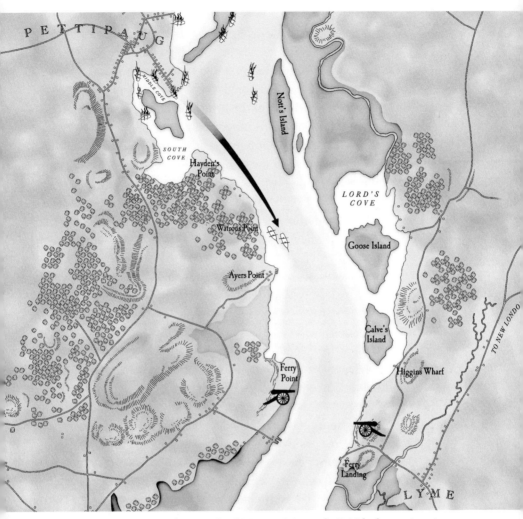

At 12:30 p.m. Young Anaconda grounds off Watrous Point as the British observe American forces gathering at the narrows downriver. (LCG/CRM.)

above the narrows—appraising the evolving situation. By this time, perhaps one o'clock in the afternoon, he would have clearly seen the mobilization that was already underway. Men and guns were gathering there, digging in for the kill. The wooded shore directly adjacent to the British position was quiet for the time being but Coote knew that would soon change. Decisions needed to be made quickly. The momentum of the British withdrawal had come to an abrupt standstill. A dead stop. As the Americans watched the schooner swing to its anchor, Ely realized he had just been granted more time, more opportunities to prepare. But what *would* the British do now?

For Coote the decision was obvious. The brig was aground on an outgoing tide. It had always been a liability, slowing any hope of a quick escape. Now it was dead weight. He decided to transfer everything and everyone to the schooner and set the *Young Anaconda* on fire. As the crew transferred men and materials with the ships' boats, fires were started within the brig's hull. The tally of American vessels that had been put to the torch in the past eight hours now jumped to twenty-six. For the Americans it was already the largest maritime loss of the war.

At this point, Coote had two rather dismal options. One was to continue downriver with the schooner and the small boats and run the gauntlet at the narrows in daylight, giving the Americans the opportunity to pound away at them from the bluffs. The other was to wait until the dark of night to continue. The second option would mean sitting, extremely exposed, in the middle of the river for several hours as the enemy's strength continued to grow.

Still, there were some positives. At their present position, the British were out of range of the enemy's guns at the narrows. Across the river on the eastern shore there were only marshy wetlands adjacent to their position. Close at hand, on the west bank, were patchy stands of trees with some cleared land. How soon would the Americans make their way here and open a direct fire against them? Did Coote gamble that there were no good roads for getting cannons into position there? Did he believe he could defend himself against any attack from the near shore? In the end, staying put offered more options and a better alternative to charging down the river in broad daylight. He decided to wait for darkness, still at least five hours away.

With all the ships' boats now tied alongside the *Eagle*, anchored not far from the burning *Young Anaconda*, 136 British officers, sailors and marines prepared themselves to sit out the afternoon, right there in the river. A few days later Lieutenant Parry wrote, "In these we lay four hours longer, eating and sleeping, within pistol-shot of the woods, in order to refresh ourselves for any further exertions which might be necessary to make." Apparently 24-year old William Parry was as unflappable as Coote.

Although exposed, Coote still had the ability to send a boat full of marines ashore to disperse any local threat along the river bank. Even if a gun crew showed up, his marines could deal with them. The schooner itself offered some physical protection and Coote still held a very concentrated and lethal force at his command. What Coote would not have guessed was that by this point, as he and his men dealt with this new set of circumstances, the American forces in New London had only recently learned of the raid, and were in the very early stages of mobilization despite the fact that it had been a full eight hours since the British had landed at Pettipaug Point and commenced the burning of the ships.

MOBILIZATION

Major Ely and the three companies of militia already in the area were part of the regular Connecticut militia system. In New London there were significant numbers of State Corps and federal troops serving under a strange command structure. As the war ramped up, Connecticut, not supportive of the war to begin with, had refused to send any of its militia units into direct federal service, as requested by the Secretary of War, to garrison federal installations like forts or take part in actions outside of Connecticut, like the invasion of Canada. But the militia had rushed to garrison Fort Griswold in Groton when Decatur arrived in New London in June 1813. After a conflict over command, the authorities worked out a strained compromise. The Governor agreed to allow men in the local militia companies to volunteer for service in federalized militia units on the condition that they serve under their own leadership, not federal officers. Therefore, the militia infantrymen and artillerymen of the State Corps in New London were under command of Major General William Williams, Connecticut State Militia, who had been appointed directly by the Governor and outranked Brigadier General Henry Burbeck, the federal commander of the military district that included Connecticut. General Burbeck commanded the federal troops manning the artillery in Fort Trumbull, and Williams deferred to him in tactical situations. The federal government supplied rations and pay for militiamen in federal service.

This detail of Official 1813 Map of Connecticut, *sanctioned by the General Assembly and created by Moses Warren and George Gillet, shows the area between the Connecticut River and New London. (Hudson & Goodwin, 1813. Courtesy of the Connecticut Historical Society, Hartford, Connecticut.)*

By the time of the British raid the relationship between Burbeck and Connecticut was already beginning to unravel, and the federalist general was losing credibility with the republican administration in Washington. He was replaced soon after the raid.

One of the hardest things to understand, by modern standards, is why it took so long for the American military forces in New London to mobilize and come to the aid of Pettipaug. Essex is only 15 miles from New London as the crow flies. It was a major seaport with two forts and three blockaded warships housing several hundred soldiers, sailors and marines under the various commands of Generals, William Williams, Henry Burbeck, and Jirah Isham, as well as Commodore Stephen Decatur with his blockaded naval forces. So where were they? Even if the lighthouse keeper had missed seeing the British, they had made their presence known at the fort on Saybrook Point by midnight on the 7th. By 4 a.m. on the 8th they had already landed in Pettipaug and started burning ships. At what point was the alarm sent to New London? In fairness we must remember that this was a world in which things generally moved by water rather than by road. Getting from Pettipaug, or even Saybrook, on the west side of the Connecticut River, to New London in 1814 was not easy. A rider would have to take the Saybrook road to the ferry, which is about four miles from either Pettipaug or Saybrook Point. Crossing the river on a ferry that was rowed or sailed, depending on conditions, could have taken at least an hour, perhaps more. Then it was another fifteen miles by road. The trip to New London could have easily taken four hours by a rider with a good horse. But the truth is everyone on the west side of the river had their hands full dealing with the immediate situation evolving around them. When help from New London was finally sent for, it was most likely requested by Major Ely in Lyme on the eastern side of the river, not from Pettipaug or Saybrook Point.

Despite all of this, even at the time, it was wondered why it took so long. According to the *Connecticut Gazette*, published in New London five days later, "Notwithstanding the enemy were on shore at 4 o'clock in the morning, it was half past 12 p.m. before the express arrived here with the information, although a report of the fact was brought by stage at 11."

General Williams own account, written the day after the raid, confirms the timing, "The stage which arrived here about 11'o'Clock a.m. of the 8th brought the first intelligence of sufferings from fellow citizens." Apparently there had been no Paul Revere dispatched after the first alarms were sounded to reach New London in all haste at all costs. By the time the first news did reach the city, the British were already weighing anchor and departing Pettipaug.

Williams logically assumed that the enemy had already departed. "It was supposed by the officers of the United States as well as myself that their work was probably completed and that they had descended the river before the Stage reached here and had arrived at their vessels, two of which were anchored just without the Bar." It took a second plea for help to prod Williams and the officers at Fort Trumbull to take action, "Soon after there arrived of the Stage one of the gentlemen from Lyme came in for assistance, and Capt. French of the artillery with his field-piece was immediately dispatched to their uses."

At last some help was on its way, but it would take time. Even if the mobilization began immediately, horses pulling wagons and artillery would not have been able to travel at more than three or four miles an hour for any distance. The *Connecticut Gazette*, makes it all sound very efficient and dashing:

> Every exertion was immediately made to send a force sufficient for the object; a body of marines from the squadron, a company of infantry from Fort Trumbull, and part of Capt. French's militia company of artillery with a field piece, and a considerable number of volunteers were soon in motion. A part of the marines and volunteers in carriages, Capt. French with his detachment and field piece, arrived at the river at four o'clock, at which time a respectable body of militia, infantry and artillery, occupied the banks on both sides.

Williams' report continues, describing a vigorous mobilization:

> Commodore Decatur ordered a body of marines from his squadron & General Burbeck a detachment from Fort Trumbull to aid in capturing the enemy. A number of officers and citizens volunteered their services, and all haste was made by taking up carriages & horses to reach the Lyme Ferry as soon as practicable. Col. Kingsbury, Captains Jones and Biddle with General Isham and myself arrived at the scene of action just before sunset.

Sunset was at 6:20 p.m.

Williams was later criticized by more than one paper for not having reacted more swiftly. In his defense, the call for help was late in being sent and by the time it arrived he and all of those in New London had every reason to expect that the British had already left the river. They could not have imagined that the British had gone aground while attempting to take two large American ships with them, and then decided to stay where they were, in the middle of the river until nightfall. After initial doubts, Williams was exonerated by the press.

> In our last week's account of the disaster, we stated in substance, among other things, that it was believed by many that the failure of the militia, to capture and prevent the escape of the enemy, was in part owing to ill-timed orders and maneuvers of Gen. Williams, who was stated to have had the command. We have since been informed by gentlemen of the first respectability, who were acquainted with the circumstances of this affair,

that the charge was unjustly made against the General. — *Columbian Register*, April 19, 1814.

"AT DEFIANCE"

By around 1 p.m. as the forces in New London were finally getting organized, the column of smoke now rising from the burning *Young Anaconda* had marked the British position even to those without a water view. A small number of Americans had begun to make their way through the woods and along the shoreline toward the enemy position in the river. No doubt some of the very men who had fled the waterfront and then spent the morning watching the British from Hayden's Point, were now cautiously approaching the scene.

As they reached a wooded area adjacent to the British position, they might have been surprised and perhaps a bit unnerved at how close they were. The burning brig was not much more than a hundred feet from the shore with the schooner anchored nearby. The question, at that point, was who was the most vulnerable? The British in the river or the Americans in the woods? Coote and his men, including forty well-armed marines were aboard the *Eagle*. This one hundred six-foot-long privateer with its thick, wooden bulwarks would have offered far more protection than the stand of trees on shore. It was still a warship after all, and these were not volunteers; this was the Royal Navy. Despite the change in plans they still represented the most powerful concentration of force on the Connecticut River.

But the Americans had recovered from the shock of being overwhelmed and invaded in the black of night. It was now daylight. This was their river. The tables had turned. Remaining within the stand of trees and being careful not to offer a concentrated target, they spread out and opened a sporadic fire of musketry that would continue off and on for the next several hours.

That morning as Coote had prepared to leave Essex and Major Ely had begun to organize his resources, the militia companies from Killingworth and Saybrook had also reached the conclusion that an assault on Pettipaug was not viable, even if they could have organized early enough to find the enemy still there. In Killingworth, Captain Amaziah Bray, in charge of the 2nd Company of the State Artillery had decided the most logical place to be was the Old Platform, the fort on Saybrook Point. He set off to reestablish an effective battery there. Despite the best efforts of people like Bray and

Ely however, even by midday, many partially assembled militia units were still understrength, disorganized and without a plan. While men had rushed from Killingworth to the defense of Saybrook, Captain George Jewett is not mentioned in any accounts as being present with his men. It is possible that he was out there somewhere trying to organize his company, but if so, it was not recorded.

The *American Mercury*'s scathing assessment of the local response was published on the 31st:

> [T]he Company of Artillery did not appear till afternoon. Unfortunately the Captain of this Company, George W. Jewett, Esq. who returned from New London county, the evening before, happened to be unusually and unpleasantly indisposed on that day, so that he was not able to ride to town until after sunrise the next morning. The first and second Lieutenants were soon upon the spot and it is believed that they collected about half a dozen men of their Company as soon as 2 o'clock p.m. At that time the invaders had left the shore but were yet in sight; and this little band of soldiers jogged along and joined the other forces near the entrance to the river. A small part of this Company however, who reside near the entrance of the river, it is understood, assembled in the forenoon on the margin of the river with the third Lieut. for the purpose of acting with other troops, assembled there from different quarters, in attacking the enemy when they descended the river.

Lieutenant Bull was one of the officers who managed to assemble part of the dispersed artillery company and make their way toward Ferry Point with its commanding bluffs overlooking the river.

As the *Young Anaconda* burned and the schooner remained anchored, Major Ely began to wonder what was going through the British commander's head. Why weren't they underway again? Was it possible they really planned to sit there until nightfall? At this point, the Americans had no guns that could reach the British where they were, further up the river. But that did not matter. One way or another, the enemy had to pass downstream between the bluffs where breastworks were already being prepared.

Time was clearly on the American side. But sometime between two and three o'clock Major Ely had waited long enough. He decided there might be an opportunity to end this now. Maybe it was time to give the British another way out of their obviously hopeless position. He scrawled out a note to the

British commander. He was diplomatic with his wording but by its haphazard penmanship, crossed out lines and misspellings it was obviously done in haste. In fact, it looked as if it had been written against someone's back. Ely was in a hurry. He probably still expected Coote to head downriver at any moment and wanted to get his message to him before they got underway. He sent Captain Charles Harrison out in a boat under a white flag to deliver it. (See facsimile of surrender note in the color section following page 116.)

Lieutenant Parry recorded the event with his now familiar mix of cool British sarcasm, wit and disdain:

> Lo, and behold, we saw a boat, with a flag of truce, coming out from Lyme, which place, with a point on the opposite side of the river, formed its narrowest part, and, we could perceive, was destined to be the grand rendezvous of their force, in their attempt to stop our going back. The boat came alongside the schooner, where we were now all assembled (having burnt the brig which had grounded); and such an officer, bearing such a letter, nobody ever heard of or saw, —a cobbler's hand, and many words wrongly spelt! It was to demand a surrender.

Coote's report was drier: "I here received a communication from the Military Officer Commanding in that district of which I have the honor to enclose herewith a copy."

Ely's note followed:

> To The Officer Commanding the detachment of his Britannic Majesty's Marine forces now gone against the Shipping lying near the mouth of the Connecticut River.
>
> Sir,
>
> To avoid the effusion of human blood is the desire of every honorable man. The number of Forces under my command are increased so much as to render it impossible for you to escape. I therefore suggest to you the propriety of surrendering your selves prisoners of War and by that means prevent the consequence of an unequal conflict which must otherwise ensue. Captain Charles Harrison is the bearer of this dispatch & will receive your communication.
>
> I am Sir with sentiments of the highest esteem your most obedient servant, (signed) Marsh Ely, Major Commanding the forces at Lyme & Saybrook.
>
> *NB* [*nota bene*, note well]: an immediate answer is expected.

Coote's report: "My reply was verbal, and merely expressed my Surprise at such Summons, assuring the bearer, that tho' sensible of their humane intentions, we set their power to detain us at defiance." This was a very British way of saying no.

Captain Harrison must have felt quite awkward standing there in the small boat in the middle of the river alongside this bastion of Royal Navy power and confidence. Their position was hopeless and everyone knew it. He may have expected to receive Coote's sword, but certainly not a dismissive rebuff. He would have saluted Coote and told his oarsmen to pull back to shore to deliver Coote's message to Major Ely. But as he left the *Eagle* behind, his lesson in indefatigable Britishness in the face of potential doom was not quite complete.

Parry elaborated, "The style in which this was demanded was enough to make us hold it in the greatest possible contempt. Three cheers for Old England, before the boat was out of hearing, was the most expressive answer to their presumptuous demand."

Marsh Ely received the rebuff which was not even dignified with a written response. The atmosphere was thickening. The stage for the next act in this strange drama was being reset. The reinforcements from New London were on their way with Captain French's artillery detachment and some of Decatur's marines in the vanguard. On both sides of the river people were getting better organized.

Throughout the afternoon, as the British waited for darkness, the men on the adjacent bank maintained their sporadic musketry fire. It was a nuisance but not worth sending a boat ashore. The British accounts do not mention returning the American's fire but new archeological evidence suggests they did. It seems that at least one round of canister shot was fired at the shore and a few British muskets and pistols were discharged. It was not a pitched battle by any means. The British were probably just making sure the Americans did not assemble a concentrated force this close to their position. If a field piece had shown up, things would have been different. Parry writes, "Whilst daylight lasted, they were afraid to bring anything against us where we then lay, for we would have landed immediately, and dispersed them."

Meanwhile, a mile and half downstream, the Americans continued to strengthen their positions, getting men and field pieces into the best possible locations to hit the British whenever they made their move. But the afternoon was wearing on.

At around 3:30 p.m., back aboard HMS *La Hogue* with the squadron off

New London, Captain Capel would have expected Coote and his men to have already made their way back to their ships if all had gone as planned. But signals from *Sylph* revealed that they had not. At 4 p.m. Capel decided to send the *Maidstone* with her thirty-eight guns to the mouth of the river to provide better communications and fire support in case a stronger show of force should be required off Saybrook Point. In fact, Capel put a special pilot with local knowledge aboard on the off chance that *Maidstone*, or at least her ships' boats, might need to try and go further in. The ship's log shows that she weighed anchor at 4:40 p.m. and ran along the coast to close with *Sylph* and *Borer*.

Earlier in the afternoon, and after learning that Captain Bray was at the fort on Saybrook Point with artillery, Ely had dispatched a messenger across to coordinate efforts on the west side of the river. Bray was told to bring his company further north to the bluffs across from Higgins Wharf. This would have been Ferry Point, which offered a perfect line of sight up the river to the British position. They would still be out of range, but everyone knew they would have to come down sooner or later. According to the *Salem Gazette*, quoting the Gentleman from Lyme:

> On the return of the messenger, Gen. Williams, Gen. Isham, Col. Kingsbury, Captains Jones and Biddle, with a number of Commodore Decatur's marines, had arrived, and numbers of volunteers, U.S. officers, and privates.

At last the troops had arrived. Not just troops but the navy and marines. The Gentleman from Lyme continued:

> Capt. Biddle, with the marines and volunteers, manned a sloop, and took a station a few rods below the wharf, near the point, on which also two pieces were placed.

Captains Biddle and Jones actually commandeered three sloops from Higgins Wharf and Ferry Landing and set about getting them equipped for action in the river. In the end, they were only able to arm and crew one of them, which Biddle got into the river below Calves Island just north of the breastworks Ely's men had been preparing. The United States Navy was in the river.

The reinforcements from New London offered a huge influx of leadership and manpower. The positions that Ely had organized were reinforced. On the 1868 Beers map of Old Lyme, the 1812 breastworks were indicated as still

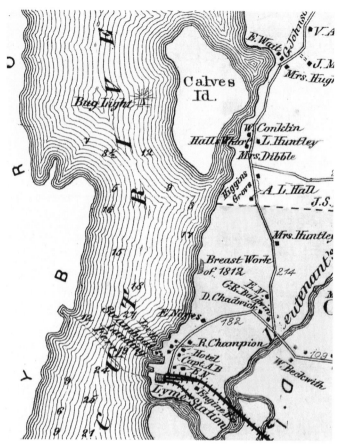

Detail of Old Lyme from Beers Atlas of New London County 1868 shows "Breastwork of 1812," located just south of the Baldwin Bridge site. Fifty-four years after the British Raid on Essex, the remains of the gun battery were still intact enough to be included on this map. (F.W. Beers. New York: A.D. Ellis & G.G. Soule. Courtesy of the New London County Historical Society, New London, CT.)

American militia with a six pounder of the State Corps of Artillery rush to engage the British position in river. (Courtesy of Victor Mays.)

being there, over fifty years later. There was now considerable manpower on both sides of the river. With two generals, two navy captains and several other officers in addition to Major Ely who had been on the scene all day, there was certainly no shortage of military brainpower. But the day was running out, the afternoon had turned to evening and the light was beginning to fade.

Hundreds of Americans and probably at least eight field pieces were now in position to blow the British out of the water. But they were still there, above Ayers Point, clearly marked by the smoldering hulk of the *Young Anaconda* and the masts of the privateer *Eagle*. It had become increasingly clear that Coote was going to wait for nightfall to come down the river. In the blackness of the overcast night there was a very real possibility that the British could get through the narrows relatively intact. As the clocks ticked and the light continued to fade it looked like time was now on Coote's side again. All he needed was darkness, and it was coming.

There was a sudden sense of urgency in the American camp. With time running out something had to be done to dislodge the British and force them down the river. Whether on the initiative of General Williams, who had just arrived, or more likely a bit earlier through Major Ely, a messenger was rushed across the river with urgent orders for Captain Bray to get one of his company's guns at Ferry Point up stream and into a position to engage the British before sunset.

It is easy to ask why they didn't send a gun upriver several hours earlier, but the Americans knew the British would have to pass the narrows at some point. They clearly thought it was best to concentrate all of their armament where they knew it would do the most good. However with darkness approaching, it was now a race to get something up the river that could cause serious damage to the British, or at least force them to come down before daylight ran out. Lieutenant Bull and his ad hoc gun crew were dispatched with their brass six pounder to head north and bring some American firepower to the enemy at last.

From Bull's own account:

> Your memorialist being 1st Lieutenant in the first Company of Artillery in the State Corps having volunteered his Services, with one of the Field pieces belonging to said Company – was directed by the Senior officer of Militia then present to move with said piece to a certain Point of land contiguous to the Barges and open a fire on them.

He did.

CHAPTER EIGHT

The End Game

[A] field piece was moved from one of the first positions, and about sun-set placed on a point in Saybrook, higher up the river, so as to reach the schooner. — A GENTLEMAN FROM LYME

As Lieutenant Bull's gun crew rushed their team north the British were making preparations to resume their escape. When Coote had made his decision to stay where they were until darkness it had meant that when they *did* head for the mouth of the river they would not be in the schooner. Coote realized that trying to get a ship out of the river after dark was an unachievable ambition. As demonstrated by the grounding of the *Young Anaconda*, tacking back and forth in the narrow channel had proven extremely problematic, even in daylight. After dark it would be impossible. So as they had waited out the day, their plan was to get everyone back into the barges at sunset, torch the *Eagle*, and proceed downriver as they had come, in their small flotilla of ships' boats.

By the time Bull and his crew reached the river adjacent the enemy position the British were already moving men and equipment from the schooner to the boats and perpetrations were being made to set it afire. It would be their final act of destruction in what had already proven to be a very destructive day.

The sun set at 6:22, and there would be no moon until 10:13. But not until nautical twilight, with the sun well below the horizon at 7:20 would the total blackness of the overcast night descend on the river. Coote was ready for it, timing his departure to have full darkness as they ran the gauntlet. As they were putting torches to the schooner and transferring into their boats for the final run down the river they were fired upon by musketry and at least one cannon from a stand of trees close abreast them.

At 7 o'clock the *Eagle* was set on fire, and the Boats formed in regular order . . . here a brisk fire was opened from the Wood which had partially annoyed us during the day, but where they had prudently concealed their Cannon 'till darkness (which) rendered it impossible for us to get possession of them. Coote.

American gun crew of the State Corps of Artillery with six-pound field piece. This is the type of weapon used by Lieutenant Bull and his crew who finally hit the British in the river. (Courtesy of Victor Mays.)

Three days later Parry recalled, "[As] soon as it was dark, and we were just on the point of leaving her, they commenced a heavy fire of field-pieces and musketry from the woods, close abreast us."

Lieutenant Bull and his team had gotten into position and unleashed their six pounder from the nearby shore at point-blank range. Glover who had been confined aboard the schooner had just gotten into the *Maidstone's* barge when a three and a half-inch round shot ripped into the boat killing two marines right next to him. A seaman was hit in the head with a musket ball.

Nearly twenty hours after it had all begun, the Americans had finally struck back with lethal force. Five and a half miles to the south, off the mouth of the river, HMS *Maidstone* reached the *Borer* and *Sylph* at 7 p.m. and anchored nearby. Her log recorded hearing the "report of muskets and great guns." Every officer and seaman aboard the three British warships were now fully aware that Captain Coote's battle to escape the river had begun.

Royal Marines Thomas Smith and Joseph Griffin were dead; Seaman William Pyley was wounded. The iron and lead continued to fly as the American gun crew reloaded and fired again as rapidly as they could. The men who had been maintaining their harassment fire throughout the afternoon now joined in with everything they had. For the British, there were no more options. Coote ordered his men to pull away from the burning schooner as fast as possible and get out of range.

Bull and his crew continued to reload and fire but it was getting dark and thus difficult to sponge the barrel, reload and keep pulling the improvised, red-hot brand from the coals to touch off the powder. After the fourth or fifth round someone got careless. Perhaps Bull was in the act of taking a bag of powder from the cartridge box. Perhaps he still had the glowing firing brand in his hand. Suddenly twelve cartridges containing eighteen pounds of powder exploded!

Eighteen pounds of black powder would have produced a violent explosion and a brilliant illumination in the darkness. The ammo box was blown apart and more than just a few rounds of iron shot would have rolled off into the darkness.

Bull was seriously injured but recovered and lived another thirty-two years.

THE GAUNTLET

As the British continued to pull away, Bull's six pounder was out of action and the militia, still firing their muskets from the woods, were soon out of range. Once clear, Coote ordered his men to ship oars and get back into stealth mode for the run down the river. As soon as the boats were out of gunshot," Glover reported, "the commander told his men that he would run his sword through the first man that spoke a loud word. They then drifted down as slow as possible."

On the bluffs further down the river the hundreds of men manning their positions would have heard, and perhaps seen, all the firing of the cannon, discharging of muskets and the explosion of the powder. After waiting all afternoon, they now knew that their moment had come, or was about to.

The darkness was now punctuated by fires along the banks, set on both sides of the river so the British boats might be seen from one side as they passed the fire on the other. A few small boats were in the river with armed men and torches along with the sloop commandeered by Captain Biddle of the *Macedonian* and crewed by marines from Decatur's squadron.

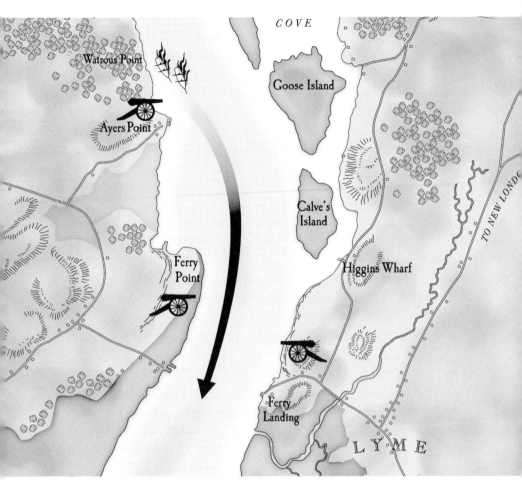

From 7:00 to 7:45 p.m. the British burn the Eagle *and run the gauntlet through the narrows in their ships' boats. (LCG/CRM.)*

But where were the British? It was a mile from the point where they had left the *Eagle* in flames to the bluffs where hundreds of men awaited them. How soon would they reach the gauntlet? Men strained to make out any shape in the blackness of the river. Officers hushed their excited troops and listened for any sounds that might reveal the enemy's location. Then a shot rang out. Had someone seen or heard something in the darkness? Others joined in sporadically from both sides of the river as individuals and groups of men thought they saw something passing by.

With the freshet running at roughly three miles per hour the British did not even have to row. They were no longer burdened with trying to maneuver two large ships against the wind without steerageway. All they had to do was keep their heads down and their boats in the middle of the river. The current would carry them through the narrows. Coote was under no illusions as to what he was now up against:

> The most formidable preparations were made near the town of Lyme and on the opposite bank of the river which is there not more than three quarters of a mile wide, here they were provided with several pieces of Cannon, and from my own observation confirmed by Major Ely's statement, I feel confident that their Military Force amounted to many hundred men.

Coote was not wrong. With the arrival of the large contingent from New London and the influx of local units there were probably upwards of 500 Americans waiting to prevent their escape.

Coote and his officers would have been making sure their men remained calm and silent. All that could be done now was to stay low, stay quiet; stay dark. Coote:

> "By waiting 'till the Night became dark, and then allowing the Boats to drop down the Stream silently, we got nearly abreast of this part of the passage unobserved," Coote recorded. But they were now entering the crucible and he knew it. "Every precaution within the Compass of their Military Skill had here been taken to arrest our progress, large fires were alight on each side to show the situation of the Boats, and Vessels filled with armed Men were anchored in the River."

And then the real shooting began. It must have been unnerving down there in the boats, but Coote's report kept its stiff upper lip as he recalled entering the gauntlet of American guns:

> All these commenced a brisk but ill directed fire at the same instant, and from the short space which separated the Parties, I have reason to suppose it must have proved much more destructive to their friends than to their Enemies.

It must have been surreal; Americans on both sides shooting into the blackness of the river, nothing to aim at, no indication if shots were hitting their marks. In fact the small flotilla was being riddled with shot, to the extent that pieces of wood were found floating along the river the next day. Muskets continued to discharge, cannons belched fire and sharp reports echoed between the bluffs as round shot whistled across the water. But hunkered down in their hulls, the British continued to drift downstream. Coote's report continues:

> Tho' I believe no Boat escaped without receiving more or less shot, by a degree of good fortune which I can only ascribe to providential care, on our side there was only one Man wounded.

Seaman Stephen Pyke in one of La Hogue's boats had been hit and seriously injured but they were all still afloat and the current soon carried them through the worst of it.

By 8 p.m. they had run the gauntlet between Ferry Point on the west and Noyes Hill on the Lyme side. Now they could pull to their oars again through a mile-wide stretch of river devoid of gun positions. For the next mile this widest stretch of the river is lined on both sides with wetlands, making it impossible for the defenders to get men or equipment close to the water. It was a welcome reprieve while it lasted. But the British were now approaching the stretch of river commanded by the fort on Saybrook Point. It had not been armed the night before but there was no doubt it would be now.

Coote's report to the Admiralty was accompanied by a colored hand-drawn map, which showed where ships were burned, where the Brig had gone aground and from where American gun positions had fired. It was perhaps drawn by Coote himself—showing his clear understanding of his theater of operations.

As Coote's men reached the area of the Old Platform the Americans had one last chance to extract a measure of revenge for the burning of the ships in Pettipaug. They tried.

> At ½ past 8 we were abreast of the lowest Fort, and that which we had found dismantled on the preceding Evening, guns however had been provided for this Fort also during the day, and here they made final and equally ineffectual effort to detain us. Coote.

They had made it out, and even the unflappable Richard Coote could not help but gloat a little as he recounted the moment in his report:

> The Boats passed in triumph leaving our Enemies to lament, their acknowledgement of being provided with a force which they had the leisure

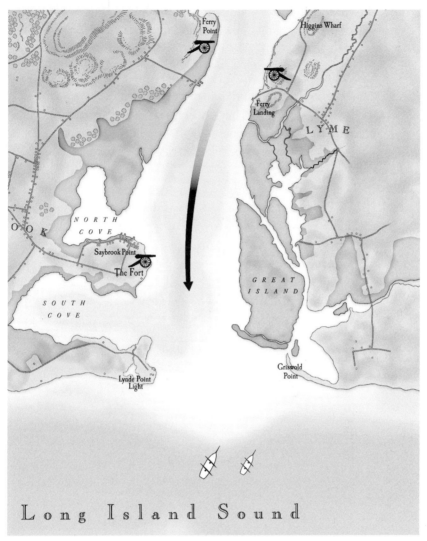

At 8:30 p.m. the British pass the fort on Saybrook Point. (LCG/CRM.)

of a whole day to collect in one of the most populous parts of America, from which they thought it impossible for us to escape.

On April 13th the *Norwich Courier* reported, "Our people kept the best look out a dark night would allow—but to their utter astonishment, about 9 o'clock, three loud cheers from the enemy announced their escape."

Captain Richard Coote and all but two of his 135 men had made it out after a 24-hour adventure that would have made Nelson himself proud, and I suspect even Decatur must have recognized as a feat of daring, professionalism and leadership.

General Williams put it bluntly, "I cannot sufficiently express the deep mortification which I feel that such an attack should be made upon us & under such circumstances, and that the assailants have escaped unpunished."

Soon the boats reached the three warships now anchored off the bar. Here Coote and his men would have returned on deck to a round of "Huzzahs" from the hundreds of seamen aboard the three warships. For the cost of two men killed and two men injured, Captain Coote had carried out Capel's plan flawlessly; destroying or damaging twenty-seven American ships, six of them newly built privateers which would now never prey upon British merchantmen.

The British raid on Pettipaug was over.

CHAPTER NINE

After the Battle

Once the British were gone, the people of Pettipaug Point were left with cleaning up the mess, salvaging what they could and moving on. Several ship owners lost numerous vessels. The Hayden, Pratt and Starkey dynasties were particularly hard hit. Estimates of the value of the financial loss from the raid vary, but accounts seem to range between $150,000 and $200,000. In today's economic equivalence we are looking at tens of millions of dollars. Imagine the cost of replacing twenty-seven vessels, many of them large ships, as well as the economic burden on the town that had built them. The impact was staggering, driving Pettipaug and several of the shipbuilding dynasties into years of economic peril.

For the British, the raid was a major success. On Coote's recommendation, Lieutenant Harry Pyne was promoted to commander. Commander Richard Coote was rewarded with his commission to full post captain, virtually guaranteeing he would one day make the admirals' list. Lieutenant Parry would go on to make his mark in Arctic exploration, leading several famous expeditions, which included Lieutenant Matthew Liddon who also participated in the raid on Pettipaug. Parry became an admiral in 1852.

In 1848 the Royal Navy authorized The Naval General Service Medal to retroactively award those involved in specific campaigns or operations from 1793 to 1840. These medals included the men who had served at Trafalgar and the other great naval operations of the golden age of British Sea power as well as those in special operations like the raid on Pettipaug. They were distributed to those involved who were still living at the time at the time of issue. For this action the clasp on the ribbon reads, "8 April Boat Service 1814." Twenty-four of the British officers and men involved in the British Raid on Essex received the special boat service medals. Lieutenants Fanshawe and Farrant each received medals with five clasps in recognition of their service in other campaigns. Fittingly, Admiral Thomas Bladen Capel, veteran of Trafalgar and the man who ordered the raid on Pettipaug, was one of the members of the board that authorized the medal.

On the American side, the first response was an outcry for protection. From the *New England Repertory*, Boston, April 16, 1814:

Alarms of War! A general alarm is spread from New Orleans to Maine from apprehensions that what has lately been dreadfully realized at Saybrook or Pettipague, in Connecticut, will be experienced in all our accessible seaports.

There was good reason for concern. After the raid on Pettipaug, British activity along the coast continued unabated and there were several actions and exchanges of gunfire off the mouth of the Connecticut River. In June 1814, Admiral Cochrane was encouraged by General Sir George Prevost in Canada to increase the raids on America, and especially New England, in retaliation for United States depredations north of the border. Once he received 5,000 troops later that summer, Cochrane went after Washington and Baltimore, even as the Royal Navy was cracking down from Connecticut to Maine. Calls for increased preparedness spread along the Atlantic seaboard as did the question, how did this happen and who is to blame? In a correspondence to Connecticut's Governor John Cotton Smith, Major-General Ebenezer Huntington of Norwich expressed the general mood:

The late desultory movement of the enemy into the Connecticut River to the village of Pettipogue, the delay at that place with impunity for nearly twenty four hours, & their safe return after having destroyed so much property, cannot fail to excite much apprehension for the safety of the vessels in our bays & rivers, particularly for those which are in the River Thames & Norwich Landing.

From the *Alexandria Gazette* on April 14, 1814:

To whose fault ought to be ascribed the loss of the property destroyed by the British at Pettipaug! The defenseless state of the mouth of the Connecticut, one of the most important rivers in the United States, was well known to the government.

From the *American Mercury*, May 31, 1814:

The ostensible object in rising a State Corpse of 2500 enlisted men, at such a great expense was 'to repel invasion, suppress insurrection and compel observance to the Laws of this state and of the United States.' Hope and Charity oblige us to suppose that the framers of this Law had no other views in raising this force: — Then no one will doubt but this force ought to have been in such a situation as at dare to execute the objects required of it: especially at this alarming and momentous season. Add to this, Connecticut is always boastful of her courage and strength, and implying not only a readiness and willingness, but a fierce determination to repel every invasion.

Although some initial blame was placed on General Williams, it soon became apparent that the problems went far beyond his control. There was plenty of blame to go around concerning the general state of unpreparedness on this important coast a full two years into the war. From the very local level, including Captain George Jewett's apparent absence and the basic shortages of black powder and shot, to the failure of state and local governments to have taken the protection of the coast more seriously, the papers were full of finger pointing. While the rhetoric continued, the real issue was the need to quickly ramp up defenses. On April 12th the selectmen of Saybrook, including Jewett himself, petitioned Governor John Cotton Smith for more protection including the arming of Fort Fenwick. On April 22, less than two weeks after the raid, the Governor issued orders for a detachment from the 7th Regiment, Connecticut Militia to garrison the fort on Saybrook Point and to replace the guns that had once been stationed there, but had been removed six months prior to the raid. Smith wrote to Secretary of the Navy William Jones suggesting that gunboats be stationed to protect the most exposed and vulnerable coastal areas.

The federal Government also ordered that a small guard be stationed at the mouth of the Connecticut River while Smith took additional measures to insure that the state militia forces along the coast were better armed, directing that stores of arms, ordinance and ammunition be placed in strategic points. These included New Haven, Bridgeport, Killingworth, Saybrook, Pettipaug, Middletown, New London and Stonington Point. Smith also recommended the equipping of Flying Squadrons of artillery to be available for swift deployment where needed.

Chain of command and communications issues between state and federalized militia units were improved and additional armament and resources were allocated along the coast. As a result of the experience at Pettipaug, when Stonington was attacked four months later, there were two nine pound cannons already in town and the coordination between state and local militia was much better organized. Stonington was bombarded for four days, but its defenders fired back with skill and tenacity. When the British tried to send marines ashore to subdue the American guns, they were turned back with deadly force.

POSTSCRIPTS

Two months after the raid, in the June 8th edition of the *Connecticut Spectator*, wedged in between columns of other news, was this poignant reminder of what had taken place in this now peaceful river,

> One day last week, the body of a dead man floating on the surface of the river, was discovered by ferry-men at Saybrook ferry. It had on a red coat, Sergeant's knot and sword belt. Supposed to have been a sergeant in the detachment which came to Pettipauge on the 8th of April last, and probably one of those killed in the boat, mentioned in Capt. Glover's affidavit.

Royal Marines wore red coats and this was probably the body of Corporal Thomas Smith or Joseph Griffin. Whoever it was they were likely to have been buried in an unmarked grave in one of the old cemeteries nearby.

On May 9th, Decatur finally gave up getting *United States* out of New London and traveled overland to take command of the forty-four-gun frigate USS *President* in New York Harbor. In January, 1815 he once again found himself blockaded by a powerful British squadron. Despite sustaining structural damage due to grounding at the mouth of the harbor, Decatur managed to get *President* to sea only to be captured on January 15 by the blockading squadron, which ironically included HMS *Endymion*, one of the ships that had blockaded him in New London. Within weeks the war was over. On February 22, 1815, Decatur was returned to New London from detention in Bermuda aboard HMS *Narcissus* and was warmly welcomed back to the city where he had been blockaded for so long. The following evening he found himself attending a "peace ball" celebrating the end of the war along with several other officers, both American and British. As the festivities proceeded there were five British warships at the mouth of river, now welcomed guests.

When Decatur had headed for New York back in May, James Biddle and USS *Hornet* had remained in the Thames River above New London until November, when they were able to escape and traverse through Long Island Sound to New York. They began a cruise in December that would take them to the South Atlantic, famously capturing HMS *Penguin* in March and finally learning the war had ended more than two months after the declaration of peace. Biddle was made post captain and would play an important role in the post war Navy.

Ironically, just weeks after the British raid, Major Marsh Ely, who had shown so much energy during the raid on Pettipaug, was indicted for having sold two shipments of beef to HMS *Valiant* of the British blockading squadron in the fall of 1813. A week before the indictment Ely's "summons" to Coote was published in the papers. It is not clear if this was to support Ely by demonstrating his strength of command, or by his opponents to suggest that he showed leniency to the enemy by offering Coote another way out. The *American Mercury* suggests Ely was part of the general dithering that resulted in a failure to prevent the British escape, ". . . sending flags of truce, waiting for reinforcements, contriving, &c, &c. delayed a bold attack till it got to be quite dark."

Although the case against Ely was strong, and attorney George W. Jewett was prepared to defend him, in September 1815, with the war over, the charges were dropped. If he had in fact sold supplies to the British he would not have been the first, or the last. It was an odd war in which men of valor could fight the enemy when necessary yet do business with them when convenient.

The British raid on Pettipaug was not something people wanted to remember. No statues were erected. Four months later the Battle of Stonington gave the state something to be proud of and the papers something better to write about. Less than three weeks after that, on August 24th, the British burned Washington eclipsing any national interest in what had happed in Pettipaug. On January 8th, 1815 General Andrew Jackson defeated the British at the Battle of New Orleans. A few weeks earlier, the Treaty of Peace and Amity between His Britannic Majesty and the United States of America had already been signed in Ghent, Belgium, officially ending the war on Christmas Eve, 1814. The British raid on Pettipaug had already begun to slide into obscurity and the realm of folklore—the forgotten battle of the forgotten war.

THE TRAITOR UNMASKED

Who was Torpedo Jack? Clearly this was a question that nagged us throughout this project. At last we found him hiding in a place we had looked many times before. We just hadn't known what to look for. It was Connecticut River

Museum curator Amy Trout who finally caught the traitor. In the muster book of HMS *Borer* on the line just above the April 8th entry that had exonerated Jeremiah Glover once and for all, there was another name entered on the 7th. It was the smoking gun. There, transferring aboard the *Borer* on the afternoon before the raid was a man named Ezekiel Jackson. The notation says that he came from the *Maidstone* with the line, "supposed to have brought a torpedo." According to Parry, Torpedo Jack was captured by the *Maidstone* on the night of Jeremiah Holmes' torpedo attack on *La Hogue*. But that's not all. Whereas Glover was listed as a prisoner, Jackson is listed as "pilot."

They both were here, one above the other—one exonerated, the other damned.

We could not help but wonder what happened to Ezekiel Jackson, AKA, "Torpedo Jack" after the raid. What did he do with the $2,000? Where did he live? Did he have a family, a wife, children? We looked through census records throughout the state and could not pin down from where he had come or to where he went. Still a phantom? In the end he turned up in the same place we had found him logging in on April 7th as the prisoner turned pilot for the British: in the muster list of HMS *Borer*. Moving ahead a few pages he showed up again on April 29th. Here, three weeks after the raid, we find Jackson transferring from the *Borer* to the *Loup Cervier*. That may not seem to mean much at first glance, but here is what it tells us. He stayed with Coote and the *Borer* for another three weeks after the raid. With $2,000 in his pocket and some possibility that he might be recognized as the traitor he was not about to flaunt his newfound wealth.

Jackson's transfer to the *Loup Cervier* has little bearing on our story but it had a dramatic impact on his life. Ironically the *Loup Cervier* had been USS *Wasp* before being captured by the British in October 1812. She was renamed *Loup Cervier* when put into service with the Royal Navy in 1813. In 1814 she was renamed HMS *Peacock* to honor the previous ship of that name that had been sunk in battle. It was this second HMS *Peacock*, originally built as an American warship, which Coote was given command as part of his promotion to post captain after the raid. All indications are that Jackson stayed with Coote, transferring with him to his new command. Clearly Jackson had decided that his future was linked to Coote and the Royal Navy, not Connecticut or anywhere near the general vicinity of Pettipaug. That's where his paper trail ends.

ADMIRAL RICHARD COOTE?

Of course we all wanted to see what became of this story's true leading man, Captain Richard Coote, a rising star in the Royal Navy. We fully expected to see him rapidly climbing through the ranks and making the admirals' list just as Lieutenant Parry eventually did. But we could not find him. That was strange. An officer like this, who had achieved so much in such a short time, should have left a pretty strong footprint within the Royal Navy. But we could not find him twenty years out, or ten, or to our astonishment, we could not even find him a year after the raid that had made him a post captain overnight. Something was wrong. So we looked for him in the last place we had seen him, in command of HMS *Peacock*. That is when we learned why we never found an Admiral Richard Coote. On July 23, 1814, just three and a half months after the British Raid on Essex, the *Peacock* was lost at sea with all hands in a gale off the Virginia Capes. The man who had led one of the most daring, and certainly the most successful, small boat actions of the war—who had survived running the gauntlet of American musketry and cannon fire on his way down the Connecticut River, had been lost at sea in a storm.

I will tell you that all of us who had been working on this project had grown to admire Coote, even though from an American perspective he was the enemy. We truly felt a bit stunned and even sad to learn of his death at thirty-two years of age, in the prime of his naval career.

Anyone with an ounce of compassion can also imagine the grief sustained by Coote's fiancée Mary Elliott back in England. She would have been elated to learn that her future husband had achieved a major victory, and that her younger brother had been a part of it, but then crushed when news later arrived that they had both been lost at sea. She had lost the younger brother she had sent to sea, and the man she had hoped to spend the rest of her life with. She never married.

We do not feel so badly about Ezekial Jackson. If in fact he was still aboard HMS *Peacock* on July 23, 1814, it would seem Torpedo Jack finally received exactly the reward that he deserved.

Six months later, HMS *Sylph*, the other ship that had accompanied *Borer* to the mouth of the Connecticut River in support of the raid on Pettipaug, met a similar fate. At about 2 a.m. on January 16th, 1815 the ship struck the Southampton Bar at the east end of Long Island. The surf pounded the grounded vessel causing it to be laid over on its side where it broke up by morning. Despite the best efforts of people on shore, who risked their own lives attempting to rescue the enemy crew, all but six of the one hundred and seventeen officers and seamen aboard *Sylph* drowned. Captain George Dickins, like Coote himself, had survived a career of high-risk combat in the service of the Royal Navy only to be lost at sea.

STONINGTON

The British Raid on Essex is often compared to the Battle of Stonington. They are the two most significant "battles" which took place in the state of Connecticut during the War of 1812. Stonington and those who defended it deserve all the glory that has been heaped on them. In the face of the overwhelming might and firepower of the Royal Navy, they not only withstood several days of bombardment, but a small group of men fought back at great personal risk and showed the British what a handful of determined Yankees could do.

But the raid on Pettipaug and the bombardment of Stonington were entirely different operations from the British perspective. Whether instigated by Jeremiah Holmes' attack on HMS *La Hogue*, or the serendipitous exploitation of the capture of Torpedo Jack, the British raid Pettipaug was a strategic attack on a military target. The British went in equipped and determined to land, occupy the village and burn a large number of vessels, including several privateers.

The bombardment of Stonington, on the other hand, was a punitive action. Hardy had been ordered by Admiral Cochrane to make an example of an American coastal town in retaliation for American transgressions against civilians in Canada. Stonington was the most exposed target of opportunity within Hardy's jurisdiction. He never intended to land troops or occupy it. He just wanted to make an example of it. In the end he did exactly what he set out to do. He hurled over fifty tons of round shot, exploding shells and Congreve rockets into the village for three days and then left. What he hadn't figured on, probably *because* of the British experience in Pettipaug, was a group of men remaining in town and shooting back. Despite the punishing attack, the example set at Stonington was not the one Cochrane had in mind.

"Surrender Note." Some time around 2 p.m. on the 8th, Major Marsh Ely sent Captain Harrison to deliver this handwritten note to Captain Coote who was aboard the schooner Eagle *anchored in the river. Coote dismissed the suggestion that he might surrender with the line: "We held their power to detain us at defiance." (Courtesy of the Connecticut Historical Society, Hartford, Connecticut.)*

The Abula, *built in Haddam in 1805 and sailed out of New York, is typical of the larger three-masted ships built in Pettipaug and other ship building towns along the lower Connecticut River. (Painted in 1806 by Nicolas Cammillieri. Courtesy of Mystic Seaport.)*

The H.M.S. *Sylph* and H.M.S. *Maidstone* attacking off of Horton Point, Southold, Long Island, NY, during the War of 1812 *(after the painting by B. J. Phillips).* The *Sylph* *accompanied* Borer *to the mouth of the Connecticut River on the night of the raid.* Maidstone *was dispatched to join them from the blockading squadron off New London the following afternoon. (Courtesy of the Southold Historical Society, Southold, NY.)*

This watercolor by Victor Mays illustrates a topsail schooner with a brig in background, both typical of vessels built in and sailed from Pettipaug. (Courtesy of Victor Mays.)

The seventy-four gun HMS Ramillies—*depicted here buying fish off Block Island—was Captain Hardy's flagship for the blockading squadron off New London. Although* Ramillies *was twenty years older than Captain Capel's HMS* La Hogue, *the scale and example of British sea power is comparable. (Courtesy of Victor Mays.)*

Kip Soldwedel's 1964 painting shows the British landing at Pettipaug Point. Although dramatic, the image is inaccurate in that it shows the village on fire and the British landing with large ship's guns and field pieces. This painting originally hung in the Griswold Inn. (CRM.)

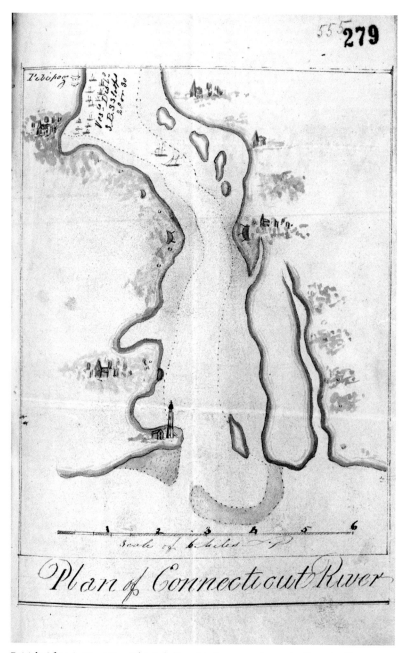

British After Action Map. *This is believed to be a map drawn by Captain Coote or one of his officers. Produced to accompany Coote's report to Captain Capel after the raid, it clearly depicts where the ships were burned, where the captured brig and schooner spent the afternoon of April 8th and the positions on shore from which the British were fired upon. The lighthouse and Saybrook Bar are depicted at the mouth of the river. (Courtesy of British National Archives.)*

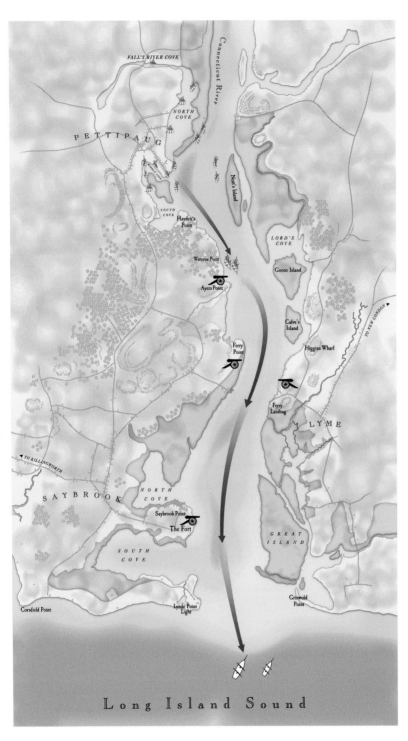

Getting Out. *At 11 a.m. the British departed Pettipaug with two captured privateers. After running aground off Watrous Point at about 12:30 p.m. the British remained there until sunset. At 7 p.m. the British were hit by an American field-piece on shore, killing two marines. They ran the gauntlet of intense cannon fire as they passed American gun positions on the bluffs. At 8:30 p.m. they were fired on again as they passed the old fort. By 9:30 p.m. the raiding force reached their ships anchored off the mouth of the river. (LCG/CRM.)*

This 1804 pattern Royal Navy Boarding Cutlass was recovered from Essex Harbor. These were the standard issue sailor's fighting swords that would have been carried ashore by the seamen taking part in the raid on Pettipaug. (Photograph by Jerry Roberts.)

Souvenir piece of wood from the Osage. (Courtesy of the Essex Historical Society.)

Musket ball found in the Ephraim Bound House on Main Street Essex. (Courtesy of the Paul Foundation.)

In 1987–88 a field team from Wesleyan University headed by John Pfeiffer excavated portions of the seventeenth-century Lay's Wharf, Ebenezer Hayden's ship's store, and the 1812 bulkhead, which runs through the parking lot of the Connecticut River Museum. Pictured here is Essex town historian, Don Malcarne. (Courtesy of the Connecticut River Museum.)

MPMRC Battle Site Project archaeologists working in summer of 2013 near site of old Fort Saybrook overlooking the mouth of the River. (Photograph by Jerry Roberts.)

In autumn 2013, the Mashantucket Pequot Museum and Research Center archaeological team worked on the ballast pile off Watrous Point trying to determine if in fact they were looking at the ruins of the American privateer Young Anaconda. (Photograph by Jerry Roberts.)

Battle site archaeologists found several coins and buttons in the vicinity of the fort on Saybrook Point. (1) 1728 Spanish Reale, (2) 1798 American Liberty penny, (3) 1806 King George penny, (4) 1812-era American naval officer's button. (Courtesy of Mashantucket Pequot Museum and Research Center.)

Ship's barge with carronade in bow. (Courtesy of Victor Mays/CRM.)

This twenty-four pound round shot is said to have been fired into the town by the British on April 7, 1814. It is being used as a doorstop in the Dauntless Club located in the Uriah Hayden homestead on the Essex waterfront.

In 1848, Great Britain introduced its Naval General Service Medal to honor surviving officers and seamen who had taken part in battles between 1793 and 1840. The Special Boat Service medal was issued to twenty-four officers and men who had taken part in the British Raid on Essex. (Courtesy of A.H. Baldwin & Sons Ltd, London. www.baldwin.co.uk.)

Section of the muster log from HMS Borer showing both Ezekiel Jackson and Jeremiah Glover logged in—one as a pilot, the other as a prisoner. (Courtesy of the British National Archives/KEW).

CHAPTER TEN

Fighting for the Lost Battle

I came to Essex in July 2006, after eighteen years at the Intrepid Sea Air Space Museum in New York to take over as executive director of the Connecticut River Museum, located on the Essex waterfront. I knew nothing of the British raid. My wife had googled Essex before we came and told me about Loser's Day. We joked that any town that had the chutzpa to hold an annual parade to mark the worst day in its 300-year history must have pretty thick skin and strong self-esteem. Ironically, even in the museum, which stands right on the waterfront, precisely where the British had come ashore, there were no exhibits about the raid, just a handful of cannonballs and a few charred ships timbers, all packed away in storage.

The Connecticut River Museum building is relatively new by Essex standards. It was constructed in 1878 as a steamboat dock and three-story warehouse for loading and offloading cargo and passengers to and from the massive side-wheeled steamships that connected Hartford to Manhattan during the golden age of steam navigation. When the steamboats left the river in 1931, the building survived the next several decades through adaptive reuse as a general store, marina, dance hall, tea room, roller rink, restaurant, and at last a pretty dodgy bar and disco in the early 70s. By 1974 it had gone bust for the last time. The grand old building which had once been the heart of this maritime community was most likely destined to be torn down and the land used for condos, or god knows what. But a group of locals, lead by Bill Winterer and Herb Clark, rallied the community, pooled their resources and bought the place. At first they had no plan; they just wanted to make sure it didn't become anything worse. In the end, largely due to the influence of maritime historian Tom Stevens, who donated his archives, they decided to make it into a museum.

Its galleries now tell the stories of the river. Among the exhibits is a working replica of the world's first combat submarine, *Bushnell's Turtle.* The original was built a few miles down the road in what is now Westbrook and first launched into the Connecticut River at Ayers Point. It was used against the British in New York Harbor in September and October of 1776. The *Turtle* had long been one of my favorite stories so upon my arrival I sank my teeth into building new exhibits around this incredible example of Yankee ingenuity. I did ask about the Commemoration Day parade and the burning of the ships, and was handed the slim, yellowed booklet written by Albert Dock and Russell Anderson, published by the Essex Historical Society back in 1981. I skimmed through its pages and was intrigued but put it aside as I submerged myself deeper into the story of the *Turtle*.

By the following year, in the summer of 2007, we finally got around to building an exhibit about the British raid. We dug out the charred timbers, dusted off the cannonballs and created some text panels that told the story. We commissioned artist Russell Buckingham to paint a twenty-two-foot mural of the British landing and actually photographed local boatyard workers storming the town with push brooms and sticks, which he then transformed into Royal Marines and fighting tars carrying muskets and boarding swords. To top it off we built a little diorama of the river complete with burning ships and a timeline of the raid.

In the summer of 2009 I attended a maritime history conference just up the coast at Mystic Seaport. Of the many programs offered, the one that caught my eye was a session hosted by the United States Navy's History and Heritage Command about the upcoming bicentennial of the War of 1812. They had created a Maritime Heritage Trail, including such obvious locations as Fort McHenry in Baltimore and the USS *Constitution* in Boston. I made my way into the crowded room to see how Connecticut was being represented. In fact there was only one War of 1812 event mentioned and that was the battle of Stonington.

Stonington certainly deserved to be on the map. With its tattered battle flag and cannons mounted in the town park, still pointing out to sea, Stonington was the perfect counterpoint to Essex with its Loser's Day parade, where the perception was that the townspeople had capitulated without firing a shot and stood back as the British burned the ships upon which their livelihoods depended. But I had read Commander Dock's booklet. We had built an exhibit. We had cannonballs and charred wood. So how did we get left out of the bicentennial mix?

I stood up in the room full of my peers, and asked why Essex had quite literally been left off the map. I reiterated the fact that the British had burned twenty-seven ships, including six American privateers, a much greater loss than the half dozen wooden houses they had managed to flatten in Stonington. We did not capitulate, we fired back and the British took casualties. The Navy officer did not seem all that interested in going off script. He basically responded that the British Raid on Essex was not on their list. Officially, it had never happened. Ironically, at that point, even I did not yet know that the United States Navy had been directly involved.

Everyone was looking at me standing there, the guy from Essex. Poor sap. The Stonington contingent in the room shook their heads. They had the cannons, the battle flag, and the book by James Tertius de Kay, *The Battle of Stonington*. It was sometimes referred to as the bible, at least in Stonington. We did not have a book. We had a twenty-page pamphlet with a stapled binding, and Loser's Day. I sat down.

Outside, after the meeting I button-holed the officer and asked what we had to do to correct this omission. There *had* been a battle, a big one, involving hundreds of American sailors, soldiers, marines and militia. He told me that nothing could be done. I asked how we had not made the list in the first place and I was informed that it had been compiled by the American Battlefield Protection Program (ABPP), which was part of the National Park Service in Washington. They had done a survey of War of 1812 battle sites in 2007 and we were not part of it, we were never mentioned, never considered. We, apparently, did not happen. He suggested I might try to contact Paul Hawke in DC, the head of the program. But he warned me not to get my hopes up.

I returned to Essex pretty riled up. I briefed our curator, Amy Trout, my partner in interpreting the history of the river. I'm not sure she knew what she was in for. I was now on a crusade. The next day we did get hold of Mr. Paul Hawke. The ABPP had been set up to catalogue Civil War battle sites and prioritize the need for protection as big-box stores and housing developments were rapidly overrunning the once peaceful fields of Pennsylvania and Virginia where tens of thousands of Americans had been killed or maimed for their respective causes. The program had been expanded to include Revolutionary War sites and as the bicentennial of the War of 1812 approached some of these sites were being included as well. I asked why we were not part of the 2007 list. He explained that the ABPP had asked each State Historic Preservation Office (SHPO) for nominations and Connecticut's SHPO had nominated only one site: Stonington.

OK, we asked, how do we now get onto the bicentennial list? Once again we were told it was too late. The survey was over and there would not be another one. There was no follow-on funding. There it was: I was sitting in my office on the very site where the British had come ashore yet I was being told it was too late. Our little booklet might be nice, the charred ship's timbers were all well and good, our exhibit was a great addition to our local history, but officially there was no battle, no battle site and no recognition by the State of Connecticut, the National Park Service or the United States Navy's History and Heritage Command.

Apparently the second battle for Essex had just begun.

OFF THE RADAR

So now it was time to get serious. The bicentennial of the war was approaching. We had the charred wood and some round shot but we were way behind the eight ball. Stonington was secure in its role as the flag bearer of Connecticut in the War of 1812. Essex apparently did not exist. The Navy did not want to know. The American Battlefield Protection Program said it was too late. Our own state SHPO had not even thought about us when it counted. We needed to reboot and fast. We needed to convince all of these people that there really was a battle and that it had state and national significance.

We realized we had to start with the people whose radar screen we had apparently not shown up on back in 2007, our State Historic Preservation Office. But first we needed some ammunition. We needed to go armed to the teeth. We needed to gather facts, do some research, get our ducks in order and go to battle. So we went back to the source, that obscure little booklet published in 1981. We dug it out of the files, dusted it off and read it again, this time with priority and purpose.

Stonington may have their *bible*, but we would soon come to refer to our thin little booklet as the *Holy Grail*. As it turned out, it was the Rosetta Stone which held the keys to unlocking the doors we needed to pass through to rediscover this forgotten battle and bring it into the light of day.

BATTLE SITE ESSEX

Having now revisited the Admiralty documents, and initiating some new research of our own, we were ready. We invited our deputy State Historic Preservation Officers Mary Donohue, Senior Survey and Planning Grants Coordinator and Stacey Vairo, National Register Coordinator, to come and hear our story and perhaps help us get back in the game. We explained that in addition to British documents we had found indexes for the over ninety newspaper articles written in the days and weeks that followed the battle. There were also dozens of leads that we needed to follow up both here and in England. This was looking like a much bigger story than previously imagined. They listened.

Perhaps there was a touch of guilt for passing Essex over in 2007, or perhaps it was because the ramp up to the 1812 bicentennial was becoming tangible. They agreed that this was not only an important Connecticut story, it was a missing chapter in our national maritime narrative that needed to be written. At last we had allies.

Best of all, they helped us secure a $20,000 Survey and Planning Grant in June 2011. This would allow us to follow through on our research and fully document the raid to the standards of the Secretary of the Interior, a requirement for an eventual nomination to the National Register of Historic Places as a federal War of 1812 battle site. But could we get all this done within two years? Our concern was that once the bicentennial of the war had passed, all interest in stories like this would fade away just as the original battle had.

As we geared up for this more comprehensive research phase, that we hoped would lead to national recognition by 2014, we asked Stacey and Mary how we might become a state battle site in the meantime. This was the million-dollar question. They gave it some thought. As far as they could tell, the SHPO had never actually created a battle site before, at least not on their watch. What SHPOs are good at is getting old buildings on the State and National Registers of Historic Places based on the merit of their architectural style and significance. An old church, a mill, a colonial house; no problem. But a battle site? That had never been done. There was no form or format. Battles have very little architectural significance, even old ones. This was going to take some outside-the-box thinking. So they asked the painfully obvious question. Do we have any old houses?

Yes we have old houses! This is Essex, Connecticut! But we wanted to create a battle site not a list of the colonial and federal architectural elements on Main Street. But this was all they had. This is what they did. We did not have time to reinvent the wheel. So we switched gears and thought about it. Yes, there are still twenty-four structures on Main Street that were here when the British came to town in 1814. There are actually dozens more in the outlying areas of the village; but within the confines of the peninsula that we believe the British occupied there are twenty-four, including the homes of sea captains, ship builders, and of course the Bushnell Tavern, AKA the Griswold Inn.

So we worked out a strange deal. Instead of creating a battle site based on the actual battle, we were able to create one based on the modern property lines of the existing pre-1814 houses and the waterfront where the colonial docks lay. This just happens to be under the current parking lot of the Connecticut River Museum, which was built on "modern" 1840's landfill meant to push the waterfront out into deeper water to accommodate the steamboats that docked here from the early 1800s to the 1930s. In 1987 Essex town historian, Don Malcarne, and archaeologist John Pfeiffer had discovered the original colonial wharves as a new septic system was being installed under the lot. A second dig was done in 1989. Hundreds of artifacts and some intriguing charred beams were found. To bring the project up-to-date, State Archaeologist Nick Bellantoni brought in a team with ground penetrating radar (GPR) in 2011 to track the 1812-era bulkhead that curved around the eastern end of town. He signed off that, with this and the artifacts in the museum and scattered about town, there was enough physical evidence to prove the battle had in fact taken place here.

Meanwhile, under the planning grant, we put out a Request for Proposal (RFP) to secure an approved academic historian who would conduct six months of intensive research along with our team and create an official report that would support both State and National Register nominations. This would require a vast amount of legwork, physically combing all the archives that might hold clues to the battle. Some would be digitized and indexed, but most would be old-school hard copy, typed or handwritten documents, or endless microfilm spools containing newspaper accounts and personal memoirs. This meant visiting a number of local historical societies, the State Archives in Hartford and the National Archives in Washington.

We contracted historian David Naumec to be our lead researcher here in New England. As he began to dig into the large task list we created, we realized we were also going to need boots on the ground in England to sift through the myriad of Admiralty documents and ships' logbooks in the British National Archives. We put out an RFP in the UK and after reviewing a host of responses we selected a woman named Rosalie Spire who seemed to know her way around the centuries-long paper trail of the Royal Navy.

The first information overload that began to come in was those ninety newspaper articles, which had to be tracked down one by one. They arrived as photocopied pages printed from microfilm reels. Some were almost impossible to read. Finding the bits and pieces that might fit our story amongst the other war news and all the other news that filled the pages of the papers was a challenge. This required hours and hours of tedious handheld magnifying glass work. We set about transcribing the most relevant articles into MS Word documents so that we could effectively read and edit them into a useful context. Only by reading all of these documents could we correlate stories and figure out which were supported by other accounts, or which were just badly written speculation and hearsay churned out to fill an editor's daily column quota in the aftermath of the raid.

By the fall of 2011 we had collected enough new information that we felt it was time to go back to Paul Hawke at the American Battlefield Protection Program again and see what they could do for us. He suggested we apply for a site identification grant.

Where the SHPO grant was to document the story of the raid, the ABPP grant was to actually define the battle site using the documented narrative, the existing physical landscape, and selective archaeology to map out the various sites upon which the British Raid on Essex was played out. This would be no small task involving six miles of river, three colonial villages and the roads and landscape that connected them. Kirsten McMasters ran this program for ABPP and would shepherd us through the process.

While all this research was going on, Stacey and Mary were pushing through the Connecticut state battle site nomination. There was a very tense day in March 2012 when I had to go to Hartford and make our case in front of the panel of people who had the power to decide if we had proven our case or not. Fortunately they were able to think beyond the beaten path of architectural significance. We were approved to be added to the State Register of Historic Places. On April 5, 2012, three days before the 198th anniversary, and after a great deal of work by our expanding team, we were designated as the State of Connecticut's first War of 1812 battle site, officially the British Raid on Essex Battle Site District.

On Commemoration Day that year, when the Sailing Masters of 1812 and all the other fife and drum corps gathered by the waterfront next to the Connecticut River Museum, Main Street was packed. The parade that once confused even those who lived in the village, the parade no one attended except for the families of those who marched, was now attended by hundreds (a lot of folks for a tiny town like Essex). Governor Dannel Malloy, a great believer in history, and the heritage tourism it attracts, read his proclamation naming us an official state battle site, the first that anyone knew of. He was clearly proud. We were all proud. This was not the end of our battle, not by a long shot, but it was a great day in Essex. No one even whispered the words, Loser's Day.

Three months later, in July, we were informed that the American Battlefield

Protection Program had approved our project and we now had $29,000 to define and map the battle site. This was a giant stepping-stone toward achieving our goal of a successful nomination to the National Register of Historic Places, which in essence meant becoming a battle site recognized by the National Park Service. To define the battle site we needed to take our documented narrative, a work still in progress, overlay it onto the landscape, match it up with the existing features that were here in 1814, and field test certain areas to see if we could find new physical evidence of the battle 200 years after the fact. In addition to a good story and a theater of operations complete with colonial roads, old houses and the river itself, we now needed to find some buttons, bullets and cannonballs. As my six-year-old son liked to say, "Indiana Jones stuff."

CHAPTER ELEVEN

The Problem with History

BATTLEFIELD ARCHAEOLOGY

By this time we had distilled the documents, old maps, newspaper accounts and other research into a comprehensive narrative. But now we needed more. We needed to define and map the battle site with solid battlefield archeology. We needed the physical evidence of a battle.

To accomplish this we needed a field team with specific experience in this kind of work and as it turned out, the only logical choice was already at work just down the road. When the Pequot tribal elders used some of their Foxwoods earnings to build their two hundred million dollar museum in the hills above Mystic it included a state-of-the-art research center complete with archives, computer labs, and a world-class archaeological facility. To run it they hired University of Connecticut Anthropologist Dr. Kevin McBride, who put together an amazing team of bright young archaeologists to carry out research into the several battles of the Pequot Wars. Some of these took place right down on Saybrook Point where the original fort once stood, and where an important part of our story had taken place as well. They were the obvious choice. Before long Kevin and his team were at work on Saybrook Point looking for, and often finding, artifacts from both the 1814 British Raid and skirmishes between the first English settlers and the Pequot in the 1640s.

I am an historian, a storyteller. My goal has been to research and document an event and then transform the results into a contextual narrative in order to produce a museum exhibit, a book, or a documentary, that makes the story accessible and hopefully compelling to the average person. Through this project, working with Kevin and his team, I learned something that should have been obvious. Archaeologists are all about the *stuff*, AKA the artifacts. Historians are all about the story. It is one of those chicken and egg things. An historian will tell you that artifacts without the story are just objects. Archaeologists, on the other hand, will tell you that without artifacts you cannot prove it happened. No bullets, no battlefield. The National Register agrees and requires a certain amount of physical evidence . . . at least it weighs heavily in their evaluations. They want to see a marriage of both the story *and* the stuff.

What I did not know is that there is a third way to define a battlefield. They call it KOCOA. It stands for **K**ey terrain, **O**bservation, **C**oncealment and Cover,

Obstacles, and Avenues of Approach and withdrawal. KOCOA puts the documented story and the artifacts in context with the landscape upon which the battle was fought. This means the rivers, hills, villages, colonial roads, the view corridors, the lines of advance and retreat, fields of fire, etc. It coaxes the story out of the book, the artifacts out of the glass cases and adds the real world of the battlefield to into the mix. It was first used by the Army War College after the Second World War as a way to teach military officers how to analyze a battle by asking how the terrain features shaped the planning and influenced the outcome. It is based on the theory of Inherent Military Probability, which suggests that by understanding what a trained soldier would have done in given circumstances you can understand how a battle would unfold.

KOCOA has now been adopted as an important tool by the American Battlefield Protection Program for analyzing battle sites. This was good news. It meant our battle site would not be measured solely by what was found in the ground, but would be defined by the story, the archaeology and the landscape.

By September 2013, after weeks of working down on Saybrook Point digging up buttons, coins, beer and soda pull tabs (and a musket ball or two) it was time to move north and deploy the team to Ayers Point. This is the area where we believed Lieutenant Bull had fired the six pounder that killed two Royal Marines as the British waited for darkness to continue their escape down the river. This meant securing more permissions to work on several private properties. I am always amazed that people, especially those with rather exclusive estates along the river, will allow Kevin's team to come in with metal detectors and then start digging holes in their manicured lawns looking for buttons and musket balls. But they do.

For two weeks Kevin and his team intensively "pounded" all four properties on Ayres Point with an army of pros, grad students and experienced volunteers equipped with metal detectors. With commanding views of the river in all directions, it was clear this was the place. But they found nothing. No bullets, no battlefield. They kept looking.

BALLAST STONE & DROPPED BALLS

About this time a man named Andy Carr who lived nearby came to hear one of my British Raid on Essex presentations at the Connecticut River Museum. He mentioned that he thought he knew where the wreck of the *Young Anaconda* was. Really? Where is it? "It is right under my dock. Would you like to come and see it?" He was referring to a pile of rocks, which he figured might be the ballast stones of a ship.

I like to think that I am reasonably open-minded, but I have to admit that I put little stock in Andy's theory. First off, we all knew the *Young Anaconda* had gone aground near Ayers Point, a quarter mile downstream. We also knew it would not be that close to shore. But I invited Kevin to meet me at Andy's place at the end of Watrous Point Road just to tick the box. Getting to Ayers Point is pretty straightforward. The convoluted road through the woods that lead to Andy's property was a bit off the beaten path to say the least. It did not even exist in 1814.

When we arrived, we found the house he had built in the 1980s, a lawn sloping down to the waterfront shaded by several large trees and a long dock jutting out into the river. Halfway out and under the dock there was indeed a pile of stones visible above the surface at low tide. It did look like ballast stone. These are basically fieldstones varying in size, from that of a cantaloupe to a large watermelon. They were loaded by hand into the bottoms of the hulls of wooden sailing vessels to provide stability and a lower center of gravity to counter the weight and leverage of masts and sails. Long after a shipwreck has rotted away, the stones remain, marking the site for hundreds and sometimes thousands of years. However the ballast stone off of Watrous Point could have belonged to any vessel from colonial times through the late 1800s. It was also in the wrong place. It was too close to land, and too far from Ayers Point. Or was it?

Part of my job as the project's battlefield historian was to work with Kevin to decide where best to look for evidence of the battle based on research, and then to figure out how whatever he and his team might find may or may not be related to the battle. In playing devils' advocate to my own doubts about the property, I revisited the relevant primary documents.

I looked at the first-hand accounts written by several people directly involved. Captain Glover, the American prisoner, said the brig went aground a mile and a quarter south of Pettipaug Point. That is where the ballast stones were. Captain Coote said that the schooner *Eagle* anchored, "half a musket shot" from shore. Parry called it, "a pistol shot." Either way, this is about a hundred feet. The ballast stones are about the same distance off the riverbank. This was leading down a path that did not fit well with our long-standing assumptions.

Meanwhile Kevin had gone back to Andy's property with one of his metal detecting crews. Over the next several weeks they found nearly thirty musket balls of various calibers in the lawn adjacent to the dock.

The pieces began to fit. The brig went aground within half a musket shot of the shore, a mile and quarter south of Pettipaug Point. The ballast stone fit this location. Now the team had found musket shot adjacent to this position. The mixture of calibers didn't make sense at first. Although we know the Americans were firing at the British, the British reports do not mention the marines returning fire. However, an analysis of the shot recovered seems to suggest they did. As expected there are unfired "dropped rounds," indicating that Americans were dropping musket balls as they were reloading. The American rounds fit with the fact that local militia supplied their own weapons which were often fouling pieces.

The team did find a distinct pattern of identical shot that may represent at least one round of canister shot fired by the British, while a few other balls fit the caliber of British muskets and sea service pistols. There are several impacted balls that do not seem to have been fired by the British but which could represent American misfires or poorly aimed shots that hit trees or the ground. We do not believe that all of this represents a pitched "battle" but probably indicates that the British were making sure the Americans did not assemble a concentrated force adjacent their position as they waited for darkness to proceed downriver. It did not all make sense, but it certainly looked like something major had happened there.

Our attention shifted back to the ballast pile; and Kevin's team spent several days trying to get down beneath the stone and mud to the hull, which would still hold clues to the ship's identity even after 200 years. But this project did not have a budget for underwater archaeology, and as October turned to November the work on the river had to end. Nothing conclusive had been found. We had not proven the vessel was the *Young Anaconda*, but we certainly had not proved it wasn't. We probably never will. No matter what is under the pile of stones it will not have ship's papers or a name board, just wood and construction characteristics that may or may not fit the profile of an American vessel built in the Connecticut River in the early 1800s.

But combined with the location of the wreck, the first-hand accounts of those who had been there, and the musket balls on the adjacent bank, it certainly made us realize that the action we had always assumed was on Ayers Point, might well have taken place on Watrous Point, a quarter mile closer to Essex. In all this we had to remember that the Americans were not shooting at the *Young Anaconda*, it had been set on fire. They were shooting at the schooner that would have anchored close by. The *Eagle* was salvaged after the British left it, so there is no wreck to mark its anchorage.

The truth is we do not know for sure exactly how all these pieces fit. That happens sometimes in this business. It would be tempting to conclude the action had taken place at Watrous point after all. Except history is not always that easy. Back in the 1960s a swivel gun had been found on Ayers Point. These are small cradle-mounted cannons meant to be mounted on the bulwarks of ships and ships' boats. A photo of the gun was printed in the *Old Saybrook Pictorial* on August 2, 1967, but like the sword left behind across from the Griswold Inn, the gun itself has disappeared. Adding to the mystery is the fact that fifteen years ago a three-and-a-half-inch cannonball was found in the garden of the adjacent property. This measures out to be six-pound round shot, the same size ball that Lieutenant Bull's cannon was firing when his powder box exploded, no doubt sending several balls rolling off into the bushes.

Was Bull at Watrous Point adjacent to the ballast stone and musket balls, or was he on Ayers Point where the six-pound ball and the swivel gun were found? Were there two cannons? Lieutenant Parry seems to have thought so. Did Captain Bray follow Bull with a second gun crew? As I have often said, like history itself, this project is a work in progress.

BATTLE SITE REVISITED

While many areas of the battle took place on what is now private land, there are four locations where the public can experience the scope of the landscape upon which the British Raid on Essex was played out and view many of the artifacts associated with the raid. Interpretive panels mark each site.

ESSEX (PETTIPAUG)

The village of Essex is worth a visit in its own right. As previously mentioned, many of the houses on Main Street, including the Griswold Inn, were there when the British took possession of the town. Along the length of this picturesque street are twenty-four houses that were there when the British occupied the village. At the foot of Main sits the Connecticut River Museum and the town boat landing where the British came ashore. From here you can look out into the harbor and imagine the arrival of the ships' boats, the exchange of gunfire with the militia, the burning of the ships and the departure of the captured privateers *Eagle* and *Young Anaconda*.

The Connecticut River Museum is located in the 1878 Steamboat dock, which had not been built at the time of the raid. In 1814 the wharves ran through what is now the museum's parking lot. The defenders gathered on high ground on the lawn of the 1732 Samuel Lay House, which is also part of the Museum Complex. Inside the main building is a permanent British Raid on Essex exhibit that includes many artifacts associated with the raid, the mural of the British landing and an interactive diorama of the battle site. Artifacts include charred pieces of the ship *Osage*, cannon and musket balls, and the Royal Navy boarding cutlass that was found in the river.

Just north of the Village is Osage Trails, maintained by the Essex Land Trust. From here you can look across Falls River Cove to the north bank where Williams shipyard once stood. It was in this cove that the *Osage* and the *Atlanta* were burned.

To find Essex take exit 65 or, 69 off I-95 and follow signs to the village and the waterfront. Osage Trails Park can be reached via North Main Street at the top of Main. Take Maple Avenue onto Foxboro Point.

OLD LYME

The best place to capture the panoramic scope of the battle is to visit the small park overlooking the river just north of the Baldwin Bridge on I-95, and just south of the site of Higgin's Wharf, now the Old Lyme Marina. From an overlook sixty feet above the river, visitors can see all the way up to Hayden's Point and Essex to the northwest and across "the gauntlet" to Ferry Point on the Saybrook side of the river. To reach the park, turn off of Route 156 onto Old Bridge Road. Go all the way to the end and you will come to a gate. Park and walk through the gate. Straight ahead is the vista with Essex to the northwest. To the left is a small park with some historic markers. This place is one of the best-kept secrets in the area.

SAYBROOK

Although the Old Platform and Fort Saybrook are long gone you can visit a small park located approximately where they once stood. Drive down Old Saybrook's Main Street through the modern part of town and proceed all the way to the end. You will pass Cypress Cemetery on your right where Lady Fenwick's tomb is visible, enclosed in its own wrought iron fence. On your right will be a large statue of Lion Gardiner, the English officer who built the original fort in 1635. Right next to Gardiner is a park with a symbolic recreation of the fort, but this was not its original location.

Proceed to the end of this road and turn left into the parking lot for Dock-n-Dine restaurant. Beyond the restaurant is a small waterfront park known as Gardiner's Landing and a rough gravel beach. This is approximately the location of the Old Platform, the natural mound upon which the second fort and 1812 gun battery was built. These were destroyed when a railroad was built there in 1873. It was removed in 1924. From this little park you can see the mouth of the river. Looking north you can see the railway bridge with the Baldwin Bridge beyond. These mark "the gauntlet" through which the British proceeded before passing the fort and finally reaching their ships at the mouth of the river.

APPENDIX ONE Primary Documents

While many of these documents are quoted or referenced throughout the course of this book, the opportunity to read them in their full and intact format helps shed a great deal of light on the mood of the times in which they were written, adding nuances of detail for those who want to read between the lines. In addition to Captain Coote's official report and other documents from the Admiralty papers, there were several personal accounts and memoirs written, and nearly 100 newspaper articles were published about the British raid in the days and weeks that followed. There have also been some interesting accounts written over the past 200 years that are informative in their specific content. I have here included a handful of the most important primary documents and some of the more interesting and informative other accounts. I have left the original spellings, styles, odd capitalizations, punctuation and grammar intact including all the variations on Pettipaug. Archivists' notes are included, also unedited. My own notes are shown in brackets. Many of the accounts had some of the basic facts wrong and modern writers have repeated some of these mistakes, making it even more difficult for future historians to sort fact from fiction. Despite the numbers quoted in some of these documents, we now know that there were 136 British directly involved in the raid and that they burned 27 vessels, although several of these were extinguished and salvaged. I hope that these documents and the narrative itself will help set the record straight and lead future historians down new paths of research to fill in some of the remaining mysteries surrounding the British Raid on Essex.

FROM THE BRITISH ADMIRALTY DOCUMENTS

———

The Report of Captain Richard Coote to Captain Capel

(ADM 1/506, pp 274–280)
(From) Commanding Officer, H.M.S. BORER
To his senior officer, Captain Capel in which he describes in detail, from his log, the raid on Essex Harbor.

His Majesty's Sloop Borer
Off Saybrook 9th April 1814
Sir,

I have the honor to acquaint you that in obedience to your Order of the 7th instant, directing me to take charge of a detachment of Boats belonging to the Squadron under your command for the purpose of taking or destroying a number of vessels building and equipping as Privateers and Letters of Marque in Connecticut River, I proceeded to His Majesty's Sloop under my command on the evening of that day to put those Orders in Execution, and I have now the pleasure of informing you that thro' the steady and indefatigable exertions of the officers and Men who you did me the honor of placing under my Orders, the Service has been accomplished in a more effectual way than my most sanguine hopes could have led me to expect.

The Borer anchored off Saybrook bar at 1/4 before 10, and the Boats, consisting of a Barge, Pinnace, and Gig, under Lieuts Pyne, Parry and Acting Lieut Fisher from La Hogue, a Barge from the Maidstone under Lt. Liddon, a Barge from the Endymion under Lieut Fanshaw, and the Borers Gig, with the Seamen and Marines selected for the expedition under their respective Officers immediately proceeded up the River.

The wind being Northerly, and a very rapid outset of the Current (notwithstanding its being flood tide) prevented us from making as steady a progress as we desired, but even this difficulty tended in the end to render our operations more deliberate, the first object being that of destroying a Battery on the West Side of the Entrance, a division landed for that purpose, and meeting no opposition in entering the Fort from which was found the Guns had been removed.

The distance from the Entrance of the River to Petty Pogue where the Vessels lay is only 6 miles; we did not arrive at that place till 1/2 past 3 in the morning of the 8th, on approaching it we found the town alarmed, the Militia all on the alert, and apparently disposed with the assistance of one 4 lb. Gun to oppose our landing, however after the discharge of the Boats' Guns, and a volley of Musketry from our Marines, they prudently ceased firing and gave us no further interruption.

The Marines were formed immediately on landing and under the skilful direction of Lieut Lloyd of that Corps, took up such a position as to command the principal Street and to cover the Seamen which employed in their respective duties. The Vessels alongside the Wharf were then warped out into the Stream, and those on the Stocks and aground near the Town were instantly burned.

As the day opened many others were seen on Slips and at Moorings higher up the River, and those were as promptly set fire to by a small detachment under Lieuts Pyne and Fanshaw to whom we are greatly indebted for the serious damage the Enemy has sustained in this respect.

Several Stores were found to contain large quantities of Cable, Cordage, Sails & Spirits which were either destroyed or removed to the Young Anaconda *Brig and* Eagle *Schooner, each ready for sea and which I at first deemed practicable to bring out, and the object of the expedition being fully accomplished by every Vessel within 3 Miles of the Town being either destroyed or in our possession, the party were at 10 o'clock embarked with the most perfect order and regularity in presence of a very numerous population, not an exception to the character of discipline and sobriety having arisen tho' surrounded by temptations and even urged by the inhabitants to indulge in Liquor.*

At 11 AM we weighed with the Brig Anaconda *and* Eagle *Schooner and proceeded with them some distance down the River, the Wind however blowing strong directly up, and the Channel being extremely narrow, the former grounded with a falling Tide, and I so perceived from the preparations which were making to annoy us on all sides, that it would be expedient to destroy both these vessels, the Party all were accordingly removed to the* Eagle, *and before we lost sight of the brig we had the satisfaction of seeing her burnt to the water's edge. I then determined to defer our retreat 'till after dark, as tho' at the Schooner's present Anchorage, we were exposed to a fire of Musquetry from a Wood within half a Musquet Shot, by far the greatest preparations were making on the banks of a still narrower part of the River which we had got to pass, I here received a communication from the Military Officer Commanding in that district of which I have the honor to enclose herewith a copy.*

———

Major Ely's Surrender Note to Coote

Major Marsh Ely to Coote
To The Officer Commanding the detachment of his Britannick Majesty's Marine forces now gone against the Shipping lying near the mouth of the Connecticut River.

Sir,
To avoid the effusion of human blood is the desire of every honorable man. The number of Forces under my command are increased so much as to render

it impossible for you to escape. I therefore suggest to you the propriety of surrendering your selves prisoners of War and by that means prevent the consequence of an unequal conflict which must otherwise ensue. Captain Charles Harrison is the bearer of this dispatch & will receive your communication.

I am Sir with sentiments of the highest esteem your most obedient servant,
(signed) Marsh Ely, Major
Commanding the forces at Lyme &
Saybrook.
NB [nota bene, note well]: an immediate answer is expected.
A copy verbatim **(signed)** *Richd. Coote*

Coote's Report Continues

My reply was verbal, and merely expressed my Surprise at such Summons, assuring the bearer, that tho' sensible of their humane intentions, we set their power to detain us at defiance.

Every arrangement being made for effecting our retreat, at 7 o'clock the Eagle *was set on fire, and the Boats formed in regular Order, commenced dropping down the River, here a brisk fire was opened from the Wood which had partially annoyed us during the day, but where they had prudently concealed their Cannon 'till darkness rendered it impossible for us to get possession of them, this encounter I am sorry to say deprived us of the lives of two valuable Marines, and wounded one Seaman in the* Maidstone's *boat, but did not in any degree disturb the regularity of our movements.*

The most formidable preparations were made near the town of Lyme and on the opposite bank of the river which is there not more than ¾ of a mile wide, here they were provided with several pieces of Cannon, and from my own observation confirmed by Major Ely's statement, I feel confident that their Military Force amounted to many hundred men.

By waiting 'till the Night became dark, and then allowing the Boats to drop down the Stream silently, we got nearly abreast of this part of the passage unobserved.

Every precaution within the Compass of their Military Skill had here been taken to arrest our progress, large fires were alight on each side to shew the situation of the Boats, and Vessels filled with armed Men were anchored in the River, all these commenced a brisk but ill directed fire at the same instant, and from the short space which separated the Parties, I have reason to suppose it must have proved much more destructive to their friends than to their Enemies, for tho' I believe no Boat escaped without receiving more or less shot, by a degree of good fortune which I can only ascribe to providential care, on our side there was only one Man wounded, at ½ past 8 we were abreast of the lowest Fort, and that which we had found dismantled on the preceding Evening, guns however had been provided for this Fort also during the day, and here they made final and equally ineffectual effort to detain us. *The Boats passed in triumph leaving our Enemies to lament, their acknowledgement of being provided with a force which they had the leisure of a whole day to collect in one of the most populous parts of America, from which they thought it impossible for us to escape.*

Having thus, Sir, detailed the particulars in performing a Service, which from the secrecy with which it was decided on, the clear and judicious instructions with which I was furnished, and the effective means with which you put it in my power to execute your Orders, I felt the fullest confidence of succeeding in. I should neither do justice to my own feelings, or to the characters of the brave Officers and Men who acted under me was I not to express in the strongest terms the high sense I entertain of their individual merit.

The Zeal and exertions of Lieut Pyne where conspicuous on every occasion and some of the Vessels which he handsomely undertook to destroy were lying more than a Mile above the Town, he was principal instrument employed in using the destructive torch and successfully accomplished every enterprise which he undertook.

The Zeal, Activity and Judgment of Lieuts W.G. Parry, M. Liddon and A. Fanshaw were displayed in executing every arrangement of which they had the charge, the two former after getting possession of the Anaconda and Eagle, loaded them with Stores from the Shore, and got them ready for sea in the course of a few hours, the latter destroyed several Vessels and a quantity of Naval Stores in the Town, and together with Acting Lieut Fisher of La Hogue whose conduct was highly conspicuous evinced all the steadiness which might be expected from much older Officers.

To Lieut Lloyd of the Marines and Lieuts Tenpler, Atkinson and Buston who acted under his Orders the Service is greatly indebted for their steady and Soldierlike conduct, the whole surrounding Country was literally kept in awe by the vigilance and discipline which was observed among this small Party. Messrs. Smith, Bodwall, Dunstor and Hopner, Mids of La Hogue, Mr, La Neve of the

Maidstone, *Mr. Heyland of the* Endymion, *and Mr. Elliott of the* Borer *all proved themselves worthy of confidence which was placed in them, and together with them I beg leave strongly to recommend Mr. Bowden, Assistant Surgeon of the* Endymion *who handsomely volunteered to accompany the expedition and was extremely useful.*

In fact the merit of every Seaman and Soldier employed individually recorded, it would not do more than justice to the good conduct and discipline which was observed among them, for when it is considered that this Service was performed in open daylight, and almost in the heart of the Enemy's Country within a few miles of New London, where there is so large a Naval and Military force stationed, I think, Sir, it will appear evident to you, that nothing than such coolness, bravery and discipline as I have represented in these Officers and Men, could have so completely effected the object which we had in view.

Lieut. Ferrant of this Brig, who it was necessary to leave on board as Commanding officer, was truly desirous of being more actively useful and could his Services in that capacity have been dispensed with, I have no doubt but his Zeal & Valor would have been strongly exemplified.

Herewith I have the honor to enclose a list of killed and wounded together with a statement of Names, and description of the Vessels destroyed in Connecticut River, which I find has hitherto been the general (undecipherable) of that Class of Vessels which are calculated to annoy our commerce.

I have the honor to be, Sir,
With every Sentiment of Respect
Your very humble Servant
Richard Coote, Commander

To/ The Hon'ble T.B. Capel
Captain HM Ship La Hogue
& Senior Officer off New London

A List of Men killed or Wounded in the Boats of His Majesty's Ships La Hogue, Maidstone, Endymion, *and* Borer, *in an attack on Ships and Vessels in the Connecticut River.*

Ship's Name	Killed	Wounded
La Hogue	None	One
Maidstone	Two	One

Endymion	*None*	*None*
Borer	*None*	*None*

Names of Men Killed or Wounded

La Hogue	*Stephen Pyke,*	*Severely Wounded*
Maidstone	*Thomas Smith,*	*Killed*
Do.	*Joseph Griffin,*	*Do.*
Do.	*Willm Pyley,*	*Slightly Wounded*

Captain Coote's list of ships destroyed which was included with his report to Capel. [also found in text]
From ADM 1/506, p 280. Document 3 – D

List of (27) Vessels destroyed in Connecticut River on the 8th of April (1814) by the Boats of His Majesty's Ships La Hogue, Maidstone, Endymion, Borer

Name	Rig	Tons	Built For	Guns	State & Condition Location
Young Anaconda*	Brig	300	privateer	18	Completely Fitted, Lying at the town
Connecticut	Schn	325	privateer	18	Completely Fitted, Lying at the town
Eagle*	Schn	250	privateer	16	Completely Fitted Lying at the town
Not named	Schn	180	privateer	16	Ready for launching (on the stocks)
Not named	Schn	150	privateer	14	Planked up & frame laid (on the stocks)
Not named	Sloop	90	packet		Ready for launching (on the stocks)
Not named	Brig	250	Merchantman		Ready for launching, (on the stocks)
Factor	Schn	180	Merchantman		Ready for launching (on the stocks)
Osage	ship	400	E. India Trade	20	Masted & housed over, at wharf a mile above town
Atalante	Ship	380	E. India Trade		Masts & spars on board, at wharf a mile above town
Superior	Ship	320	letter of marquee	16	new & housed over, at moorings above the town
Guardian	Ship	320	letter of marquee	16	Masted & housed over, at moorings above the town
Unknown	Ship	250	Merchantman		Masted. Spars on board, at moorings above town
Unknown	Ship	300	Merchantman		Masted. Spars on board, at mooring above the town
Felix	Brig	240	Merchantman		Masted. Spars on board, at moorings above the town
Cleopatra	Brig	220	Merchantman		Masted. Spars on board, at moorings above the town
Unknown	Brig	150	Merchantman		Completely rigged & fitted
Hatton	Schn	200	Merchantman		Completely rigged
Emblem	Schn	180	Merchantman		Lower masts in Lying below the town
Emerald	Sloop	55	Cargo of wood		Ready for sailing Lying below the town
Mahrata	Sloop	50	Ballast		Ready for sailing Lying below the town

[*vessels Coote says were taken down the river by the British and later burned]

Name	Rig	Tons	Built For	Guns	State & Condition Location
Nancy	Sloop	25			Ready for sailing Lying below the town
Mars	Sloop	50			Ready for sailing Lying below the town
Comet	Sloop	25			Ready for sailing Lying below the town
Thetis	Sloop	80			Ready for sailing Lying below the town
Unknown	Sloop	70	Ballast		Ready for sailing Lying below the town
Unknown	Sloop	70	Ballast		Ready for sailing Lying below the town
Total: 27		Total tonnage: 5,110			Total of Guns pierced for: 134

A number of boats, cables, cordage, sails, Moulds, shipwrights tools, working sheds destroyed

signed Richard Coote Commdr.

[Note: in the copy of ADM 1/506, p 280 that this came from, the date was wrongly listed as April 9th.]

———

Captain Capel to Captain Talbot, HMS Victorious

(ADM 1/506, p. 272–273)

Report of 13 April 1814 from Thomas B. Capel, Captain of H.M.S. *La Hogue*, and Senior Officer of the British squadron blockading Long Island Sound and New London to Captain John Talbot, commanding officer of *H.M.S. Victorious*. This report was forwarded by Talbot to Vice Admiral Cochrane, Commander in Chief of British Naval Forces in North American waters.

His Majesty's Ship La Hogue
Off New London 13th April 1814

Sir,

I have great satisfaction in transmitting to you a letter I received from Captain Coote of His Majesty's Sloop Borer, *under whose directions I placed a division of Boats from His Majesty's Ships named* La Hogue, Maidstone, Endymion, *and* Borer, *for the purpose of destroying a number of large Privateers and letters of Marque, building and equipping in the Connecticut River, and which Service by the judicious arrangements of that Officer, aided by the exemplary good Conduct, steadiness and gallantry of every Officer and Man employed with him, has been attended with complete success.*

The Zeal, activity and abilities of Captain Coote, have been most conspicuous on all occasions connected with this Blockade, and is well known to every Officer under whom he has served on this part of the Station, and I am most highly gratified in assuring you that in the present enterprise, he has fully justified the confidence I placed in him.

I am informed from undoubted authority that a Force of more than a thousand Troops and Militia Men aided by detachment of Seamen and Marines from the Enemy's Squadron in New London, lined the banks of the river, and were in Boats to oppose his return, and by the Enemy's summons to surrender, they must have been themselves convinced of their overwhelming force, but nothing could intimidate him and his gallant Associates, his cool decision in waiting 'till dark, before he returned; his judicious arrangements then dropping down the Stream (without rowing) baffled all the vigilance of the Enemy, and he passed thro' the heaviest of their fire; his men giving three cheers.

I request of you to recommend Captain Coote to the notice of the Commander in Chief, and make known to him in the most favorable terms, the good Order, regularity and discipline with whom every individual employed in this service conducted himself, underneath I subjoin a Statement of our force employed on this occasion.

I am Sir, Your most obedient Servant

(signed) *Thomas Bladen Capel, Captain*

& *Senior Officer off New London*

P.S. The Enemy's loss in shipping amounts to upwards of Five thousand tons and Vessels, capable of carrying more than One hundred and Thirty Guns, and is estimated by them at least Two hundred thousand Dollars.

British Force

Ship's Names	No. of Boats	No. of Men
La Hogue	Three	68
Maidstone	One	30
Endymion	One	31
Borer	One	7
Total	SIX	136

Vice Admiral Cochrane to Croker

(ADM 1/506, p. 269–271)
Dispatch to John Wilson Croker, Secretary to the Lord Commissioners of the Admiralty, London

Bermuda 10th May 1814
Sir,

I have much pleasure in transmitting to you, to be laid before my Lords Commissioners of the Admiralty, a Copy of a Dispatch from the Honorable Captain Capel of His Majesty's Ship La Hogue, (addressed to Captain Talbot of His Majesty's ship Victorious, the senior Officer of the Squadron off New London and Rhode Island) detailing the particulars of a most gallant and successful attack that was made on the Evening of the 7th of April, with a division of Boats under the command of Captain Coote of His Majesty's Ship Borer, upon the Enemy's Shipping in the Connecticut River, by which was effected the destruction of twenty seven sail of Ships and Vessels, of various descriptions; three of which were large privateers completely equipped and ready to put to sea.

I know not whether to admire most the judicious arrangement of the Honorable Captain Capel who ordered this Expedition, the skilful steady and determined manner in which Captain Coote carried his plan into execution or the gallantry discipline and (undecipherable) which marked the conduct of the Officers, Seamen and Marines under his command: it was such as to call forth the encomium even of the Enemy, while they lamented it as the greatest calamity that had befallen the United States since the commencement of the War, and in justice to Captain Coote I should not omit to mention that the Force sent to cut him off in Retreat, which he so judiciously and bravely conducted, is represented in the American Papers, as infinitely superior to what is stated in the Honorable Captain Capel's Dispatch.

Captain Talbot bears testimony to the exertions and abilities of Captain Coote, as represented by the Honorable Captain Capel, and strongly recommends him to my notice, which I beg leave to submit to their Lordships for their consideration as well as the Statement Captain Coote makes respecting the officers serving under him, all of whom appear to be highly deserving their Lordships' protection.

I have the honor to be, Sir,

Your most obedient humble servant Alex Cochrane
Vice Admiral and Commander in Chief

Lieutenant Parry's Transcription

From the *Memoirs of Rear Admiral Sir W. Edward Parry: By his son the Rev. Edward Parry*, 5th edition, 1858.

In the following spring, Lieut. Parry was engaged in a successful boat-expedition, attended with considerable danger. On more than one occasion, the enemy had endeavoured to destroy the British ships by means of "torpedoes," a species of "infernal machine;" and, during one night in April, an attempt of this kind was made on La Hogue, *then lying off New London. "This," he writes, "ended in smoke, or rather in no smoke at all, for all the effect was the ducking of half-a-dozen people by the column of water forced up in the explosion." At the same moment, a boat was detected by the* Maidstone *frigate, containing one man, who pretended to have come off for the purpose of selling provisions. The lateness of the hour, however, and his muffled oars, combined with something uncommon in the appearance of the man himself, raised the suspicions of the Captain, who detained him in irons. The man would not allow that he had any share in the attempt to blow up the ship, but after a few days, offered, in consideration of being set at liberty, to pilot the boats of the squadron up to Pettipague Point, in the river Connecticut, where several American privateers and letters of marque were lying. "Torpedo Jack," as the sailors had dubbed their captive, was willing to prove the honesty of his intentions, by going himself, handcuffed, in one of the boats. An expedition was planned accordingly, consisting of six boats from:* La Hogue, Maidstone, *and* Endymion, *under the orders of Captain Coote, of the* Borer *brig. Parry commanded one of the boats, being third in seniority of the officers engaged; and the account of his gallant exploit, for which a medal was afterwards awarded, may be given in his own words: ----*

"We proceeded in the Borer *to the mouth of the river, where she anchored, and we left her, at 10 o'clock at night, in six good boats, containing 120 men, of whom 40 were marines. We had only six or eight miles to row, but, on account of the tide, which, this season of the year, always runs out of the river, did not get up to the shipping till break of day, and landed without opposition, after warning the inhabitants, that, if a single shot were fired in the neighbourhood, the town should be burnt. To make a short story of it, we were employed in burn-*

ing vessels from daylight, at about half-past four, till noon, when we hauled off into the stream of the river, in two of the finest vessels that were afloat. In these we lay four hours longer, eating and sleeping, within pistol-shot of the woods, in order to refresh ourselves for any further exertions which might be necessary to make; when, lo, and behold! We saw a boat, with a flag of truce, coming out from Lyme, which place, with a point on the opposite side of the river, formed its narrowest part, and, we could perceive, was destined to be the grand rendezvous of their force, in their attempt to stop our going back. The boat came alongside the schooner, where we were now all assembled (having burnt the brig which had grounded); and such an officer, bearing such a letter, nobody ever heard of or saw, -a cobbler's hand, and many words wrongly spelt! It was to demand a surrender. The style in which this was demanded was enough to make us hold it in the greatest possible contempt, which the answer that Captain Coote gave him was sufficient to show. Three cheers for Old England, before the boat was out of hearing, was the most expressive answer to their presumptuous demand; and I verily believe that there was but one mind amongst us upon the occasion. Captain Coote determined upon our remaining where we were in the schooner till dusk, then to set fire to her, and push down the river. She made the twenty-seventh which we destroyed. Whilst daylight lasted, they were afraid to bring anything against us where we then lay, for we would have landed immediately, and dispersed them; but, as soon as it was dark, and we were just on the point of leaving her, they commenced a heavy fire of field-pieces and musketry from the woods close abreast us. The tide was running at the rate of three or four miles an hour in our favour, and we were soon away from the schooner. The grand point, at which their chief force was collected, as I before mentioned, was near Lyme, and its opposite bank (about two miles and a half below us), and thither we drifted silently, without rowing, which would have warned them of our approach. We observed them lighting their fires on the beach, which enabled them to see when we passed the ferry, not by the light which they threw on the water, which was inconsiderable, but they could see when any object passed between them and the fires opposite. This was very quickly the case with us, and a heavy fire commenced. We pulled rapidly past them in a few minutes, and then considered ourselves safe enough. When we went up the night before, we landed at a fort at the mouth of the river, and, finding no guns, merely threw down the flag-staff, to let them know we had been there. We knew, however, that they would have had time enough to get guns here now. When we came abreast of it, they *opened a third fire, but with no effect. Our only loss, in this truly well conducted retreat, has been two killed belonging to the 'Maidstone,' and one wounded of 'La Hogue'. Several privateers, which would very soon have been ready for sea, were destroyed. Reckoning at a rate of 10£. per ton, the value of the damage done would be near 50,000£; and, as an immense quantity of stores were also burnt, it will not be above the mark to value the whole at 60,000£. sterling. We have not yet seen the New London account of it, but we hear that they are astonished. Independently of the stir we made there (five or six leagues from this place), we have also been actually the means of driving the American squadron from their anchorage several miles up the river. We imagined they must have gone up for the purpose of sending a large force from thence, round to Sayboro' to cut us off in our retreat; if they did go, they were a day behind. Such is the outline of this little, but well conducted affair, of which you will soon see the official account."* **

In the summer of 1814, Sir J. B. Warren was succeeded in his command by Sir A. Cochrane, and a more vigorous blockade of the American ports commenced. La Hogue was still stationed off New London, and, with the rest of the squadron, kept the whole coast in a state of alarm. Little, however, was actually done, the American ships of war in the Connecticut river not venturing out to sea. At length Commodore Decatur, finding it had been impossible to break the blockade, even in the winter, and despairing of effecting it in the summer, prudently relinquished his inactive situation, and sent the crews of his ships round by land to man the "President" and others elsewhere.

*The brave leader of this expedition, Captain Coote, was shortly afterwards lost at sea, greatly regretted by all, and by none more than Parry, who spoke of him as a "pattern to all the Captains of His Majesty's Service."

The prospect of peace, held out by the abdication of Napoleon, was hailed with joy by Parry, though it seriously impaired his expectations of promotion, so long delayed.

AMERICAN FIRST HAND ACCOUNTS

Captain Jeremiah Glover

-Copy of April 14, 1814, Court Affidavit of Captain Jeremiah Glover,
    Purporting to Explain his Actions During the British Raid
-Letter from Justice of the Peace

-Letter from Captain Glover to the *Connecticut Spectator* (newspaper) correcting their account.

April 21, 1814 (Thursday)

Mr. Dunning,

The following is an exact copy of the affidavit of Capt. Glover, which was taken by his request and inserted agreeable to his wishes in his own language.

It is a simple narration of occurrences that were all within his knowledge, and are a plain statement of facts which he is willing the public should be made acquainted with. He is in my opinion, a plain, honest and upright man.

Joseph Hill (signed)
Saybrook April 14, 1814

Affidavit

I, Jeremiah Glover, of Saybrook in the County of Middlesex, being duly sworn depose and testify as follows, to wit:

That at Saybrook on the 8ᵗʰ April inst. While the enemy were burning and destroying vessels, at and near Pettipauge Point, I was induced by the advice of my neighbors and friends, to take a white flag and go aboard of my small sloop to endeavor to prevail with the commander not to have her burnt, which I accordingly did. When I came along side of my sloop which was lashed to the cutter built schooner that was in possession of the enemy, the commander demanded of me what I wanted or wished? I told him that the sloop was my property - that I was a poor man, and that I had no other means of support myself and family, but by what I could earn in that vessel; and that I hoped and trusted that he had feelings for the poor and unfortunate, and that he would restore me to my vessel. His answer was "Well, old man, if you behave well, perhaps we shall let you have her." Soon after I was on board, I was solicited to pilot the schooner down the river. I told them I was no pilot - that I had always been in a small vessel or boat and did not know the channel. They still insisted on my complying, which I shortly refused to do; and told them I would abandon my vessel and requested that I might be permitted to go on shore, which request they refused to grant, and commanded me to come on board the schooner. I was obliged to comply. They immediately left the sloop after robbing her of her license and property worth fifty dollars and got the schooner under way and proceeded down the river. When the brig got aground the schooner was immediately anchored 1 ¼ miles *below Pettipauge Point where the brig was burnt. The enemy came all aboard the schooner and their boats were fastened to her. I was confined below. Just at the dusk of the evening they set the schooner on fire and commanded me to get into the boat. Just before the boat left the schooner, a shot from a field piece on the shore killed two men on board the boat which I was in, one man wounded in the head by a musket ball. Orders were immediately given to cast off and pull away. As soon as the boats were out of gunshot, the commander told his men that he would run his sword through the first man that spoke a loud word. They then drifted down as slow as possible until they received the first fire from Ferry Point; when the captain ordered them to pull away, which was done until they got out of gunshot, when they were ordered to give three cheers. Several balls struck the boats, but none was killed at that time to my knowledge. They arrived on board the ships and brig just as the moon rose. I was kept on board the brig until Tuesday the 12th, when I was landed on Fisher Island – and further say not.*

Jeremiah Glover (signed)

State of Connecticut

Saybrook, County of Middlesex, April 14, A.D. 1814

Personally appeared Jeremiah Glover and subscribed to the foregoing affidavit; and made solemn oath to the truth of the Same before me.

Joseph Hill

Justice of the Peace

Connecticut Spectator, MAY 5, 1814 (Thursday)

Saybrook, April 26, 1814

Captain Glover, in addition to the preceding affidavit, stated to the post rider that the enemy passed down near the fort, not suspecting any force was there and received a fire which in his opinion killed 15 or 20 of them, and that on Monday there was an interment on Plumb Island, the ceremonies of which indicated the loss of some character on board of very considerable official respectability. He was no able to ascertain how many of the enemy were killed or wounded – on his departure he was told he might tell the Yankees they killed TWO.

Mr. Dunning,

Sir, — In your paper under affidavit is a statement taken from SPECTATOR stating to be information which I gave the Post-rider. It is a fact that I have seen no Post Rider since I left the enemy - neither have I given such kind of infor-

mation to any person – nor have I any knowledge of any person being killed in passing the fort – or of any such interment on Plumb Island or elsewhere.

> *From your obt. Servant, Jeremiah Glover*

———

Lieutenant Bull's Account

May 16, 1814 – 1st Lieutenant William C. Bull Account. Primary Account
Citation: Connecticut State Library, Connecticut Archives, War of 1812 –
  II: 93A

> . . . *The Memorial of William C. Bull of Say Brook in Middlesex County respectfully Shewith – that on the 8th day of April last while the British barges were lying in Connecticut river about Six miles from its mouth – Your Memorialist being 1st Lieutenant in the first Company of Artillery in the State Corps having volunteered his Services, with one of the Field pieces belonging to said Company – was directed by the Senior officer of Militia then present to move with said piece to a certain Point of land contiguous to said Barges and open a fire on them – That in the performance of said duty, being destitute of proper match rope, said piece was fired with bands or Coals of fire – And not having the necessary compliment of men to work the Field pieces your memorialist was obliged to assist in loading the piece so that about the fifth or sixth fire as he was in the act of taking a Cartridge from one of the Side boxes which was five or six paces in the rear, and to [illegible] of the Piece the same box took fire and blew up with twelve Cartridges containing about Eighteen pounds of Powder. By this accident your Memorialist was badly burned and wounded & from which he has not yet wholly recovered . . .*

———

General William Williams' Account

April 9, 1814 – Major General William Williams Account to Governor
  James Cotton Smith
[Williams was the highest-ranking American officer involved in the
  response to the British raid and came from New London to Lyme after
  mobilizing the forces there.]
Citation: Papers of John Cotton Smith, Collections of the Connecticut
  Historical Society, Vol. II: 1813–1814 (226–228) page 226
Extract of a letter from Major General William Williams to Governor
  Smith, April 9, 1814

New London April 9th 1814

Sir

The enemy in several barges carrying about 200 men appeared yesterday morning at day-light In front of Pettipaug just above Saybrook, to which place they had been attracted by a number of vessels there laid up for security. A company of marines formed and exercised in the principal street of the village as I understand, and gave notice to the inhabitants that they should not be disturbed, nor should their dwellings be injured, as the sole object of the expedition was the destruction of the navigation there collected.

Their promises were faithfully executed both in the protection of the inhabitants and their houses as well as in the compete destruction of about twenty sail of vessels which with the property on board of them are valued at $100,000 and upwards. The loss has fallen upon citizens of the state of New York as well as inhabitants of this state. What adds to my regret is that the British continued in front of Pettipaug & five or six miles with the mouth of Connecticut river from day light yesterday morning until after sunset last evening without receiving any annoyance from us. The Stage which arrived here about 11'O'Clock A.M of the 8th brought the first intelligence of the sufferings from fellow citizens. It was supposed by the officers of the United States as well as myself that their work was probably completed and that they had descended the river before the Stage reached here and had arrived of their vessels, two of which were anchored just without the Bar to further the object of the expedition. Soon after, there arrived of the Stage one of the gentlemen from Lyme came in for assistance, and Capt. French of the artillery with his field-piece was immediately dispatched to their uses. Commodore Decatur ordered a body of marines from his squadron & Gen. Burbach a detachment from Fort Trumbull to aid in capturing the enemy. A number of officers and citizens volunteered their services, and all haste was made by taking up carriages & horses to reach Lyme-ferry as soon as practicable. Col. Kingsbury, Capt. Jones & Biddle with Gen[l] Isham & myself arrived at the scene of action just before sunset, and the artillery from this town together with that from Lyme and Saybrook was placed in the most advantageous position to cut off the retreat of the barges, which at this time were along side a schooner at anchor about half way between Lyme and Pettipaug and without the reach of artillery from either side. On board this schooner the whole British force well armed was prepared for effectual resistance. Owing to the lateness of the hour when aid was requested many of the marines and the detachment from Fort Trumbull did not arrive until sunset, and before a sufficient number of men *properly armed could be collected and the necessary arrangements made, it was dark. The British seized the first moments afterwards & silently took to their barges. The rapidity of the current at this season of the year would soon have carried them beyond our reach without the aid of oars, and so favoured were they by the night that not a person knew when they passed. I cannot sufficiently express the deep mortification which I feel that such an attack should be made upon us & under such circumstances, and that the assailants have escaped un-punished.*

This expedition together with the report that Admiral Cochrane, who is to command on the American Station has a body of troops under him, make it my duty to State to your Excellency the unprepared condition of this quarter to re-ceive the enemy should any future attack be made.

―――

A Gentleman from Lyme

April 20, 1814 – A Gentleman From Lyme (eye witness account from
   Higgin's Wharf)
Citation: *Salem Gazette*, Salem, MA. April 29, 1814. Volume XXVIII,
   Issue 34. P. 2.

Middletown, April 20
THE PETTIPAUGE CATASTROPHE
A gentleman from Lyme has stated to a Friend in this city that he lives about a mile from Higgin's wharf in Lyme: that on the 8th inst. About 7 o'clock, A.M. he was informed that the British were at Pettipauge: that he immediately repaired to the wharf, where were a ship belonging up the river, and sundry other vessels: that on his arrival he discovered the vessels at Pettipauge on fire, at the distance of about three miles, and the enemy on board a schooner, apparently intending to return immediately, the vessel, men and movements being clearly discernible with a glass: that the first object of the inhabitants at Lyme was to secure the ves-sels lying there: that they immediately provided a field piece and two ship guns – the militia collected expeditiously, and suitable preparations were made to wait on the enemy on their return, which was expected every moment that the people were assembling on the opposite side of the river at Saybrook, on the Point. A messenger was dispatched to propose measures to be adopted, that the inhabi-tants might act in concert in intercepting the enemy: that Capt. Bray had just arrived at the fort, and by request instantly removed to the Point opposite the

wharf, taking the most advantageous post with his pieces for co operating with the force on the Lyme shore in annoying the enemy as they came down the river.

On the return of the messenger, Gen. Williams, Gen. Isham, Col. Kingsbury, Captains Jones and Biddle, with a number of Commodore Decatur's marines, had arrived, and numbers of volunteers, U.S. officers, and privates. Capt. Biddle, with the marines and volunteers, manned a sloop, and took a station a few rods below the wharf, near the point, on which also two pieces were placed. That this arrangement precluded all doubts of intercepting and capturing or destroying the barges on their return, which would have taken place immediately had they not been delayed by attempting to take the schooner our of the river. The wind, at length, being ahead, and the enemy delaying to come down, and the afternoon nearly spent, a field piece was moved from one of the first positions, and about sun-set placed on a point in Saybrook, higher up the river, so as to reach the schooner, and by several well directed discharges did such execution that the enemy abandoned her with precipitancy after attempting to burn her, which was prevented by the immediate extinguishment of the flames by the inhabitants who hastened on board. It soon grew dark, the atmosphere was cloudy, and threatening rain, and no object could be seen: - the enemy were still, not a motion to be heard, and though they were supposed to be floating down, they could not be detected. Conjecturing once or twice that they were passing, sundry discharges were made –

When passing the old fort, they were fired upon with some effect – an oar floated ashore, and a piece of a barge. 22 vessels of various descriptions were destroyed by the enemy at Pettipauge: - they were ashore about two or three hours, and the inhabitants were not out of their beds before the enemy had landed and taken possession of the village. – Loss estimated at 150,000 dollars.

———

Selectmen of Saybrook to Governor Smith

April 12, 1813, Selectmen of Saybrook to Governor Smith
Citation: Papers of John Cotton Smith, Collections of the Connecticut
    Historical Society, Vol. II 1813–1814, (235–236) April 12, 1814, page 235.
[This is a letter from the selectmen of Saybrook to the Governor
    complaining of the lack of protection preceding the British raid.]

From the SELECTMEN OF SAYBROOK
To Governor JOHN COTTON SMITH

April 12th, 1814

To His Excellency,

Sir, *In pursuance of a Vote of this Town, in a legal Town meeting assembled —
the unsigned Select Men of said Town, and in behalf thereof; — take the liberty
to State to your Excellency, that on the Morning of the 8th Instant, the Inhabitants of Pettipauge Point (Seven miles from the light house), were surprised by
a detachment of the Enemy, from the Squadron in the sound; consisting of between 2 and 3 hundred Seamen and Marines; commanded by Cap Coote, of the
Brig* Borer.

*So few of the Inhabitants had any notice of their approach; and so sudden was
the landing, that the marines were in many of the House[s] before the Inhabitants were out of their beds — After having destroyed nearly all Shipping in Port,
they retired on board a Schooner, which they hauled off into the Stream below
the Point, and remained there until Dusk, when they were routed by Leut. Bull
with a fieldpiece; in which they lost two men killed, and one wounded — they
then took to their Barges and escaped in the dark; not however without being
briskly fired on by the Militia on either Side the river. — The number of Vessels
burnt by them was twenty-one, beside Several Boats; those remaining are two
new Vessels on Stocks — One Schooner and a Small Sloop — The property destroyed is estimated to have been worth, one hundred forty thousand Dollars.
This very Serious misfortune, is as we conceive, to be attributed, to the total
neglect, which the Government has manifested toward this Town and Port, the
winter past — Had there been a guard of Fifty or even Twenty Men at Saybrook;
this event we verily believe would not have happened; / and had there been a
Supply of Ammunition, especially for the Field Pieces — though that would not
have prevented the landing, yet would certainly have enabled us to have routed
them from Pettipaug before night: and in Such Case, they must have suffered
severe loss if not a total Capture — They escaped under cover of Darkness —
There being no Cannon Ammunition at Pettipauge, and but few Cartridges
at the Platform — It was very late before a few could be got to serve the piece,
which routed them as above stated — / Your Excellency must be sensible that the
Inhabitants of this Town feel Indignant at the General Government; for declar-
ing a war of Offence, & then leaving a Section of the Country so important, as
the Mouth of the Connecticut River, and its Neighborhood; wholly unprotected,
without the means of defence, and under the very Guns of a large Squadron
of the Enemy — To that Government they have applied in vain; Their repeated
applications have been treated with total neglect, From that, they expect no re-*

lief—It is true that at present there is but little in this Port, to tempt new incursions of the Enemy—but if the embargo should be removed many,—and if not—some vessels will collect in this Port—and as this instance of success will Inspire them with boldness and assurance; It is but reasonable to suppose, that we shall frequently be disturbed by them, and it is prudent that we should be in readiness to repel them—

The Inhabitants of this Town, therefore, look up to the State Government, thro its chief Majistrate; for that protection & assistance which they need; and which they have a right to expect from the Government of the United States; but for which they have anxiously looked in vain—And they do hope that no motive of Economy, will prevent a trifling expenditure, for so important an object; or operate even as a procrastination. In behalf of this Town therefore and at its particular request, we pray your Excellency would be pleased to place a respectable guard near the Mouth of the river, to keep ward & watch, with power to stop, examine, and detain, if necessary, all vessels, boats navigating said River.—We also pray that a Magazine of Ammunition may be established in the Neighborhood well supplied with Suitable Items for Ordinance, and Muskets, and such other things as may be thought needful by the Wisdom of Your Excellency;—Please Pardon the liberty we take in praying Speciffe [specific] relief—The anxiety and Solicitude of the Inhabitants are our apology

Signed, John Ayre, George W. Jewett, Jonathan Warner

AMERICAN NEWSPAPER ACCOUNTS

Connecticut Gazette

Connecticut Gazette, New London, April 13, 1814

[One of the first papers to get the story out was the *Connecticut Gazette* published in New London, Wednesday, April 13, 1814, just five days after the raid. It was a fairly accurate account of the raid and many other papers simply reprinted or re-edited parts of it. We know now that there were 136 British involved, not 200, and they set fire to a total of 27 vessels and some smaller boats. We also know that the British did lose two men killed and one severely wounded. Despite the claim made in this account, there are no other reports or documents to support the idea that the British left the schooner and hid behind an island before proceeding down the river. Interestingly, while searching the Admiralty records in

England we found a hand written verbatim copy for this article. Clearly Captain Coote, Captain Capel and all the other officers of the blockading squadron had the paper in their hands within a day or two of its publication.]

Disaster of Pettipauge

It is with grief and mortification, we perform the task of announcing to our readers, that on Friday morning last, four of the enemy's barges and two launches commanded by Capt. Coote of the brig Borer, with 200 men proceeded up the Connecticut River to Pettipauge Point, and destroyed upward of twenty sail of vessels, without sustaining, probably, the loss of a single man.

We have ascertained on the unfortunate stop the following facts. – The boats first landed at the fort at Saybrook, where they found neither men nor cannon; from thence they proceeded directly to Pettipauge Point; landed at 4 o'clock in the morning and were paraded in the principal street before the least alarm was given. The inhabitants were, it may well be supposed, in great consternation; but Capt. Coote informed them that he was in sufficient force to effect the object of his expedition, which was to burn the vessels; and that if his party were not fired upon, no harm should fall on the persons of the inhabitants, or the property unconnected with the vessels, and a mutual understanding of that purport was agreed to. The enemy immediately after commenced the act of burning the vessels. Such as exposed the buildings on the wharves they hauled into the stream.

A party of 14 men in the meantime were sent a quarter of a mile above the point, who put fire to several vessels which were on the stocks. At 10 o'clock they left the shore entirely, and took possession of a brig and a schooner, which were built for privateers; these they attempted to beat down the river, but the brig getting on shore they burnt her, and the schooner was so light as to be unmanageable.

They continued in her and the boats alongside, until about dusk, when Lieutenant Bray with a field piece from Killingworth, commenced firing on them. After the second shot they left the schooner and took shelter under a small island opposite the point, and at half past 8 o'clock it being very dark made their escape from the river. Their conduct towards the inhabitants was unexceptional, except that some clothes and plate were taken by a person supposed to be American, who it was conjectured acted as a pilot and guide;

and had frequently been there with fish for sale. This wretch, without orders, destroyed a large new cable by cutting it with an axe.

Notwithstanding the enemy were on shore at 4 o'clock in the morning, it was half past 12 P.M. before the express arrived here with the information, although a report of the fact was brought by stage at 11. Every exertion was immediately made to send a force sufficient for the object; a body of marines from the squadron, a company of infantry from Fort Trumbull, and a part of Capt. French's militia company of artillery with a field piece, and a considerable number of volunteers were soon in motion. A part of the marines and volunteers in carriages, and Capt. French with his detachment and field piece, arrived at the River at 4 o'clock, at which time a respectable body of militia, infantry and artillery, occupied the banks on both sides, in the momentary expectation that the enemy would attempt to descend.

It was, however, soon perceived that it was not their intention to attempt going out before dark; and that the only chance of taking or destroying them was by a joint attack by land and water. Timely measures for this purpose were prevented by a want of water craft, a misfortune which could not be remedied in the very short period required. A strong freshet, an ebb tide, and thick mist, enabled the enemy to escape down the river unheard, and unseen, except by a very few who commenced a fire, which was followed at random by many who discerned no object to direct their aim.

The troops from the garrison and marines on foot did not arrive until after night fall.

This ended an expedition achieved with the smallest loss to the enemy, and greatest in magnitude of damage that has occurred on the seaboard since commencement of the war.

List of Vessels destroyed by the enemy

Ships

    GUARDIAN, 380 tons, Hayden & Starkey, owners of Pettipauge

    OSAGE, 346 tons, Horatio Alden & Co., Hartford

    ATLANTA, 280 tons, F. Hayden & Others, Pettipauge

    SUPERIOR, 290 tons, A. & J. Pratt and others of Pettipauge

Brigs

    CLEOPATRA, 180 tons, J. Hill and others of Pettipauge

AMAZON, 180 tons, Middletown
(NEW PRIVATEER), 350 tons, W.C. Hall and others of Middletown
FELIX, 200 tons, J. & E. Lyman, New York

Schooners

EMBLEM, 150 tons, J. Hill & others, Pettipauge
BLACK PRINCE, 318 tons, Richard Hayden & others Pettipauge
(On stocks, unnamed), 130 tons, Hayden & Starkey, Pettipauge
And Hall & Goodman, New York
(On stocks, unnamed), 150 tons, H. Hayden & Bros., Pettipauge

Sloops

MOHALA, 50 tons, Hayden & Starkey & Tucker, Pettipauge
COMET, 30 tons, Hayden & Starkey & Tucker, Pettipauge
_____, 70 tons, Middletown
_____, 50 tons, Middletown
EMERALD, 40 tons, J. Platts & others, Pettipauge
THETIS, 75tons, J. Pratt & others, Pettipauge
ROXANA, 50 tons, S. Peck & Barber, New London
(On stocks, unnamed), 80 tons, R. Hayden & others, Pettipauge

Also a sloop from Long Island, name unknown, and several pleasure boats. A brig and a schooner on stocks above the point were on fire and extinguished.

The enemy had stowed in the hold of the privateer schooner, which they left, a considerable quantity of cordage and sails. Before leaving her they put fire in her hold, and cut her masts half off. The fire was extinguished before it had done much damage.

Seven hogs heads of rum were stove in a store the property of Wm. C. Hall. The loss sustained is estimated at various sums. It may amount to $100,000 or upwards.

The village of Pettipauge Point forms a part of the Town of Saybrook and contains about 50 dwelling houses. It is situated on the west side of the Connecticut River, 6 miles from the light house and 19 miles from New London. The STATIRA was off the mouth of the Connecticut River during Friday, and BORER all day Saturday.

Middlesex Gazette

Middlesex Gazette, Middletown, April 14, 1814

April 14, 1814 (Thursday)

About half past 3 o'clock on Friday morning last, information was given at Pettipauge Point, Saybrook, that the British Barges were in the river, and probably bound there and at 4 o'clock six barges, with about 200 sailors and marines commanded by Capt. Coote, of the British Brig BORER, arrived, and rushed into the village, posted sentinels and took possession of the place before many of the inhabitants were out of their beds.

The commanding officer said that his orders were to burn the vessels in the harbor, and not molest the inhabitants, but if any of the soldiers were insulted or killed, they had orders to burn every house in the village – having met with no opposition, they fired every vessel in the harbor to the number of twenty-three, which have been valued at 150,000 dollars – several articles of plate were stolen, but were returned by the officers – they stove 7 hogsheads of Rum and carried off about 5,000 dollars worth of Cordage, the property of Samuel Hayden. The principal part of the vessels were on fire by sunrise or soon after.

After remaining at the village until about 10 o'clock they went on board their boats, and vessels that they had hauled off; they finally got the vessels all aground and burned them, except one schooner which they anchored below 6 Mile Island, nearly out of reach with small arms – they were driven from her about dusk, by a field piece which was brought to bear upon her, when they took to their boats and by the help of their oars and the freshet they passed the narrow passes of the river, where many hundred guns were fired at them by great numbers of people stationed on each side of the river, but with what effect cannot be determined as it was very dark.

LIST OF VESSELS DESTROYED.

Ship "Osage" – 350 tons - owned by H. Alden & Co. Hartford

Ship "Atalanta" – 250 tons – owned by E. Hayden and others, Pettipauge.

Ship "Guardian" - 318 tons – owned by Hayden & Starkey, Pettipauge

Ship "Superior" – 300 tons –owned by A. & J. Pratt and others, Pettipauge

Brig "Cleopatra" – 180 tons – owned by J. Hill & others, Pettipauge

Brig "Felix" – 250 tons – owned by J. & E. Lyman, New York

Cutter Brig – 340 tons – owned by W. C. Hall and others, Middletown

Brig "Amazon" – 170 tons – owned by W. C. Hall, Middletown

New Schooner on stocks – 130 tons – Hayden & Starkey & others, Pettipauge

New Schooner on Stocks on stocks - 160 tons – H. Hayden & brother, Pettipauge

New sharp schooner "Black Prince – 318 tons – R. Hayden & others, Pettipauge

Schooner "Emblem" – 150 tons – J. Hill and others, Pettipauge

Sloop "Thetis" – 75 tons – L. Belden & others, Hartford

Sloop (?) "Emerald" - 60 tons – J. Platts, Jr. & others, Pettipauge

New sloop on stocks - 75 tons – A. Jones & others, Pettipauge

Sloop "Commet" – 30 tons – R, Hayden and others, Pettipauge

Sloop "William" – 70 tons – Tryon, Hartford

Sloop (?) "Washington" – 60 tons – J. & E. Layman, New York

Sloop "Mars" – 60 tons – Wm. Scovel, Middletown

Sloop "?" - 60 tons – Long Island

Sloop (?) "Sally Ann" – 60 tons – Bacon, Middletown

Pleasure boat, E. & S. M. Hayden, Pettipauge

Pleasure boat – Noah Scovel – Pettipauge

Sloop "Mahala" – 50 tons – Hayden & Starkey, Pettipauge

One brig and two schooners were set on fire, but extinguished by the inhabitants. Large quantities of sails and rigging were taken from the stores and burnt with the vessels.

The inhabitants were treated with civility by the officers and generally by the soldiers.

One or two men, with the enemy, whose countenances were recognized by the inhabitants as those who had several times called at the point to sell fish or clams, did considerable damage, by robbing the inhabitants and wantonly destroying property.

———

Connecticut Spectator

[This is the article in which the citizens of Pettipaug defended themselves from attacks in several newspaper accounts.]

Connecticut Spectator, Middletown, May 17, 1814—Essex Account

Middletown, May 18.

By the politeness of sundry gentlemen, we have been favored with an official account of the circumstances which occurred at the time the British landed and burnt the shipping at Pettipauge. We are happy to have it in our power to lay before the public a correct statement of this affair. Various accounts respecting the transactions have been published and some have replete with infamy. We sincerely hope, that those who have given publicity to former accounts will give the following a place in their respective papers. By complying with this request, they will sensibly oblige, the inhabitants of this unfortunate village, and the lovers of truth.

We the under signers, inhabitants of Pettipauge Point and the vicinity, having heard of many incorrect assertions from individuals, and several strong statements published in Newspapers respecting the unfortunate affair that happened at this place, on the 8th day of last April, take this opportunity of making a fair and candid statement of the circumstances which took place at that time, from our personal knowledge, and from the best information we have been able to obtain.

Before 11 o'clock, on the evening of the 7th of April, six British boats were discovered coming into the mouth of Connecticut river, by the keeper of the Light-House, who immediately gave notice to the inhabitants of Saybrook Point, or platform, which is about one mile above the light-house. By 12 o'clock, a considerable number of the enemy were seen in the old fort at Saybrook Point where it appears they found nothing, neither met with opposition. They soon went on board their boats and proceeded up the river for Pettipauge Point, which is near six miles above the said fort. But by reason of a strong northerly wind and a great freshet running down, they did not arrive at Pettipauge Point, until about four o'clock on Friday morning.

The inhabitants had no knowledge that the enemy were in the river, not more than thirty minutes before they were landed and had possession of the Point; and several of the inhabitants had no information that the enemy were near until some of the Vessels were on fire; there was not time after the alarm was given, to get the women and children off from the point, before the enemy were landed and amongst us, and commenced the burning and destroying vessels on the stocks, and on the water. Picket guards searched houses and stores, for arms and ammunition, taking all they could find. After finding that a sufficient force could not be collected in time to save the property from destruction, some of the inhabitants, whose buildings were much exposed to the fire, went back to the Point, to try to save their buildings from the general conflagration with the vessels. Mr. Richard Powers, whose house had just taken fire from a vessel being on the stocks, made enquiry of the commander whether he might endeavor to save his house? His request was granted by the officer. Capt. Timothy Starkey, jr. asked the officer if he should spare the houses and stores from the flames? His answer was, that he did not know what might happen. We do not know of any others who conversed with the officer on the subject. At about 10 o'clock, they called in their guards and proceeded down the river with a brig, a schooner, and two sloops; but the wind shifting at that time, from N.E. to the S.E. they set fire to all but the schooner, and anchored her about a mile and a quarter below Pettipaug Point, where they lay till dark, and then set fire to her and departed down the river. We have heard that it has been stated; by some individuals, that the inhabitants of Pettipauge Point, made an agreement or compromise with the enemy not to resist, if they would spare their houses and other buildings. No such agreement, we believe, was ever made; neither was it heard by the inhabitants of Pettipauge Point, until some time after the affair happened. And we think every such assertion ought to be treated with contempt.

The force of the enemy consisted to two launches, each carrying 9 or 12 pound carronades and about 50 or 60 men each, and 4 barges which it is supposed had about 25 men in each. They were completely fitted for an expedition in every respect. They were furnished with torches and combustibles to set fire instantly.

Pettipauge Point contains about 30 families and is about 35 rods wide, with a road running through the centre, east and west, bounded easterly on Connecticut River; north and south by large coves. The vessels destroyed were lying at wharves at the east end of the Point, and in the river near it, and in the north and south Coves.

Ebenr. Hayden, 2d.	Horace Hayden,
Joseph Hill,	Augustus Jones, jr.
Richard Powers,	Phillip Toncker, jr.
Timothy Starkey, jr.	Richard Hayden, 2d.
Saml. M. Hayden,	Ethan Bushnell,
Judea Pratt,	John C. Hayden,

Asabel Pratt,
Saybrook, May 14, 1814.

———

New York Commercial Advertiser

New York Commercial Advertiser, April 9, 1814—Lyme Account

We were yesterday, politely favored with two letters from Lyme, from which the following extracts are taken. The letters came to hand at too late an hour to be published in our paper last evening.

Lyme, (Con.) April 9,

Yesterday was a distressing day to every friend of commerce in this quarter. The enemy having approached the entrance of Connecticut River, the night before last, with the brig Borer and a sloop of war, they sent into the river six of their barges with about 230 men. They proceeded to Pettipague, without attempting any injury below; and having landed their men, commenced setting fire to the vessels at that place. They took possession of a brig and schr. Bent their sails, and attempted to get them under way; but the wind being unfavorable, and perceiving that the militia were collecting with field pieces on both sides of the river, they set fire to the brig and abandoned her. Of the schr. they kept possession until the evening, when they set her on fire and left her. The flames were soon extinguished. This schooner, and a small sloop preserved by the entreaties of the poor man who owned her are the only vessels to be seen out of about 25 which, the enemy found at that place.

We had entrenchments and several small pieces on each side of the river; and, in the course of the afternoon, Capts. Jones and Biddle and other navy officers, with a large number of men, arrived from New London. Finding the enemy intended to remain above until dark, we made an attempt to fit out 3 sloops to go up in pursuit of them. We succeeded in getting one ready, and a number of us volunteered on board and dropped her in the stream; but finding that the others could not be prepared, we were obliged to abandon the enterprize. Between 8 and 9 o'clock last evening, it being so dark we could not distinguish the enemy across the river, they came down, and were not discovered until they had passed our encampment some distance. Several rounds were then fired, but it is generally supposed without much effect. It was truly aggravating to behold such destruction of property, and not be able to rescue it. I am happy to say, that the most sacred respect was paid to the houses and property on shore. Indeed, several houses, which accidently took fire, were extinguished by the British. Mr. H. is now at Pettipauge, and will be able to give you more correct information, than I can at present, as to the amount of property destroyed and the persons by whom the losses were sustained.

The British vessels remain at anchor a little to the westward of the light-house; and a 74 which joined them yesterday is now lying off Four Mile River.

———

American Mercury

American Mercury, Hartford, CT, May 31, 1814

[This is perhaps, the most comprehensive, but also the most scathing, account of the raid. The *Mercury* published a series of attacks on Pettipaug to which the people of the village defended themselves, pointing out several exaggerations. It went back and forth for some time. The *Mercury* did print a partial retraction, clarifying some of the details. It is generally an accurate account and paints a vivid picture of the lack of organization early in the day.]

May 31, 1814

Who then, let us inquire, would have indulged the remotest fears that only about 150 sailors and marines of the enemy (and only about 50 of them were marines) would have met with such a dishonorable reception at Pettipague. Not a gun was fired nor a bayonet charged upon them while they remained at the point, a time at least of six hours. It is true the enemy came about four o'clock in the morning and probably we could have made but an ineffectual resistance at the time of their landing as we had but about 30 minutes warning of their approach. A few patriotic citizens behaved like men. They seized their arms and accoutrements and repaired immediately towards the scene of action, singly, by pairs, and half dozens; but want of union, regularity and officers, rendered their services ineffectual, so they generally returned as they came, only not quite so swift.

About half dozen individuals, who resided the most contiguous to the scene of danger, exhorted submission and non-resistance. They said "to oppose them would only exasperate and provoke them to burn houses;" and said,"the enemy agreed not to burn buildings, if they were not opposed but threatened it if they were." The Military Officers and some other men were duped enough to assent to this kind reasoning; as little or no kind of preparations were made to repel them, till they had been here some hours. At length after being entreated and urged by the inhabitants, the officers began to make some shew of preparations. It is (or ought to be) well known that there is in this Town, one company of the celebrated State Artillery (raised in pursuance of the above sited act of the legislature) with 2 brass six pounders belonging to it, and the officers and soldiers composing it mostly reside within two miles of the place invaded. And also, by some unaccountable neglect, no fixed ammunition, and in fact no kind of ammunition was provided except some balls and canister shot, and they were about four miles distant: yet it is acknowledged by all that had practicable exertions been made, the Cannon might have been placed in a commanding position and a sufficiency of ammunition procured as soon, at least, as half an hour after sunrise, and had this been done, there is not the least doubt but it would have saved 'most' of the shipping that was destroyed, as they did not burn many vessels till two or more hours after sunrise; yet strange to tell, the Company of Artillery did not appear till afternoon. Unfortunately the Captain of this Company, George W. Jewett, Esq. who returned from New London county, the evening before, happened to be unusually and unpleasantly indisposed on that day, so that he was not able to ride to town until after sunrise the next morning. The first and second Lieutenants were soon upon the spot and it is believed that they collected about half a dozen men of their Company as soon as 2 o'clock P.M. At that time the invaders had left the shore but were yet in sight; and this little band of soldiers jogged along and joined the other forces near the entrance to the river. A small part of this Company however, who reside near the entrance of the river, it is understood, assembled in the forenoon on the margin of the river with the third Lieut. for the purpose of acting with other troops, assembled there from different quarters, in attacking the enemy when they descended the river. We will mention but one circumstance relative to the Militia Company here, (consisting of considerably over 100 men) and that is this; instead of being ordered by their officers to assemble forthwith, at some contiguous place to the scene, they were ordered to meet at 10 o'clock A.M. at the usual place of parade; which place is about two miles from the place invaded. They marched down toward the point about noon, or a little before, about that time the enemy completed their work of destruction and abandoned the shore. By the operations and manoevers of the enemy they gave us a good opportunity to capture them. They divided into parties, forty-eight muskets were stacked on the point, and only eight marines guarded them a number of hours, whilst other parties were busied in ascending each cove and destroying the vessels in them and in the river. Some detachments went entirely unarmed excepting one or two Cutlasses and hatchets : and here were from 2 to 400 men capable of bearing arms idle spectators, and by our inactivity and submission, as it were, inviting them to burn and destroy without reserve. Considerable preparations were made below to cut off their retreat; but sending flags of truce, waiting for reinforcements, contriving, &c. &c. delayed a bold attack till it got to be quite dark. They were then ready to annoy the enemy, and Lieut. W. C. Bull began to play upon them with his field piece, which made them hasten away as fast as possible. But the cloudy atmosphere and want of a moon prevented much damage which otherwise might have happened to them.

These facts the public may be assured are substantially correct – and believing that the public ought to be made acquainted with them, that truth may prevail, is the only motive which induces the writer to make this simple statement for their benefit. By an eye witness."

———

Connecticut Spectator

Connecticut Spectator, Middletown, June 8th, 1814
[In response to the Mercury's attack on May 31st, George Jewett placed
   this "Advertisement" in the *Connecticut Spectator* the following week.
   Although he vigorously attacks the motives and credibility of his
   accusers, he again makes no mention of where he was the night of the
   raid. This was not the end of the public exchange of barbs and counter
   barbs as Spencer and Dickinson continued to maintain the basic truth
   of their accusations even while publishing a partial retraction. All of this
   must have helped sell a lot of newspapers.]

Advertisement
*In the American Mercury of last week, there is a publication relative to the
affair, at Pettipauge, on the eighth of April Last; signed "By an eyewitness," professing to have no other end in view, but to state facts correctly, that truth might
prevail, &c.*

*There is however, no person of the least candor or discernment, but will at
once perceive that the real object is slander. It shoots its envenomed shafts of
malice, at the state at large, at its Institutions, its officers, its citizens, with the
consequence and authority of a Roman dictator. The distinguished citizens, who
were the authors of that modest article, the public at large ought to know, and
surely if its objects are, what they profess to be, the authors could have no objec-*

tion, to being known. Yet true it is, the authors of that vile production, neither wished that their names, or designs should be discovered; while they, under the mask of a slanderous, anonymous publication, like the Bohen Upas should scatter their poison around them ; but, "murder will out," and the public are hereby informed, that the piece in questions, was written by, and between, a couple of low bred, obscure, illiterate, lying wretches ; resident in Pettipauge, by the names of Obadiah Spencer, and Gideon A. Dickinson, who until this time have remained to the public, quite unknown, but who, at present, are in a hopeful way, to a regular introduction.

Why these foul Bipeds, should level so large a share of malice at me, I know not ; But so it is, that in the short notice, which they take of me, and the company I command ; there is no less than eight distinct falsehoods ; indeed, there is not one circumstance, which is related of me, that either of them had the least possible knowledge of : although they say they were an "eye witness." Happening to be at Hartford the day the piece was published, a friend of mine put the paper that contained it into my hands. I repaired to the office, whence it issued, and there learned the names of the distinguished gentlemen who wrote it.

After I returned, I made Spencer acquainted with my knowledge of his rascally conduct. He endeavored to palliate, by saying that he had written that part of the publication relating to me very different from what it now appeared ; but before he sent it away he showed it to his friend Dickinson, who desired to alter that part of it, and put something in about me that would read a little "Cuter ;" and that Dickinson altered it, so as to make it read as it now stands. In a moment or two I saw Dickinson coming up. I asked him if he knew who was the author of the peace in the Mercury, signed by an eye witness. He very readily, and very seriously, replied, he did not. I let him understand, in plain terms, that although he had added to the catalogue of his former lies, he had not deceived me.

Thus these truth professing Hypocrites are somewhat like the two thieves, who went into a butcher's shop and stole a piece of meat ; while one swore he did not take it ; the other swore he had not got it.

I therefore take this method, to caution the public not to believe, or circulate that false and scandalous publication ; and do at the same time declare, the said Obadiah Spencer and Gideon A. Dickinson to be a brace of lowbred lying rascals.

Geo. W. Jewett. Pettipauge, June 6.

[Despite all the controversy, Jewett was later promoted from captain to major.]

APPENDIX TWO Order of Battle

BRITISH RAID ON ESSEX, APRIL 7–8, 1814
Compiled by David Naumec for CT SHPO report,
and amended by the author and Andy Germen.

I - Total Number of Combatants Engaged: (US: 400–600 / British: 136)
United States Armed Forces in the area: Approx. 700–1,000
    US Regular: Approx. 150–200
    Connecticut State Militia & volunteer: Approx. 550–800
It is not known precisely how many Americans were deployed to the
    river but it is believed there were between 400 and 600 although some
    estimates are higher.
British Armed Forces deployed into the Connecticut River in the ships'
    boats: 136

II - Casualties: (US: 2 WIA, 1 Captured / British: 2 KIA, 2 WIA)
United States Armed Forces: Two wounded in action
    1 man wounded in action, Saybrook (Pettipaug) Militia / Volunteer
        (George Harrington)
    1 man wounded in action, 1st Co. Bray's, CT State Artillery (Lieutenant
        William C. Bull)
    1 man captured, Sea Captain Jeremiah Glover, Saybrook
British Armed Forces: Two killed in action, two wounded
    2 Royal Marines, killed in action (Corporal Thomas Smith &
        Joseph Griffin, HMS *Maidstone*)
    2 Royal Sailors, wounded in action (Stephen Pyke, HMS *La Hogue* &
        William Pyley, HMS *Maidstone*)

III – United States Forces
United States Armed Forces — Regular Forces:
Officers:
    General Henry Burbeck, commandant of US forces stationed at
        New London (Fort Trumbull, New London, CT)

Colonel, Inspector General Jacob Kingsbury, commander of US forces
in RI and CT

Colonel A. Benjamin, 37th Regiment United States Infantry

Captain Stephen Decatur, USS *United States*

Captain Jacob Jones, USS *Macedonia* (Detached to take command of
US Marines and US Sailors from Macedonia and Hornet)

Master Commandant James Biddle, USS *Hornet* (Detached to take
command of US Marines and US Sailors from Macedonia and
Hornet)

Units:

1 Company (Approx. 60–80) 37th Regiment US Infantry,
Fort Trumbull, New London, CT

"Detachment" (Approx. 40–50) US Marines, Decatur's Fleet,
Gales Ferry, CT

"Detachment" (Approx. 60–80) US Sailors, Decatur's Fleet,
Gales Ferry, CT

United States Armed Forces – Connecticut Forces:

Officers:

Major-General William Williams, Third Division, Connecticut Militia,
New London, CT

Brigadier-General Jirah Isham, Third Division, Third Brigade,
Connecticut Militia, New London, CT

Colonel Marsh Ely, 33rd Regiment, Third Division, Third Brigade,
Connecticut Militia, Lyme, CT

Captain John French, 3rd Regiment, Third Division, Third Brigade,
Matross Company, Connecticut Militia, New London, CT

Captain George W. Jewett, 1st Company, Connecticut Artillery Corps &
Saybrook Militia, Saybrook, CT (Pettipauge Quarter)

Captain Amaziah Bray, 2nd Company Connecticut State Artillery
Company, Saybrook & Killingworth, CT

Units:

Exact number of Connecticut forces brought to bear on the British is
unknown as both militia and private citizens responded to the alarm
throughout the day. The following figures are based on estimated troop
strength of state and federal forces deployed during the Essex Alarm.

East Side Connecticut River:

150–200 Lyme, Connecticut Militia and volunteers, and 3 cannons

(1 brass 6 lb. gun, 1 iron 4lb gun and 1 iron 6 lb. gun). (Present towns of Lyme, East Lyme, and Old Lyme)

200–300 New London, Connecticut Militia and volunteers. (Present towns of New London, Montville, and Waterford)

1 Field Piece (brass 6 lb. gun) Captain French's Artillery Company (approx. 15–20 men), 3rd Regiment, Third Division, Third Brigade, Matross Company, CT Militia, New London, CT

West Side Connecticut River:

2 Field Pieces (brass 6 lb. gun) Captain Bray's Artillery Company (Approx. 40–60 men), 1st Company Artillery, Connecticut State Corps, Killingworth, CT

2 Field Pieces (brass 6 lb. gun) Captain Jewett's Artillery Company (Approx. 20–30 men), 2nd Company Artillery, Connecticut State Corps, Saybrook, CT

100–150 Saybrook, CT militia and volunteers, and 1 cannon (iron 4lb gun at Pettipauge) and 1 cannon (iron 6 lb. deployed to Fort Fenwick) [Present towns of Old Saybrook, Deep River, Essex, Centerbrook, and Ivoryton]

60–80 Killingworth, CT militia and volunteers (Present towns of Killingworth and Clinton)

IV – British Forces

Officers:

Captain John Talbot, MHS *Victorious*, Senior Officer off New London and Rhode Island

Captain Thomas B. Capel, HMS *La Hogue*, Senior Officer off New London

Captain Henry Hope, HMS *Endymion*

Captain George Burdett, Esq, HMS *Maidstone*

Captain George Dickins HMS *Sylph*

Captain Richard Coote, HMS *Borer*, in command of all British forces during the raid

Lieutenant William Edward Parry, HMS *La Hogue*, in command of one Pinnace from the *La Hogue*

Lieutenant Fisher, HMS *La Hogue*, in command of one Gig from the *La Hogue*

Lieutenant Arthur Fanshawe, HMS *Endymion*, in command of one Barge from the *Endymion*

Lieutenant Mathew Liddon, HMS *Maidstone*, in command of one Barge from the *Maidstone*

Lietuenant Henry Pyne, HMS *La Hogue*, in command of Barge from HMS *La Hogue*

Lieutenant Walter Griffith Lloyd, *HMS Endymion*, in command of all Royal Marines

Lieutenant Atkinson, Royal Marines

Lieutenant Buston, Royal Marines

Lieutenant Templer, Royal Marines

Other Personnel:

Pilot for expedition – Ezekial Jackson

Pilot for HMS *Maidstone* – Unknown Swedish sailor from *Ann Maria**

Quartermaster James Chialleborough, HMS *La Hogue*

Gunner Robert Chiene, HMS *La Hogue*

Quarter Gunner Joseph Masterman, HMS *La Hogue*

Master Edward F. Bedwell, HMS *La Hogue*

Midshipman Bodwall, HMS *La Hogue*

Midshipman Smith, HMS *La Hogue*

Midshipman Dunstor, *La Hogue* [Coote names him]

Midshipman James Heyland, HMS *Endymion*

Midshipman Hopner, HMS *La Hogue*

Midshipman Frederick L'Estrange, HMS *Maidstone*

Midshipman Basil Eliott, *Borer*

Midshipman Anselm Peter La Neve, HMS *Maidstone*

Mate John Skinley,

Mate Stephen Pyke, HMS *La Hogue* (WIA)

Mate William Pyley, HMS *Maidstone* (WIA)

Assistant Surgeon Bowden, HMS *Endymion*

Yeoman of Sheets Francis Fowler, HMS *La Hogue*

Orderly Francis Harrison, HMS *La Hogue*

L.M. John Jameson, HMS *Borer*

Private Isaac Elliott, Royal Marines, HMS *Maidstone*

Private Evan Jones, Royal Marines, HMS *La Hogue*

Thomas Smith, Royal Marines, HMS *Maidstone* (KIA)

Joseph Griffin, Royal Marines, HMS *Maidstone* (KIA)

---

*"Evening Post Marine List," *Evening Post* (New York, NY), April 21, 1814, Issue 3653. p. 2.

Units:

HMS *Borer*, 12-gun *Bold*-class gun brig (launched 1812), crew of 80 (deployed to CT river on April 7th)

HMS *Slyph*, 22-gun sloop of war (launched 1812), crew of 117 (deployed on April 7th)

HMS *Maidstone*, 32-gun 5th rate *Apollo*-class frigate (launched 1811), crew of 264 (deployed on April 8th)

HMS *La Hogue*, 74-gun 3rd rate *Vengeur*-class ship of the line (launched 1811), crew of approx. 550 (remained off New London)

HMS *Endymion*, 40-gun 5th rate *Endymion*-class frigate (launched 1797), crew of 340 (remained off New London)

1 Barge from HMS *Endymion*, 31 men

1 Barge from HMS *Maidstone*, 30 men

1 Barge from HMS *La Hogue*, 31 men

1 Pinnace from HMS *La Hogue*, 30 men

1 Gig from HMS *La Hogue*, 7 men

1 Gig from HMS *Borer*, 7 men

TOTAL: 136 officers, seamen and marines. Approximately 40 of these were Royal Marines.

ACKNOWLEDGMENTS

There are many people and organizations whose resources, expertise and encouragement have helped to make this book possible. I want to start by thanking Admiral Pullen, Commander Albert Dock, Captain Russell Anderson and the Essex Historical Society for tracking down and publishing the *British Admiralty Papers* and other important documents in 1981. Thanks also to the Sailing Masters of 1812 fife and drum corps for keeping the tradition of the annual Commemoration Day parade alive for over 50 years.

This project began while I was executive director at the Connecticut River Museum and I am grateful that the Museum has continued to allow the use of all research materials and many of their historic and modern images. I want to especially thank CRM curator Amy Trout who was my partner in working to bring this story to life. Our in-house research team included Margaret-Ellen Fein and Warner Lord. Lead researcher David Naumec worked tirelessly, searching archives, libraries and historical societies to compile the report, which supported the battle site nominations and provided invaluable resources for this book. In England, Rosalie Spire was commissioned to help track down ships logs and other important information in the British National Archives. I also want to thank the *Archival Angels* at the Essex Historical Society, especially Debbie Weinstein and Eve Potts, for their research assistance.

I want to thank Roy Manston, Andy German, Amy Trout, and Geoffrey Paul, who not only helped vet the manuscript but went way beyond the call of duty supplying a great deal of additional research and much appreciated advice. Victor Mays, Fellow Emeritus of the American Society of Marine Artists, has also been an integral part of my vetting and research team and has honored me by allowing the use of several images he has created over the years including many that were commissioned specifically for this project and are seen for the first time in this publication. Thank you, Victor!

I cannot thank Bob VanKeirsbilck of Long Cat Graphics enough for creating all the modern battle maps and the 1814 bird's-eye-view of Essex. Bob has been with this project from the beginning and has been a critical part of the team providing images that have supported exhibits in the Connecticut River Museum, the work of the archeological field team, and this publication.

Much thanks are due to maritime artist Russell Buckingham whose twenty-two foot mural of the British landing for the Connecticut River Museum has been reproduced for the cover of this book. Russell worked tirelessly on this ambitious project often repainting details and even uniforms prompted by the ongoing research.

I want to thank the archaeologists who have spent so much time digging up the physical evidence of the battle. This began in the 1980s with Wesleyan anthropologist Dr. John

Pfeiffer and his team including Dr. Robert Funk, Dr. Richard Gould, the late Essex historian, Don Malcarne and a host of volunteers. John Pfeiffer has continued to play an important role in the project along with Connecticut State Archaeologist Dr. Nick Bellantoni who has been a great supporter and deeply involved since the beginning.

Dr. Kevin McBride and his team from the Mashantucket Pequot Museum and Research Center (MPMRC), the UConn Field School of Anthropology and a number of dedicated volunteers conducted a six-month comprehensive investigation in 2013 of this complex six-mile long battle area. They found dozens of important artifacts and mapped the scattered sites into the GIS system all of which support the federal battle site nomination. The MPMRC team included David Naumec, Heather Manwaring, Amara Litten, Kathleen Boushee, Noah Fellman, Gena Dezi, Ralph Sebastian Sidberry, and Angel Desmarias and Dr. Kroum Batchvarov. The Yankee Territory Coinshooters metal detecting team included George Pescia, Mike Horen, Ken Gudernach, Robert Brock, and Dan Lamontagne.

I want to thank the Paul Foundation, Essex Historical Society and the British Raid on Essex Bicentennial Committee for all of their support and encouragement. Geoffrey Paul, Herb and Sherry Clark, Susan Malan, Yves Feder, Brenda Milkofsky and Joanne Masin, amongst others, have truly helped keep this project going. I want to thank Norm Needleman and the Town of Essex for supporting this effort as well as all of the property owners who allowed us to literally dig up their lawns searching for musket balls and British buttons. I particularly want to thank Andy Carr on whose lawn we found over 28 musket balls and under whose dock lays the ballast stone that may be the *Young Anaconda*. Among the many others who allowed unfettered access to their properties I would especially like to thank the Chiats, Ray Allen, Cynthia McFadden, the Pites, the Lvoffs and Charles Brittan.

I would like to thank Stacey Vairo and Mary Donohue of the Connecticut State Historic Preservation Office, Paul Hawke and Kristen McMasters from the American Battlefield Protection Program, Congressman Joe Courtney, Governor Dannel P. Malloy, Edward Baker and the New London Historical Society, Richard Buel, Chris Pagliuco, Glenn Gordinier, Gail Tubbs, Neal Kirk, Geoffrey Neilson, Nancy Steenburg and Damian Wesserbauer, all of whom helped support this project in one way or another.

I want to thank Suzanna Tamminen for believing in this project and the incredible team at Wesleyan University Press including Leslie Starr and Victoria Stahl for working so hard to get this book published by the bicentennial of the raid. Thank you.

Lastly, my greatest thanks are directed to my wife Jeni. In addition to allowing me the dedicated time to research and write this book, virtually living on the battle sites for months on end, she has directly supported this project on a daily basis through invaluable research, manuscript proofing and constant encouragement. It may sound like a cliché, but I literally could not have done it without her!

NOTES AND SOURCES

INTRODUCTION

The original purpose of this project was to document the British Raid on Essex in order to attain official state and national recognition of the battle site. All of our research was geared toward that goal. This book is a result of some of the information we collected. Each discovery has lead to its own spider web of additional information, and additional threads to this complex story. At some point I had to say, enough is enough (for now) and write this book, but I truly feel we have just begun.

The genesis of the *British Raid on Essex* pamphlet, published by Commander Dock and Captain Anderson in 1981, was the British Admiralty and Secretariat Papers and a handful of contemporary American newspaper accounts. This is where we began. We were fortunate that through a grant from the Connecticut State Office of Historic Preservation we were able to secure two professional researchers, David J. Naumec in the United States and Rosalie Spire in England. With David's and Rosalie's help, Connecticut River Museum Curator Amy Trout and I were able to compile additional British and American documents, a number of firsthand accounts and over ninety newspapers articles published within the days and months after the raid. In addition to the chapter-by-chapter sources and notes that follow, here is a quick overview of where much of the information was derived from.

British Forces and Movements

Unless otherwise noted, the information pertaining to the British movements and order of battle come from The Admiralty and Secretarial Papers, ADM 1/06, which include correspondences between Admiral Alexander Cochrane, commander in chief of the Royal Navy's North American Station; Captain Thomas Bladen Capel, senior officer off New London and the man who initiated the raid; and Captain Richard Coote, operational commander of the raid. These documents contain Captain Coote's comprehensive after-action report which includes a chronology of events, forces deployed, a list of ships burned, and casualties sustained. The Admiralty Papers, ADM 37 also includes the muster and log-books of the five British warships directly involved with the raid.

American Forces and Movements

Like the American defense and reaction to the attack, the official documentation of the raid from the American side is disorganized and incomplete. There were a small number of reports by officers directly involved including Major General Williams and Lieutenant William Bull, but for the most part official reports were not filed or have not been found.

Captain Jeremiah Glover, the American who was abducted by the British during the raid gives a unique account of his experience in an affidavit he filed after the raid. In the *Salem Gazette*, April 29, 1814, "A Gentleman from Lyme" provided an extraordinary eyewitness account of events throughout the day. A large number of other newspapers offered additional detail and perspective. The best examples of these are, the *Connecticut Gazette*, the *American Mercury*, and the *Middlesex Gazette*.

Information on the Order of Battle was compiled by David J. Naumec as part of his comprehensive and well-documented report commissioned by the Connecticut State Office of Historic Preservation in support of the British Raid on Essex Battle Site District, in 2012. The entire report is filed with CT SHPO.

Torpedo Jack "the Traitor"

Information having to do with the capture of Ezekiel Jackson (Torpedo Jack) is found in *The Memoirs of Rear-Admiral Sir W. Edward Parry*, published in London in 1857; "Blue Lights and Infernal Machines" by Goldenberg, found in the *Mariner's Mirror*, Volume 61, Number 4. London, UK: Society for Nautical Research, November 1975; and "The Battle of Stonington" by James Tertius de Kay, Parnassus Imprints, 1990.

Decatur's War

The departure of the American squadron under Commodore Stephan Decatur from New York, its transit through Long Island Sound, confrontation with British naval forces in Block Island Sound, and its retreat into New London are derived from William M.P. Dunne's, "The Inglorious First of June," Long Island Journal 2, No. 2, 1990 pages 201–220. I hope that this book at last dispels some of the myths and puts this action into its proper place within the documented maritime history of both our state and nation.

CHAPTER NOTES

Prologue

Page ix: *The rediscovery of the British raid*: the meeting is explained in Albert Dock and Russell Anderson, *The British Raid on Essex* (Essex Historical Society, 1981), 5; "Two Essex historians discover Old Saybrook had native turncoat," *The Pictorial Extra, Pictorial Gazette*, Old Saybrook, March 31, 1981, vol. 17.

Chapter 1

Page xii: *Sir, I have great satisfaction*: Capel to Talbot, Admiralty Secretariat Papers, ADM 1/506, 272–73.

Page 1: *The Light was fading*: the following reconstruction of the British situation at the climactic point of the raid is drawn from Capt. Coote's report, Coote to Capel, April 9,

1814, Admiralty Secretariat Papers, ADM 1/506 (see appendix); calculations of sun and moon rises and set come from the United States Naval Observatory (USNO) online historic calculator http://aa.usno.navy.mil/data/docs/RS_OneYear.php; references to weather and wind direction come from the logbooks of the British ships off New London and from Coote's account, and several newspaper accounts, especially the *Connecticut Gazette*, April 18, 1814 (see appendix).

Page 1: *Through his glass*: based on the account by the "Gentleman from Lyme," *Salem Gazette*, April 29, 1814 (see appendix).

Page 2: *Earlier in the day*: see Victor Mays, *The events in Killingworth Harbor, 1813–1814* (Clinton: Clinton Historical Society, 2009); "Gentleman from Lyme" (see appendix); Thomas A. Stevens, "Trinity Lodge No. 43 A. F. & A. M. Deep River, Connecticut: A History of its Founding in 1797 and the Spread of Free Masonry in Lower Middlesex Co., Conn.," address presented at Trinity Lodge No. 43, November, 1972.

Page 3: *That afternoon*: "Gentleman from Lyme" (see appendix); Williams to Smith, April 9, 1814, Papers of John Cotton Smith, Collections of the Connecticut Historical Society, War of 1812–Vol. II. (226–228) (see appendix); Memorial of Lieut. William C. Bull, Connecticut Archives, War of 1812—II, 93A, Connecticut State Library (see appendix).

Page 3: *As evening approached*: Williams to Smith (see appendix); *Connecticut Gazette*, April 13, 1814; "Gentleman from Lyme" (see appendix).

Page 3: *But as the sun grew low*: *Connecticut Gazette*, April 13, 1814; "Gentleman from Lyme" (see appendix).

Page 3: *Lieutenant Bull was dispatched*: Memorial of Lieut. Bull (see appendix); Donald E. Graves, "Field Artillery of the War of 1812: Equipment, Organization, Tactics and Effectiveness," *War of 1812 Magazine* 12 (November 2009), http://www.napoleon-series.org/military/Warof1812/2009/Issue12/c_Artillery.html.

Page 4: *Lacking proper match rope*: Memorial of Lieut. Bull (see appendix).

Page 5: *Loser's Day*: Although officially known as "Commemoration Day," or, "The Burning of the Ships," "Loser's Day," is the common terminology used by many people in Essex. Until recently most people knew little more than: the British came and burned ships after a very slight resistance at the landing site. Most do not know of the large mobilization the following day, or the musket and cannon fire, which was directed at the British through the afternoon of April 8th.

Chapter 2

Page 9: *There have been stacks of books*: for general overview this study has made reference to Jon Latimer, *1812: War with America* (Cambridge, MA: Belknap Press, 2007) and G. H. Hollister, *The History of Connecticut from the First Settlement to the Adoption of the present Constitution*, Volume II (New Haven: Durrie and Peck, 1855); the war in Connecticut is the subject of James Tertius de Kay, *The Battle of Stonington: Torpedoes, Submarines, and Rockets in the War of 1812* (Annapolis: Naval Institute Press, 1990), and Glenn S. Gordinier, *The Rockets' Red Glare: The War of 1812 and Connecticut* (New London: New London County Historical Society, 2012).

Page 10: *When the War of 1812 began*: There are a number of biographical sources on Capt. Stephen Decatur, the most recent being Spencer C. Tucker's *Stephen Decatur: A Life Most Bold and Daring* (Annapolis: Naval Institute Press, 2004).

Page 13: *On April 9th*: The reconstruction of the events that brought USS *United States, Macedonian*, and *Hornet* into New London is based on the extensive research of William M. P. Dunne, published as "'The Inglorious First of June': Commodore Stephen Decatur on Long Island Sound, 1813," *Long Island Historical Journal* 2, No. 2 (Spring 1990): 201–220.

Page 17: *Although safe within*: Joseph A. Goldenberg, "Blue Lights and Infernal Machines: The British Blockade of New London," *The Mariner's Mirror* 61, No. 4 (November 1975); Gordinier, *The Rockets' Red Glare: The War of 1812 and Connecticut*; for torpedo men, see Andrew W. German, "'To Serve Their Country and Make Their Fortunes': Connecticut Privateers and Torpedomen in the War of 1812," *Connecticut History* 52, No. 1 (Spring 2013): 47–63.

Page 17: *Blockade*: Goldenberg, "Blue Lights and Infernal Machines: The British Blockade of New London," *Mariner's Mirror*; Gordinier, *The Rockets' Red Glare: The War of 1812 and Connecticut*.

Page 18: *Yet even this*: German, "'To Serve Their Country and Make Their Fortunes': Connecticut Privateers and Torpedomen in the War of 1812," *Connecticut History* 52, No. 1 (Spring 2013): 47–63.

Page 18: *Government-sanctioned privateering*: the most comprehensive study of privateering during the war remains George Coggeshall's *History of the American Privateers, and Letters-of-Marque, During Our War with England in the Years 1812, '13 and '14* (New York: author, 1856); the most analytical study is Jerome R. Garitee's *The Republic's Private Navy: The American Privateering Business as Practiced by Baltimore During the War of 1812* (Middletown: Wesleyan University Press for Mystic Seaport, 1977); for Connecticut privateering, see German, "'To Serve Their Country and Make Their Fortunes': Connecticut Privateers and Torpedomen in the War of 1812," *Connecticut History* 52, No. 1 (Spring 2013): 47–63.

Page 20: *It was no secret*: British ships off New London received American Newspapers on a regular basses from American and neutral vessels which operated under special license.

Page 21 *On the night of March 24*: based on an interview with Jeremiah Holmes, the Rev. Frederic Denison published "The Torpedo Adventures," *Mystic Pioneer*, June 18, 1859.

Page 21: *As an American seaman*: Rev. Frederic Denison, "Narrative of Capt. Jeremiah Holmes of Mystic Bridge, Conn. 1859," VFM 390, G.W. Blunt White Library, Mystic Seaport. http://library.mysticseaport.org/initiative/PageImage.cfm?BibID=25275.

Page 21: *The torpedo used*: "The Torpedo Adventures," *Mystic Pioneer*, June 18, 1859.

Page 22: *Captain Capel*: William R. O'Byrne, *A Naval Biographical Dictionary* (London: John Murray, 1849), 167.

Page 23: *The Traitor*: Goldenberg, "Blue Lights and Infernal Machines: The British Blockade of New London," *Mariner's Mirror*; Edward Parry, *Memoirs of Rear-Admiral Sir W. Edward Parry* (London, UK: Longman, Brown, Green, Longmans, & Roberts, 1857).

Chapter 3

Page 27: *The Saybrook Bar*: regarding the *Oliver Cromwell* and *Trumbull* getting over the bar, see Ellsworth S. Grant, *"Thar She Goes!" Shipbuilding on the Connecticut River* (Essex: Greenwich Publishing Group for the Connecticut River Museum, 2000).

Page 27: *With large warships*: Rif Winfield, *British Warships of the Age of Sail, 1793–1817: Design, Construction, Careers and Fates* (Barnsley, UK: Seaforth Publishing, 2008).

Page 31: *After a two and a half hour transit*: for Lieutenant Farrant, see William R. O'Byrne, *A Naval Biographical Dictionary* (London: John Murray, 1849), 349.

Page 31: *It was an impressive little armada*: the numbers of men and names of the officers are accounted in Coote's report (see appendix); for Lieutenant Pyne see John Marshall, *Royal Naval Biography* (London: Longman, Rees, Orme, Brown, Green, and Longman, 1833), 301–04; for Lieutenants Liddon and Fanshawe see O'Byrne, *A Naval Biographical Dictionary*, vol. 4, part 1 658, 347; for Lieutenant Parry see Edward Parry, *Memoirs of Rear-Admiral Sir W. Edward Parry* (London, UK: Longman, Brown, Green, Longmans, & Roberts, 1857).

Page 31: *One member of the* Borer's *crew*: The story of Coote's fiancée, Mary Elliot and her brother Basil are from "Memoirs of Emily Elliot," written in 1889 and transcribed by her grandson, Ted Barton, in 1966.

Page 33: *The marines were equipped*: René Chartrand, *"A Scarlet Coat," Uniforms, Flags and Equipment of the British Forces in the War of 1812* (Ottawa, Canada: Service Publications, 2011); Adrian B. Caruana, *The History of English Sea Ordnance 1523–1875, Volume II 1715–1815: The Age of the System* (East Sussex, UK: Jean Boudriot Publications, 1997); Spencer C. Tucker, "The Carronade," *Nautical Research Journal* 42, No. 1 (March 1997): 15–23.

Page 33: *The first American to notice*: *Connecticut Spectator*, May 17, 1814.

Page 35: *Indeed Coote*: Coote to Capel (see appendix); "The last guard at Fort Fenwick was discharged on the 1st since which, except three windy & cold days, we have been continually menaced by the Enemy with their armed vessels & boats," 1814 "Representation from Saybrook," Letters Received by the Secretary of War, M221, Registered Series, 1801–1860, November 1812–May 1814.

Page 35: *The first fort*: "Siege and Battle of Saybrook Fort," National Park Service American Battlefield Protection Program, Technical Report, Sept. 1636–June 1637. Mashantucket Pequot Museum and Research Center (GA-2255-10-012) 16–17; William B. Tully, "Town of Old Saybrook," in *The History of Middlesex County, 1635–1885* (New York: J. H. Beers, 1885), 282–320.

Page 36: *Within eyesight*: Connecticut Gazette, July 7, 1813.

Page 36: *Local legend*: J. Stuart Rankin, *Maritime History of Essex* (Essex: Dauntless Club, 1929), 15.

Page 36: *According to local reports*: Tully, "Town of Old Saybrook," in *The History of Middlesex County, 1635–1885* (New York: J. H. Beers, 1885), 282–320.

Page 36: *Out in the river*: Coote to Capel (see appendix).

Page 39: *We do not know*: American Mercury, May 31, 1814.

Page 40: *It is fairly safe to say*: see René Chartrand, *A Most Warlike Appearance: Uniforms, Flags and Equipment of the United States in the War of 1812* (Ottawa, Canada: Service Publications, 2011), 131–38; *American Mercury*, May 31, 1814.

Page 41: *Apparently no officers*: on Jewett see Frederic Clarke Jewett, *History and Genealogy of the Jewetts of America* (New York: Grafton Press, 1908), 329–30; Selectmen of Saybrook to Governor Smith, April 12, 1814, *John Cotton Smith Papers*, vol. 2, July 19, 1813–April 14, 1814 (Hartford: Connecticut Historical Society, 1949) (see appendix).

Page 41: *The men on the waterfront*: Coote to Capel (see appendix); *The Naval Chronicle For 1814: Containing a General and Biographical history of The Royal Navy of the United Kingdom*, vol. 32, July–December (London, UK: Joyce Gold, 1814), 171; *The Columbian*, April 12, 1814.

Page 42: *In each of the larger boats*: René Chartrand, *"A Scarlet Coat": Uniforms, Flags and Equipment of the British Forces in the War of 1812* (Ottawa, Canada: Service Publications, 2011); Adrian B. Caruana, *The History of English Sea Ordnance 1523 - 1875, Volume II 1715-1815: The Age of the System* (East Sussex, UK: Jean Boudriot Publications, 1997); Spencer C. Tucker, "The Carronade," *Nautical Research Journal* 42, No. 1 (March 1997), 15–23.

Page 42: *Some reports have suggested*: Rankin, *Maritime History of Essex*, 15.

Page 42: *Did the defenders*: Coote indicates the presence of an American fieldpiece, Coote to Capel (see appendix).

Page 43: *It seems the British gunners*: Samuel Morley Comstock, "A River-Town," *New England Magazine* 20 (1899): 565.

Page 44: *What happened next*: Coote to Capel (see appendix).

Chapter 4

Page 47: *As the militia moved away*: American Mercury, May 31, 1814.

Page 48: *In simple terms*: Connecticut Gazette, April 13, 1814; Williams to Smith, Connecticut Archives, War of 1812 — III, 18, Connecticut State Library; *Boston Daily Advertiser*, April 12, 1814. *American Mercury*, May 31, 1814.

Page 50: *In addition to the whole*: American Mercury, April 12, 1814; "The Night the Boats Burned," Captain Jeremiah Whitaker, *Hartford Courant Magazine*, Sunday, April 3, 1955.

Page 51: *Jewett himself was roundly*: *American Mercury*, Hartford, CT, Volume XXX, Issue 1561, May 31, 1814. p. 3 (see appendix).

Page 51: *We thought at the time we gave the official account; Connecticut Spectator*, Middletown, June 8, 1814.

Page 52: *To make a short story of it*: Edward Parry, *Memoirs of Rear-Admiral Sir W. Edward Parry* (London, UK: Longman, Brown, Green, Longmans, & Roberts, 1857), for his full account (see appendix).

Page 52: *Parry's timeline was a bit off*: Coote to Capel, April 9, 1814, Admiralty Secretariat Papers, ADM 1/506 (see appendix).

Page 52: *Although almost everything*: for Coote's annotated list of vessels (see appendix).

Page 53: *The reference to* warping: the period definition of warping can be found in William Falconer, *An Universal Dictionary of the Marine* (London: T. Cadell, 1780), 1464.

Page 53: *From the* Connecticut Spectator: this account was written by Richard Powers, Thomas Starkey Jr., and other participants to defend the actions of Pettipaug residents, *Connecticut Spectator*, May 17, 1814 (see appendix).

Page 54: *In addition to burning vessels*: Coote to Capel (see appendix).

Page 55: *Although there is no specific evidence*: Albert Dock and Russell Anderson, *The British Raid on Essex* (Essex Historical Society, 1981); *Middlesex Gazette*, April 14, 1814. See appendix.

Page 55: *When the militia had departed*: J. Stuart Rankin, *Maritime History of Essex* (Essex: Dauntless Club, 1929), 12; "The Night the Boats Burned," Captain Jeremiah Whitaker, *Hartford Courant Magazine*, Sunday, April 3, 1955.

Page 56: *In the Williams Yard*: Oral history said to have been told by Austen Lay.

Page 56: *Although there are no*: BOUND HOUSE, Houses of Essex, Don Malcarne, 2004, Ivoryton Library Association, page 37. Bullet found by Arthur 'Bud' Lovell in the Bound House is on display in Connecticut River Museum with label by A. Lovell.

Page 56: *Even stranger*: "The Old Rope Walk," unidentified newspaper, March 17, 1898, "Rope walk" Files, Essex Historical Society; Samuel Morley Comstock, "A River-Town," *The New England Magazine* 20 (1899).

Page 60: *Now I was standing there*: for the 1804 pattern Royal Navy boarding cutlass see René Chartrand, *"A Scarlet Coat": Uniforms, Flags and Equipment of the British Forces in the War of 1812* (Ottawa, Canada: Service Publications, 2011).

Chapter 5

Page 61: *As with most events*: for Coote's annotated list of vessels (see appendix).

Page 62: *One problem is*: for the American lists of vessels (see appendix).

Page 64: *According to Lieutenant Parry*: Edward Parry, *Memoirs of Rear-Admiral Sir W. Edward Parry* (London, UK: Longman, Brown, Green, Longmans, & Roberts, 1857). For his full account (see appendix); calculations of sun and moon rises and set come from the

United States Naval Observatory (USNO) online historic calculator http://aa.usno.navy
.mil/data/docs/RS_OneYear.php.

Page 66: *Whatever the case*: In 1934 "Eugene Southworth of Riverview Street" in Essex
recalled how in his youth, Austin Lay would visit his school "from time to time" and "one
of his favorite topics was to recite the facts as he knew them concerning the raid on Essex
which he had remembered from his youth." See also, "Essex Trapper Finds Keel of Osage
Burned By British," *New Haven Register*, Friday, June 3, 1934, War Files, Essex Historical
Society.

Page 66: *The* Osage *also became*: "Essex Trapper Finds Keel of Osage Burned By British,"
New Haven Register, Friday, June 3, 1934.

Page 68: *Because Coote mentioned*: Elizabeth Putnam, *Brockway's Ferry Lyme, Connecticut, A History and Memoir*, Revised second edition (Lyme Public Hall Association,
2002), 3–4.

Page 69: *The British did not burn*: Coote to Capel, April 9, 1814, Admiralty Secretariat
Papers, ADM 1/506 (see appendix).

Page 69: *Why did the British bother*: For a complete account of the treatment of prizes
and prize money in the Royal Navy, see Richard Hill, *The Prizes of War: The Naval Prize
System in the Napoleonic Wars, 1793–1815* (Portsmouth, UK: Royal Naval Museum, 1998).

Page 70: *The American newspaper reports*: See the appendix for lists.

Page 71: *Two respected local historians*: Don Malcarne, Bulletin of the Archaeological Society of Connecticut, Vol. 65, 2003; Tom Stevens, unpublished accounting of ships
destroyed during the British Raid on Essex, on file in the Thomas A. Stevens Research
Library, Connecticut River Museum, Essex, CT.

Page 71: *Coincidentally or not, an American privateer*: Rif Winfield, *British Warships of
the Age of Sail, 1793–1817: Design, Construction, Careers and Fates* (Barnsley, UK: Seaforth
Publishing, 2008).

Chapter 6

Page 72: *While Lieutenants Parry and Liddon*: Glover's affidavit was published in the
Connecticut Spectator, May 5, 1814 (see appendix).

Page 79: *As the British prepared to leave*: In their letter, the residents of Pettipaug in-
dicate the favorable wind direction, *Connecticut Spectator*, May 17, 1814 (see appendix).

Page 80: *As the British rounded Hayden's Point*: In their letter, the residents of Pettipaug
note the change in wind direction, *Connecticut Spectator*, May 17, 1814 (see appendix).

Page 82: *The senior American officer*: Fifty-three-year-old Marsh Ely (1761–1835) was a
minor political figure in Lyme but a high-ranking militia officer, see "'Moved & Seduced by
the Instigation of the Devil': Treason Trials in Connecticut in the War of 1812," by Bruce P.
Stark, *Connecticut History* 52, No. 1 (Spring 2013): 86–98.

Chapter 7

Page 86: *And then it happened*: Glover's affidavit in the *Connecticut Spectator*, May 5, 1814 (see appendix).

Page 88: *With all the ships' boats*: Edward Parry, *Memoirs of Rear-Admiral Sir W. Edward Parry* (London, UK: Longman, Brown, Green, Longmans, & Roberts, 1857). For his full account, see appendix.

Page 89: *Major Ely and the three companies*: see Fred Calabretta, "Connecticut's Militia," in Glenn S. Gordinier, *The Rockets' Red Glare: The War of 1812 and Connecticut* (New London: New London County Historical Society, 2012), 33–37.

Page 91: *General Williams' own account*: Papers of John Cotton Smith, Collections of the Connecticut Historical Society, Vol. II: 1813–1814 (226–228), April 9, 1814, page 226 (see appendix).

Page 92: *Every exertion was immediately*: *Connecticut Gazette*, April 13, 1814 (see appendix).

Page 93: *As they reached a wooded area*: The position of the burning brig is inferred from a recently discovered pile of ballast stones.

Page 93: *That morning as Coote*: Victor Mays, *The Events in Killingworth Harbor 1813–1814* (Clinton: Clinton Historical Society, 2009); Papers of John Cotton Smith, Collections of the Connecticut Historical Society, Vol. II: 1813–1814 (226–228) April 9, 1814, page 226 (see appendix).

Page 94: *Time was clearly on the American side*: Ely to the Officer Commanding, April 8, 1814, Manuscript Collection, MS 37848, Connecticut Historical Society.

Page 95: *Lieutenant Parry recorded*: Parry, *Memoirs of Rear-Admiral Sir W. Edward Parry*. For his full account, see appendix.

Page 95: *Coote's report was drier*: Coote to Capel, April 9, 1814, Admiralty Secretariat Papers, ADM 1/506 (see appendix); since the original copy of Ely's message still exists at the Connecticut Historical Society, Coote must have had one of his officers copy it before declining the offer.

Page 96: *At around 3:30 p.m.*: Captain's log, HMS *La Hogue*, Admiralty and Secretariat Papers, ADM 51 / 2527; captains log, HMS *Maidstone*, Admiralty and Secretariat Papers, ADM 51 / 2577.

Page 97: *Earlier in the afternoon*: *Salem Gazette*, April 29, 1814.

Page 97: *At last the troops had arrived*: "A Gentleman from Lyme," *Salem Gazette*, Salem, MA. April 29, 1814. Volume XXVIII, Issue 34. p. 2.

Page 100: *From Bull's own account*: Memorial of Lieut. William C. Bull, Connecticut Archives, War of 1812—II, 93A, Connecticut State Library (see appendix).

Chapter 8

Page 101: *The sun set at 6:22*: Calculations of sun and moon rises and set come from the United States Naval Observatory (USNO) online historic calculator http://aa.usno .navy.mil/data/docs/RS_OneYear.php; Coote to Capel, April 9, 1814, Admiralty Secretariat Papers, ADM 1/506 (see appendix).

Page 102: *Three days later*: Edward Parry, *Memoirs of Rear-Admiral Sir W. Edward Parry* (London, UK: Longman, Brown, Green, Longmans, & Roberts, 1857). For his full account, see appendix.

Page 102: *Lieutenant Bull and his team*: Memorial of Lieut. William C. Bull, Connecticut Archives, War of 1812 — II, 93A, Connecticut State Library (see appendix); for field artillery equipment and practices, see Donald E. Graves, "Field Artillery of the War of 1812: Equipment, Organization, Tactics and Effectiveness," *War of 1812 Magazine* 12 (November 2009). http://www.napoleon-series.org/military/Warof1812/2009/Issue12/c_Artillery.html.

Page 102: *Nearly twenty hours after*: Captains log, HMS *Maidstone*, Admiralty and Secretariat Papers, ADM 51 / 2577.

Page 102: *Royal Marines Thomas Smith*: Coote to Capel (see appendix).

Page 103: *Bull and his crew*: Memorial of Lieut. William C. Bull (see appendix).

Page 103: *As the British continued*: Glover's affidavit in the *Connecticut Spectator*, May 5, 1814 (see appendix).

Page 105: *The most formidable*: Coote to Capel (see appendix).

Page 105: *By waiting 'till the night*: Coote to Capel (see appendix).

Page 106: *Tho' I believe no boat*: Coote to Capel (see appendix).

Page 106: *As Coote's men reached*: Coote to Capel (see appendix).

Page 108: *General Williams put it bluntly*: Williams to Smith, Papers of John Cotton Smith, Collections of the Connecticut Historical Society, Vol. II: 1813–1814 (226–228), April 9, 1814, page 226. See appendix.

Chapter 9

Page 109: *Once the British were gone*: The estimates of monetary damages appear in several newspaper accounts including the *Norwich Courier*, April 13, 1814, Vol. XVIII, Issue 22, p. 33, "The loss sustained . . . not far from $150,000"; the *Yankee*, Boston, April 15, 1814, Vol. III, Issue 16, p. 2. "valued at 200,000 dollars."

Page 109: *For the British*: Promotions; Naval History of Great Britain, Vol. VI, page 325 by Lieutenant Garland. http://www.pbenyon.plus.com/Naval_History/Vol_VI/P_325 .html; Edward Parry, *Memoirs of Rear-Admiral Sir W. Edward Parry* (London, UK: Longman, Brown, Green, Longmans, & Roberts, 1857).

Page 109: *In 1848 the Royal Navy*: Kenneth Douglas-Morris, *Naval General Service Medal Roll, 1793–1840* (reprint, Uckfield, UK: Naval & Military Press, 2001).

Page 110 *There was good reason for concern*: Ebenezer Huntington to John Cotton

Smith, *John Cotton Smith Papers*, Collections of the Connecticut Historical Society, Vol. II, 1813–1814 (4:122), 6.

Page 111: *Although some initial blame*: *Columbian Register*, New Haven, CT, Volume II, Issue 73, April 19, 1814. p. 3; The *Selectmen of Saybrook*: Papers of John Cotton Smith, Collections of the Connecticut Historical Society, Vol. II 1813–1814 (235–236), April 12, 1814; 7th *Regiment*, Papers of John Cotton Smith, CCHS, Vol. XXVII. p. 28.

Page 111: *Smith wrote to Secretary of the Navy*: Papers of John Cotton Smith, CCHS, XXVII. p. 20.

Page 111: *Chain of command*: For the details of the Battle of Stonington, see James Tertius de Kay, *The Battle of Stonington: Torpedoes, Submarines, and Rockets in the War of 1812* (Annapolis: Naval Institute Press, 1990), and Glenn S. Gordinier, *The Rockets' Red Glare: The War of 1812 and Connecticut* (New London: New London County Historical Society, 2012).

Page 112: *On May 9th*: Decatur had sent the *United States*, *Macedonian*, and *Hornet* upriver to a few miles south of Norwich, where the first two were down-rigged and laid up, while the *Hornet* remained in commission. The crew's of the *United States* and *Macedonian* then were sent to New York. Decatur's crew joined him in USS *President*, and Jones's crew went with him to Lake Ontario. *Connecticut Gazette*, April 20, May 4, May 11, 1814; for Decatur's return to New London after his capture and his presence at the peace ball attended by British officers, see *Connecticut Gazette*, February 22, March 1, 1815.

Page 112: *When Decatur had headed for New York*: for the *Hornet's* departure from New London for New York, see *Connecticut Gazette*, November 23, 1814; also see Gordinier, *The Rockets' Red Glare: The War of 1812 and Connecticut*, 81, 90–91.

Page 113: *Ironically, just weeks after*: See Bruce P. Stark, "'Moved & Seduced by the Instigation of the Devil': Treason Trials in Connecticut in the War of 1812," *Connecticut History* 52, No. 1 (Spring 2013): 86–98.

Page 113: *Who was Torpedo Jack*: HMS *Borer*, Muster List, ADM 37 / 4487, no. 446, shows Ezekial Jackson transferring to HMS *Loup Cervier*.

Page 115: *Anyone with an ounce of compassion*: The story of Coote's fiancée, Mary Elliot and her brother Basil are from the "Memoirs of Emily Elliot," written in 1889 and transcribed by her grandson, Ted Barton, in 1966.

Page 115: *Six months later, HMS* Sylph: The *East Hampton Star*, East Hampton, N.Y. October 15, 1998; Henry Thomas Dering "The Wreck of HMS *Sylph* and the Southold Historical Society's report on HMS *Sylph* compiled by Geoffrey K. Fleming which includes an eye witness account of the loss of the *Sylph*," January 18th, 1814.

BIBLIOGRAPHY

MANUSCRIPT SOURCES

Admiralty and Secretariat Papers, ADM 1/506, April 9, 1814, Coote to Capel.

Admiralty and Secretariat Papers, ADM 1/506, April 13, 1814, Capel to Talbot.

Admiralty and Secretariat Papers, ADM 1/506, May 10, 1814, Cochrane to Croker.

Admiralty and Secretariat Papers, ADM 37 /4348, *Maidstone*, 1st March–30th April; Parry, Memoirs.

Admiralty and Secretariat Papers, ADM 37 /4487, *Borer*, Prisoners at 2/3 Allowance, 1st March–30th April, 1814.

Admiralty and Secretariat Papers, ADM 37 /4487, *Borer*, "Supernumeraries for Victuals Only," No. 446.

Admiralty and Secretariat Papers, ADM 51 / 2527, *La Hogue*, Captain's Logs.

Admiralty and Secretariat Papers, ADM 51 / 2577, *Maidstone*, Captain's Logs.

Connecticut Historical Society Manuscript Collection, MS 37848, Ely Marsh.

Connecticut River Museum Collection, Thomas A. Stevens, "Trinity Lodge No. 43 A. F. & A. M. Deep River, Connecticut: A History of its Founding in 1797 and the Spread of Free Masonry in Lower Middlesex Co., Conn." Address presented at Trinity Lodge No. 43, November 1972.

Connecticut State Library, Connecticut Archives, War of 1812, III: 17, 18, 93.

East Lyme Historical Society, Charles H. Smith Journal (1828–1907), "War of 1812. Elisha Smith's Service."

"Memoirs of Emily Elliot," written in 1889 and transcribed by her grandson, Ted Barton, in 1966.

Mystic Seaport Museum, G. W. Blunt White Library, VFM 390, "Narrative of Capt. Jeremiah Holmes of Mystic Bridge, Conn. 1859," Rev. Frederic Denison. http://library.mysticseaport.org/initiative/PageImage.cfm?BibID=25275.

National Archives and Records Administration, M221, Letters Received by the Secretary of War, Registered Series, 1801–1860; November 1812–May 1814, Representation from Saybrook.

National Archives and Records Administration, RG45, Records of the US Navy, M125, R35 Captains' Letters.

National Archives and Records Administration, RG45, Records of the US Navy, M147, R5 Letters from Commanders.

Yale University, Manuscript Collection, MS 189, William Griswold Lane Memorial Collection, Box 7, 1814 April–1815 December, Charles Griswold; Box 25, 18 April 1814, Charles Griswold to Ebenezer Lane.

PUBLISHED PAPERS

American State Papers, Volume VI Naval Affairs, 13th Congress, Second Session, No. 111, "Condition of the Navy, and the Progress Made in Providing Materials and Building Ships."

Naval Chronicle For 1814: Containing a General and Biographical history of The Royal Navy of the United Kingdom, Volume XXXII July–December. London, UK: Joyce Gold, 1814.

Smith, John Cotton. Papers. Volume I, 1812–13. *Collections of the Connecticut Historical Society*, Volume XXV. Hartford: The Connecticut Historical Society, 1948.

Smith, John Cotton. Papers. Volume II, 1813–1814. *Collections of the Connecticut Historical Society*, Volume XXVI. Hartford: The Connecticut Historical Society, 1949.

Smith, John Cotton. Papers. Volume III. *Collections of the Connecticut Historical Society*, Volume XXVII. Hartford: The Connecticut Historical Society, 1952.

NEWSPAPERS, JOURNALS, MAGAZINES

Alexandria Gazette Commercial and Political, Alexandria, VA, Volume XIV, Issue 4155, April 14, 1814.

American Mercury, Hartford, CT, Volume XXX, Issue 1554, April 12, 1814. p. 3.

American Mercury, Hartford, CT, Volume XXX, Issue 1559, May 17, 1814. p. 3.

American Mercury, Hartford, CT, Volume XXX, Issue 1561, May 31, 1814. p. 3.

American Mercury, Hartford, CT, Volume XXX, Issue 1567, July 7, 1814. p. 3.

Boston Daily Advertiser, Volume V, Issue 36, April 12, 1814. p. 2.

The Columbian, New York, NY, Volume V, Issue 1366, April 11, 1814. p. 3.

The Columbian, New York, NY, Volume V, Issue 1367, April 12, 1814. p. 3.

Columbian Register, New Haven, CT, Volume II, Issue 73, April 19, 1814. p. 3.

Connecticut Gazette, New London, CT, Volume 50, July 7, 1813; April 13, 1813; April 20, 1814; May 4, 1814; May 11, 1814; November 23, 1814; February 22, 1814; March 1, 1815.

Connecticut History, Volume 52, Number 1, Spring 2013. Bruce P. Stark, "'Moved & Seduced by the Instigation of the Devil': Treason Trials in Connecticut in the War of 1812." p. 86–98.

Connecticut History, Volume 52, Number 1, Spring 2013. Andrew W. German, "'To Serve Their Country and Make Their Fortunes': Connecticut Privateers and Torpedomen in the War of 1812." p. 47–63.

Connecticut Journal, New London, CT, Volume XLVII, Issue 2425, April 18, 1814. p. 3.

Connecticut Spectator, Middletown, CT, Volume 1, Issue 1, April 20, 1814. p. 3.

Connecticut Spectator, Middletown, CT, Volume I, Issue 4, May 11, 1814. p. 3.

Connecticut Spectator, Middletown, CT, Volume 1, Issue 5, May 17, 1814. p. 3.

Connecticut Spectator, Middletown, CT, Volume I, Issue 8, June 8, 1814. p. 3.

Unknown Newspaper, Essex Historical Society, "Ropewalk" Files, "The Old Rope Walk," March 17, 1898.

Essex Register, Salem, MA, Volume XIV, Issue 33, April 23, 1814.

Evening Post, New York, NY, Issue 3653, April 21, 1814.

Gleaner, Wilkes-Barre, PA, Volume IV, Issue 12, May 27, 1814. p. 3.

Intelligencer, Portsmouth, NH, Volume 8, Issue 3653, April 21, 1814. p. 2.

London Gazette, Number 16916. London, UK: Robert George Clarke, 1814.

Long Island Journal, Volume 2, Number 2, Spring 1990. William M. P. Dunne, "The Inglorious First of June: Commodore Stephen Decatur On Long Island Sound, 1813." p. 201–220.

The Mariner's Mirror, Volume 61, Number 4, November 1975, Joseph A. Goldenberg, "Blue Lights and Infernal Machines: The British Blockade of New London."

Middlesex Gazette, Middletown, CT, Volume XXIX, Issue 1482, April 19, 1814. p. 3.

Middlesex Gazette, Middletown, CT, Volume XXIX, Issue 1486, May 19, 1814. p. 3.

Mystic Pioneer, June 18, 1859. Rev. Frederic Denison, "The Torpedo Adventures."

Nautical Research Journal, Volume 42, Number 1, March 1997. Spencer C. Tucker, "The Carronade." p. 15–23.

New England Magazine. Volume XX, March 1899 – August 1899. Samuel Morley Comstock, "A River-Town." p. 555–567.

New Haven Register, Friday, June 3, 1934. EHS, War Files, "Essex Trapper Finds Keel of Osage Burned By British."

New York Gazette & General Advertiser, Volume XXV, Issue 9967, February 8, 1814.

New York Commercial Advertiser, New York, NY, Volume XVII, Issue 6763, April 13, 1814. p. 3.

Providence Patriot, Providence, RI, Volume 12, Issue 14, April 12, 1814. p. 2.

Repertory, Boston, MA, Volume XI, Issue 21, April 16, 1814.

Repertory, Boston, MA, Volume XI, Issue 22, April 19, 1814. p. 1.

Rhode Island American & General Advertiser, Providence, RI, Volume VI, Issue 53, May 15, 1814. p. 2.

Salem Gazette, Salem, MA, Volume XXVIII, Issue 34, April 29, 1814. "The Pettipauge Catastrophe."

War of 1812 Magazine, Volume 12, November 2009. Donald E. Graves, "Field Artillery of the War of 1812: Equipment, Organization, Tactics and Effectiveness." http://www.napoleon-series.org/military/Warof1812/2009/Issue12/c_Artillery.html.

BOOKS

Anderson, Russell F., and Albert Dock, *The British Raid on Essex, April 8, 1814*. Essex Historical Society, 1981.

Barber, John Warner. *John Warner Barber's Views of Connecticut Towns 1834–36.* Hartford, CT: Connecticut Historical Society, 1990.

Beers, F.W. *Beers Atlas of New London County 1868.* New York: A.D. Ellis & G.G. Soule, 1868.

Caruana, Adrian B. *The History of English Sea Ordnance 1523–1875,* Volume II 1715–1815: *The Age of the System.* East Sussex, UK: Jean Boudriot Publications, 1997.

Caulkins, Frances Manwaring. *History of New London, Connecticut; From the First Survey of the Coast in 1612, to 1860.* New London, CT: H. D. Utley, 1895.

Chartrand, René. *A Most Warlike Appearance: Uniforms, Flags and Equipment of the United States in the War of 1812.* Ottawa, Canada: Service Publications, 2011.

Chartrand, René. *"A Scarlet Coat": Uniforms, Flags and Equipment of the British Forces in the War of 1812.* Ottawa, Canada: Service Publications, 2011.

Coggeshall, George. *History of the American Privateers, and Letters-of-Marque, During Our War with England in the Years 1812, '13 and '14.* New York: Coggeshall, 1856.

DeKay, James Tertius. *The Battle of Stonington: Torpedoes, Submarines and Rockets in the War of 1812.* Hyannis, MA: Parnassus Imprints, 1990.

Douglas–Morris, Kenneth. *Naval General Service Medal Roll, 1793–1840.* Reprinted, Uckfield, UK: Naval & Military Press, 2001.

Falconer, William. *An Universal Dictionary of the Marine.* London: T. Cadell, 1780.

Field, David Dudley. *A Statistical Account of the county of Middlesex in Connecticut.* Middletown, CT: Clark & Lyman, April 1819.

Garitee, Jerome R. *The Republic's Private Navy: The American Privateering Business as Practiced by Baltimore During the War of 1812.* Middletown: Wesleyan University Press for Mystic Seaport, 1977.

Gordinier, Glenn. S. *The Rockets' Red Glare: The War of 1812 and Connecticut.* New London, CT: New London County Historical Society, 2012.

Hall, Verne M. and Elizabeth B. Plimpton. *Vital Records of Lyme, Connecticut.* Lyme, CT: American Revolution Bicentennial Commission, 1976.

Hollister, G. H., *The History of Connecticut from the First Settlement to the Adoption of the present Constitution,* Volume II. New Haven, CT: Durrie and Peck, 1855.

Jewett, Frederic Clarke. *History and Genealogy of the Jewetts of America.* New York: Grafton Press, 1908.

Latimer, Jon. *1812: War with America.* Cambridge, MA: Belknap Press, 2007.

Lossing, Benson J. *The Pictorial Field-Book of the War of 1812.* New York, NY: Harper & Brothers, Publishers, 1869.

Luce, Commodore S.B., U.S. Navy, *Seamanship. The Equipping and Handling of Vessels Under Sail or Seam.* New York: Van Nostrand Company, 1891.

Mays, Victor. *The Events in Killingworth Harbor 1813–1814.* Clinton, CT: Clinton Historical Society, 2009.

Mullen, A.L.T. *Military General Service Roll 1793-1814*. East Sussex, UK: Naval & Military Press Ltd, 2001.

O'Byrne, William R. *A Naval Biographical Dictionary*. London, John Murray, 1849.

Parry, Edward. *Memoirs of Rear-Admiral Sir W. Edward Parry*. London, UK: Longman, Brown, Green, Longmans, & Roberts, 1857.

Pease, John C. and John M. Stiles. *A Gazetteer of the States of Connecticut and Rhode Island*. Hartford, CT: William G. Marsh, 1819.

Perkins, Samuel. *A History of The Political and Military Events of the Late War between the United States and Great Britain*. New Haven, CT: S. Converse, 1825.

Rankin, J. Stuart. *Maritime History of the Town of Essex Connecticut*. Essex, CT: Dauntless Club, 1929.

Tucker, Spencer C. *Stephen Decatur: A Life Most Bold and Daring*. Annapolis: Naval Institute Press, 2004.

Tully, William B. "Town of Old Saybrook" in *History of Middlesex County, Connecticut*. New York, NY: J. B. Beers & Co., 1884.

Winfield, Rif. *British Warships of the Age of Sail, 1793-1817: Design, Construction, Careers and Fates*. Barnsley, UK: Seaforth Publishing, 2008.

WEBSITES

jerrypaulroberts.com
battlesiteessex.org
essexhistory.org
ctrivermuseum.org

INDEX

Page numbers in italics refer to illustrations.

Garnet Books

Jerry Roberts has had a lifelong passion for history and the sea and has been a writer, maritime historian, and museum executive for over 25 years. He served as vice president at the Intrepid Sea Air Space Museum in New York City and from 2006 to 2013 as executive director for the Connecticut River Museum in Essex. Roberts has been the driving force behind efforts to bring the British Raid on Essex to national attention and serves as the battlefield historian to the National Park Service-funded project to further research and map the battle. Roberts lives with his wife and two children in their home overlooking the Connecticut River, where he continues to write of adventures large and small.

ABOUT THE DRIFTLESS CONNECTICUT SERIES

The Driftless Connecticut Series is a publication award program
established in 2010 to recognize excellent books with a Connecticut
focus or written by a Connecticut author. To be eligible, the book
must have a Connecticut topic or setting or an author must have
been born in Connecticut or have been a legal resident of Connecticut
for at least three years.

The Driftless Connecticut Series is funded by the
Beatrice Fox Auerbach Foundation Fund at the
Hartford Foundation for Public Giving.
For more information and a complete list of books in
the Driftless Connecticut Series, please visit us online at
http://www.wesleyan.edu/wespress/driftless.